AF553881

Panorama of Buddhist Thought and Culture : 3

Archaeological and Epigraphical Sources on Buddhism

(Collection of Articles from *The Indian Antiquary*)

Compiled by
P. Mittal
Geeta Dua

Re-arranged with an Introduction by
Prof. S R Bhatt

Originals
(an imprint of Low Price Publications)
Delhi-110052

First Published In Indian Antiquary 1872-1933
Compiled and Published 2008 (Q4)

ISBN 81-88629-50-2

Published by
Originals
(an imprint of Low Price Publications)
A-6, Nimri Commercial Centre,
Near Ashok Vihar Phase-IV,
Delhi-110052
Phones: 27302453
e-mail: info@Lppindia.com
visit us at: www.Lppindia.com

Printed at
D K Fine Art Press P Ltd.
Delhi-110052

PRINTED IN INDIA

CONTENTS

Introduction

A culture is known for and creates a mark in human history by scientific and technological achievements as well as artistic excellences. Both are complementary and constitute significant facets of human life in so far as they cater to the needs and aspirations of different dimensions of human existence. The utility of science and technology lies in making life easier and comfortable. The value of arts is in respect of evoking beauty and bliss. Art is a symbolic representation of thought and culture. It elevates life to a higher plane.

Indian culture is well known for achieving great heights in artistic accomplishments in different art-pursuits right from the Vedic times. In the vast spatio-temporal span of the flow of Indian culture there have evolved various types of arts with multiple traditions and varied forms. Indian culture in this respect is like a multi-hued tapestry with innumerable shades and colors presenting a wonderful pageant. To this contributions have come both from the religious as well secular traditions. The Buddhist contribution has been immense and significant. There has been phenomenal growth of Buddhist art and culture at least from 3rd century B.C. Since then Buddhism has been playing an important tole in the development of art in India and in other Asian countries with notable impact from India. The Buddha's life and teachings, seminal Buddhist doctrines, beliefs and practices, Buddhist mythology and pantheon etc. provided main stimulus and offered prime inspiration to artists. Buddhist art was cultivated through out Greater India from 3rd century onwards till the time of Muslim invasions. The history of development of Buddhist art in and outside India is quite fascinating and it has great aesthetic value and religious significance. Buddhist art treasures are found in all parts of India and in many Asian countries in many mediums and in many forms.

The themes and subject matter of Buddhist art have been quite varied. In Buddhist art we find different postures of the Buddha depicting his glory. His life events and happenings of previous lives are also displayed on the basis of material drawn from *Jātakas* and *Avadānas*. Buddhist mythology is very rich and Buddhist pantheon is very vast comprising many gods and goddesses. All these are picturesquely depicted in the Buddhist art. The edifying legends are prominently displayed.

The Buddhist art found expression in *vihāras, stūpas* and *caityas,* cave-paintings and wall-hangings, in sculptures and bronzes, metal and ceramic images, terracotta figures etc. The edicts and inscriptions of Aśoka and other rulers provide glimpses of art products apart from describing social, political and economic state of the society in those times. Different art creations are symbols representing different facets of Buddhism as a religion and as a way of life.

The Buddhist art objects evidence a very highly developed state of art in those time. They not only display great vision and thought, they also excel in aesthetic beauty. They are exquisitely worked out and appear extraordinarily enchanting. There have been many traditions of Buddhist art in India. The Gāndhāra tradition, the Mathurā tradition, the Nālandā tradition in the North, the Pāla and Sena traditions in the East, the Cālukya, Pallava and the Āndhra traditions in the South are a few notable examples. The *stūpas, caityas* and *vihāras* present a fine form of architecture. Some of them are richly carved with scenes from Buddha's life. The *stūpas* and *caityas* are supposed to contain relics of the Buddha, Pratyekabuddhas, Arhatas and Bodhisattvas. The relics are called *'dhātus'* and they are classified as corporeal (*śārīrika*), memorial (*uddeśika*), and utility objects (*pāribhogika*). The corporeal relics are tooth, hair, bones etc. The memorial ones are connected with important events like *Dhammacakkapavattana*. The utility objects are garbs, bowls, staff etc. The *stūpas* have architectural significance where as the *caityas* have religious importance. Some of these *stūpas* and *caityas* are now extinct and some are existent in mutilated form. Only a few are in good shape. The Chinese pilgrims of ancient times have given a very vivid account of many such *stūpas, caityas* and *vihāras*. The surviving ones are regarded as places of Buddhist pilgrimage. Mention may be made of Lumbini where the Buddha was born, of Bodh Gaya where he obtained enlightenment, of Sarnath where he preached the first sermon, and Kusinagara where he attained *mahāparinirvāṇa*. All these contain rich art treasures. For the residence of monks and nuns apart from *vihāras* and *caityas* caves and rock-cut dwellings were created. These places contain beautiful paintings to display the glory of the Buddha and Buddhism. The Ajantā, Ellora, Bāgh and other caves are famous for the paintings. The Thangakā paintings and the tāntric paintings are the masterpieces of Buddhist art. This apart there are wood carvings of great aesthetic value.

Sculpture and bronze and other metal works of art present another variety of Buddhist art and these are objects of great religious veneration, aesthetic grandeur, archeological significance and iconographic importance. They represent different postures of the Buddha and the Buddhist pantheon. The stucco-head of the Buddha, the crowned and bejeweled Buddha, the standing Buddha, he reclining Buddha, the preaching Buddha, the Buddha giving protection and granting fearlessness etc. depict the air of supreme spiritual calm and detachment and yet provide presence of great compassion. The faces in these art forms are radiant with spiritual aura. The smiling countenance with downcast eyes conveys divine compassion and blessings of the Buddha for all beings. The colossal and gigantic figures are awe-inspiring and depict omnipresence, omnipotence and omniscience of the Buddha.

Originating in India Buddhism as religion rapidly spread almost all over Asia. Likewise the Buddhist art and culture also became vibrant, vital and living force in all those places where it went. There were profitable and enriching exchanges between India and those countries. The Theravāda, Mahāyāna and Tantrayāna forms of Buddhism exercised their respective influences in the countries of their locale and produced great masterpieces and wonders. The temple at Anuradhapuram, the Gal Vihara in Sri Lanka. The Borobudur in Java, the now-destroyed Bamiyans in Afghanistan, the Śvayambhunatha and Bodhanatha stupas and the mahabodhi temple in Nepal, Angkor Wat in Cambodia, Ayuthia and other places in Thailand, temples of Myanmar, the Tibetan monasteries with Thangka paintings and fine sculptures, the temples at Sanshi, caves at Lo-Yang and Lohan in China, the Zen paintings in Japan are some of the specimen of Buddhist art outside India. The Himalayan states of India are full of Buddhist art pieces. Indian museums possess a large variety of Buddhist art objects. Thus we find that Buddhist art has been magnificent and a rich contribution to world heritage.

S.R.BHATT
Former Professor and Chair
Department of Philosophy, Delhi University
MP-23, Pitam Pura
Delhi-110088 (India).
21-8-2005

1

Note on a Buddhist Cave at Bhamer, Khandesh

W.F. Sinclair

Bo. C. S. Khandesh

The fort of Bhamer, in the Nizāmpur Peṭā of Khāndesh, lies about 30 miles W. by N. of Dhulia as the crow flies, and consists of two steep rocks lying nearly at right angles to each other, and rising from the centre of a plateau which separates the valleys of the Kān and Burai rivers.

The hollow between them, facing south, is enclosed by two semicircular and concentric ramparts, within the lesser or innermost of which lies the *māchī* or cantonment, while the outer protects the town or *kasba*. Each of these has but one gate, and there is no other approach but by a steep and narrow footpath between the two hills, called the Kasai Barī. The space thus enclosed is of about 100 acres, and seems to have formerly contained about a thousand houses besides several fine wells and cisterns, but there are now about a dozen resident families, half of them Bhills and Mhārs. There are three large tanks, one of which is sacred to Mahādeva, who has here a temple of considerable size and unknown antiquity. This tank and another are dry; the only one retaining any water is a little lake called to Rāj Talāo, which local tradition holds to be bottomless, and to have an underground communication with a spring called the Gokūr Pānī, about three miles away on the further or northern side of the fort.

There are several caves visible in the eastern and larger hill, and one in the western. This latter is a small plain vihāra, resembling some of those at Junnar; the first two in the eastern or castle hill are apparently mere cellars and reservoirs of the same class as those at Lalling near Dhulia, and probably of no great antiquity; but on entering the third, above the doors of which I noticed some carving, I was surprised and delighted to find myself in a vihāra much resembling, but for its small size, some of those at Ajanṭā. I had unfortunately, no means of measurement with me; and the caves are too full of water and débris to admit of pacing, but I estimate the length of the veranda at about fifty feet, and it is five deep. This veranda terminates at each end in a cell, and communicates by three doors ornamented with scrollwork, with as many square caves. These have no inner communication. To roofs are supported by pillars about eight feet high, hewn in the living rock, of a pattern very like what I have seen at Ajanṭā. About one-third of the pillar is square (the corners terminating in a sort of leaf), surmounted by an octagonal band, as this in its turn is by a circular one; and then the same arrangement is repeated: from the base of the last circle a triangle rises into the capital. The ceiling is crossed by broad joists intersecting at right angles at, and between, the pillars. I failed to detect any image or inscription, or any sign of plaster or painting, but I had no light and my inspection was necessarily brief. The westernmost cave opens by a hole 6 inches square into a large pit or cistern, which the villagers say was a dungeon; and this hole was used to feed the prisoners through. The pit is about fifty feet long by thirty wide, deep, and open at the top along the whole of one side, but there are no steps down into it. I should think it was originally made to hold water, which is bad any scarce on the rock; but it may afterwards have been used as related. There is another cave on this southern side of the hill, and three or four on the northern; but they are all of the same class as those first entered. I know of no other Buddhist cave within sixty miles.

Statue of Comateśvara at Śravaṇa Beḷgoḷa (Facing Page 2)

2

Dr. Leitner's Buddhistic Sculptures

James Burgess

The accompanying illustration, from a photograph by Mr. Burke, represents a group of sculptures from the collection of Dr. Leitner of Lahor. They belong to various periods in Græco-Buddhistic, Buddhistic, and ancient Hindu archæology.

At the top is a brass jug on which scenes from the *Rāmāyaṇa* (the rape of Sītā and the war with Lankā), the incarnations of Vishṇu, and representations of Śiva, are most exquisitely engraved. This jug was obtained at Jelālpur (the true site of the battle of Alexander with Porus, as Dr. Leitner and others consider): the two heads on the top ledge are, the one a Baktrian, the other a most beautiful Græco-Buddhist female; whilst the fragment near the latter represents the lower part of a jovial procession, with a goat led out and followed by dancing men.

The big fragment of a group on the second ledge consists of men-dragons; in the upper row, of Buddha when still a prince; in the second row, sitting in the unusual attitude of a European on a throne; and in the main or lowest group, of Buddha as a teacher.

This fragment is supported by purely Buddhist heads, distinguished by the hair simply tied in the well-known topknot, whilst on the extreme left is the head of a Baktrian or Græco-Buddhist prince.

On the third row (from the top) are a variety of figures and groups, which arc quite an historical contribution. Beginning from the extreme right, we have Buddha meeting with the recluse; then a peculiar Hindu-Buddhist figure (transition period), obtained at Ketas, the ancient Sinhapurā[1] (?), from a female saint, in whose family it is said to have been for eight hundred years; then a Skythian (?) or aboriginal head, which, with another representing a face in deep agony, surrounds a group in which two persons carry a horse and its rider. The smaller fragments before and beyond it are too indistinct to furnish any immediate explanation, but attention is deservedly arrested at a highly elaborated and perforated bit of architecture surrounding a group in various and nobly conceived attitudes of prayer.

On the lowest ledge is a confused mass of fragments, one belonging to the fragment on the second row which represents,—beginning, on the extreme right,—the usual group surrounding Buddha followed by a well-bearded old man in a kilt, and other indistinct figures of men, dragons, &c. &c., none of which, however, are at all conceived in the grotesque spirit of Indian idols.

The whole antiquarian collection of Dr. Leitner consists of 172 pieces, of which the majority were excavated by him in 1870, at Takht-i-Bahi.

"One group presented by Dr. Leitner to the Belvedere, Vienna, is interesting as the most complete specimen of the ordinary Buddhist worship of the purest type. There were bas-reliefs showing Buddha surrounded by female as well as male worshippers. In one figure, the North Indian Rāja, with his thin moustache, and the *ṭikkā* mark on his forehead, was represented with a Greek diadem and headdress. The face showed dignity and resolution, and Dr. Leitner considered it the finest specimen in his collection. One particularly beautiful group, of which casts have been sent to both the Belvedere and the Vienna Exhibition, consists of ten sculptures, which seemed to represent almost a continuous tale. A young prince (probably Buddha) is led by an attendant holding an umbrella (the sign of authority) towards an idol, to which he appears to refuse worship, beyond which and a solitary pillar ugly dwarfs are seated. Again the boy (who appears to be the rightful prince) is led forward on to a block, in front of a stern-looking king, to be killed, whilst one of the group of attendants seems to

Buddhist Sculptures from the Neighbourhood of Peshawar (Facing Page 4)

keep back his brother, or perhaps a pretender; whilst at the side niche the boy is already on the sacrificial altar, his mother (probably that of Buddha) vehemently interceding for his life before the same stern ruler. In the next, Buddha, riding an ass, with his attendants, arrives at the gate of a town, where they meet with a writer with a tablet. At a place in the Kyang plain, in Middle Thibet, about 10,000 feet high, a similar carving is seen, where Buddha is represented riding on an ass, and preceded and followed by men wearing branches of the palm-tree (which is unknown in that region). In connection with this group Dr. Leitner mentioned a very remarkable carving, showing Indians at Olympian games. A most remarkable point about all these groups is the minuteness of the carving on the stone or slate, and the variety and completeness of historical and religious representation, which yet require much study. Of architectural fragments, the most notable is the "Buddhist railing"—the device of serpent ornamentation. Curious were the two specimens of figures in mortar (gypsum) resting on a thick base, and representing Buddha and two worshippers. The Græco-Buddhists evidently knew how to cast moulds in mortar, and the art of casting moulds in mud is still faintly preserved at Lāhor. There are also cornices, capitals, &c., of which the highest school of architecture need not be ashamed. The figure of a Buddhist hermit who has just breathed his last is a marvellous success of artistic representation. The sunken eyes and the lines in the cheeks, and the mouth, showed thought and privation. The carving had received a red daub on the forehead by some Hindu who wanted to worship it. On most of the statues, to whatever type they might belong, the *ṭikkā* was worn on the forehead. Very few, in fact only two, of the faces were bearded, and those that were so belonged either to a Muhammadan cast of countenance or to the kilted invaders (probably Skythians). Modern Hindu village gods, in clay and brass, showed that the lineaments of Buddha still lingered in the mind of the sculptor in the Panjāb, Zanskar, and Ladak."[2]

Dr. Leitner's collection is by no means a completely representative one, but the sculptures are, in the opinion of competent judges, a most valuable series, and were they and other materials, such as the so-called Græco-Bactrian sculptures in the Museums of Lahor, Delhi, Calcutta and Edinburgh University, only made accessible by adequate photographic representations, it would not be very difficult, probably, to arrange a series of Buddhist sculptures extending almost without a break from B.C. 250 to A.D. 700, which would not only be a most interesting chapter in the history of Eastern art, but would form a chronometric scale by which to test the age of other monuments, and especially of the Buddhist caves, at an age when we know, as yet, very little about the matter.

References

1. Cunningham's *Anc. Geog. of India*, pp. 124-5; but see *Ind. Ant.* Vol. II, p. 16.–Ed.
2. From report of a Lecture by Dr. Leitner in *The Building News*, March 6, 1874.

3

Notes on Some Little-Known Bauddha Excavations in the Puṇā Collectorate

G. H. Johns
Bo. C.S.

Nānoli – Shelārwāḍī – Bhāmchandra

A short time ago I visited the groups of caves at Nānolī, Shelārwāḍī, and Bhāmchandra, in the Puṇā collectorate; and, though the excavations of the last named are alone of special merit, it may not be uninteresting to give a short account of all the three sets.

The two first mentioned are in the Māwal tālukā to the north and south of the town of Talegāṁ, and the Bhāmchandra hill is in the tālukā of Kheḍ, a few miles to the north-east of Nānolī.

The village of Nānolī lies three miles to the north of Talegāṁ on the left bank of the Indrāyanī, and the caves are in the escarpment of the hill a mile north of the village. A steep climb three-fourths up the hill brought me to the base of a high scarp facing south-west, skirting which I passed first a cistern and cell, and then reached a high flight of steps rudely cut; ascending them I entered a flat-roofed cave about eighteen feet square, with a height of upwards of seven feet; this excavation is now used as a temple to Feringabāi; a small cell is caverned out of the south wall or side. Further on, the escarpment is hollowed out into two small cells.

The Shelārwāḍī excavations are high up in the hill about two miles to the south-east of Talegāṁ, and are most of them in the village limits of Gahunje, and facing south-west.

The north-west caves are in Shelārwāḍī, which is a hamlet of Talegāṁ, and consist of two or three cells only; they are nearly inaccessible, and have some fine *champaka* trees (*Michelia Champaca*) at the entrance. The south-west excavations possess more merit; at the base of the scarp out of which they are hollowed is a narrow footpath, pursuing which a two-celled cave high up in the cliff is first passed, and then a fine cistern: two cells succeed, one with an inscription of five lines cut on its outer face, close to which, but further south, is a large excavation consisting of a nave or vestibule 24 feet by 18 feet, with four cells on either side, and of an inner shrine near the end of which are what would seem to be the remains of a *dāhgobā,* viz. an abacus of four slabs, the lower the smaller, pendent from the roof, and an indistinctly traced foundation of the drum; the latter is now occupied by a *shāluṅkha* and *liṅga*. The roof is flat and about nine feet from the ground. The entrance to this cave is now walled up with two round-arched doorways as means of ingress. Further on are a cistern and a cell. The cave being flat-roofed and the top of the *dāhgobā* being an abacus would induce the opinion that it is an unfinished excavation, which would have been converted into a circular-roofed temple with a *chhatri'd dāhgobā* on completion.

The Bhāmchandra excavations are hollowed out of a hill seven miles west of Chakan, within the village limits of Sinde, close to the boundary of Bhāmbolī. The hill rises steep from the plain on the south and west, and in the escarped southern side are the caves in question. After a somewhat arduous climb from the base of the hill a cistern is passed on the right; the villagers call it 'Sītā's Bath.' A little further on, after rounding a promontary, the principal cave is reached; it is small and faces south-west, and is now dedicated to Bhāmchandra Mahādeva. There is a cistern on the left as one enters; the entrance, which is 8 feet high by 13 wide, is now built up, having a small arched doorway in the centre. The temple is very nearly square, rather more than 14 feet long by 15 broad, the height being 7 feet; the roof is flat; four pillars, two on either side, divide the cave into three compartments (it would be a straining of terms to say into nave and aisles), the side compartments being each adorned with two pilasters similar to the pillars, and having each a niche with pillared jambs and canopy. There is a trace of a *dāhgobā* in the centre,—a circular base five feet in diameter within a square mark where it once stood; and the *chhatri* carved in the roof confirms the view that a *dāhgobā* once occupied the cave. The pillars are massive and square, but halfway up are twice chamfered off so as to be octagonal; the capitals have massive projections on their four sides.

There is an inner shrine occupied by the phallic symbol, and a figure of Buddha: the latter is carved on a detached stone, and may originally have adorned the *dāhgobā*. The inner is separated from the outer cave by an elaborately sculptured doorway, the opening being two feet wide by four feet high; the carvings are mostly of human figures. There are no horse-shoe arch or Buddhist rail ornaments discernible in the cave,—contrasting in this respect with almost all the other *chaitya* excavations in the collectorate; and were it not for the *dāhgobā* I should hardly suppose it to be a Buddhist temple. Perhaps it is Buddhist *chaitya* of the Chālukyan era. The rock of which this hill is composed is of a soft nature, and the screen or doorway dividing the two shrines (the presence of the *dāhgobā* in the outer prevents my calling that a mere nave) has had to be cemented or mortared by the villagers to be kept in its place. Further on is a cell, or rather cavern; and at some little distance, in the middle of the escarpment, and therefore reached with difficulty, is a cave at the end of which is a winding cavernous road low and narrow, said to permeate the hill, and to be many *kos* in length. There are one or two inaccessible holes or caves higher up, and beyond, on the west, is also a small cave.

The *guru* of the temple is supported by a grant of inām land in Bhāmbolī.

4
Memorandum on the Buddhist Caves at Junnar

James Burgess

The caves of Junnar,[1] like those of Bhājā, Beḍsā, Talājā, Śānā, Kuḍā, and other groups, are remarkably devoid of figure ornament or imagery: in this respect contrasting strongly with those at Ajaṇṭā, Elora, Kārlā, Aurangābād, and elsewhere. The Dahgoba alone is common to all: and, on comparing the different groups, one might almost suppose that the Dahgoba and Buddhist rail were the earliest ornaments as well as furniture of the caves: that the Chaitya or horse-shoe window with its latticed aperture was next developed, both as a structural feature and an ornament,—and at Junnar there are some peculiar applications of it; and that figures of Buddha, as in the later caves at Nāśik, at Kanheri, and at Ajaṇṭā, Elora, and Aurangābād, were introduced at a later date. Or is it possible that a puritan sect of Bauddhas, objecting to all anthropomorphic forms, made the Dahgoba their only *qeblah*, while a separate school delighted in pictures and images of their Great Teacher, his Mother, and all the Bauddha Saints ? This is a point deserving the attention of archæologists in attempting to arrange the Buddhist remains in anything like chronological order. We know that in early times it was usual for one school or sect almost to monopolize the popular religious attachment of particular cities or even provinces: these sects doubtless differed in their ritual and its accessories; and this might account for the prevalence at Ajaṇṭā and elsewhere of images of Buddha, both in the sanctuaries and on the façades, and for the entire absence of such symbols at Bhājā, in the older and middle series of about ten caves at Nāśik, and at Junnar. It has yet, I think, to be decided how far the former class of caves are subsequent to the latter, or how far they may be regarded as synchronous.

Other ornament is but sparingly found at Junnar, – partly perhaps because the façades of many of the caves have peeled off in the lapse of centuries: but all instances of its occurrence are noted in the following brief descriptions.

The Gaṇeśa Pahār group of caves is about three miles north-east of the town, and about 360 feet above it. The ascent is partly by a built stair, which leads up to the front of the Chaitya. This Chaitya faces due south, and measures inside 40 ft. in length by 22 ft. 5 in. wide and 24 ft. 2 in. high. It has a verandah 20 ft. 5 in. long by 4 ft. 2 in. wide, reached by about six steps, with two pillars and two demi-pillars in front, of the style so prevalent at Nāśik, – the capitals consisting of an abacus of three, four, or five thin square tile-shaped members, each projecting a little over the one below it. Under this is a deep member resembling an inverted water-jar. The shaft is octagonal, and the base is just the capital reversed. Over the abacus are figures of elephants roughly chiselled out, somewhat in the style of those in the Vihāra to the right of the Pāṇḍu Lenā Chaitya to be noticed below. The door is perfectly plain, 5 ft. 9 in. wide, and lofty, and is the only entrance for light to the cave; for the arched window is merely indicated as a slight recess, high up in the rock, – too high to have corresponded with the arch of the cave: but its carefully smoothed area shows that it was never intended to drive it through. Over the entrance is a well-cut inscription in one long line. (No. 1).[2]

The nave is about 12 ft. 9 in. wide, and 24 ft. 6½ in. up to the Dahgoba, limited on each side by five columns and one demi-column 10 ft. 10 in. high, similar to those in the front, and with lions or tigers and elephants over the capitals, fairly well cut. In the apse round the Dahgoba, about 3 ft. from it, are six plain octagon shafts 16½ in. in diameter without base or capital. The aisle behind the pillars is 3 ft. 6 in. wide, and is ribbed over, like the roof of the nave, in imitation of wooden ribs. The Dahgoba is of the usual form, a plain circular drum of base 8 ft. 9½ in. in diameter and 6 ft. 4½ in. high, with a Buddhist-rail cornice, supporting the *garbha* or dome on which stands the *torana* or capital, consisting of a square block, representing a box ornamented with the Buddhist-rail pattern, surmounted by an abacus of five thin slab-like members, each in succession wider than the one below, until the uppermost is 5 ft. 10 in. square, with a hole in the centre of it to support the shaft of a wooden umbrella,[3] as at Kārlā, and four shallow square ones for relies: for it was on this *torana,* as on an altar, that the relics of Buddha or the Bauddha saints were deposited for adoration. In some cases, as at Bhājā, the box under the capital of the tee was hollow, for the preservation of the relics. The whole height of this Dahgoba is 16 ft. 5 in.

The next cave east of this is a Vihāra,—the door-jambs now broken away. It has two windows, is 25 ft. wide by 29 deep, and 8 ft. 2 in. high, with a bench or seat 16 ft. 10 in. wide round the three inner sides. At the back are three cells, and at each side two, for the resident monks. In the cells are high stone benches for their beds: on these they spread their quilt and enjoyed their rest,—simple beds for simple livers. Their *shāḷa* or hall, which they doubtless regarded as spacious, is now used as a goat-shed. Over the left window is the inscription No. 2.[4]

The next cave is higher up in rock and is a small square one, with a stone bench-bed at the right end. The next, still to the east, is similar, about 8 ft. square, with a bench at the left end. The next again is similar, with a bench at the left end and one large cell at the back, also a small recess—probably for a water-vessel. In the wall is a square hole into the next cave, which is 13 ft. 8 in. deep at the left or west side, but at the other has a cell about 7 ft. by 6 inside, having a bed at the east end. In front of this is a verandah, with two pillars, supporting a projecting frieze carved with the Buddhist-rail pattern as in several of the caves at Nāśik.

Returning now to the Chaitya, and proceeding westwards, an ascending stair enters under the rock and comes out in the verandah of the largest Vihāra cave here,—now known as the Gaṇeśa Lenā, because this fine cave has been appropriated by some low Brāhmaṇ in which to enshrine an image of the pot-bellied, elephant-snouted Gaṇapati.[5] This personification of the misformed is named Ashṭ Vināyaka, as being, according to the *Gaṇeśa Purāṇa,* the eighth avatāra of this *deva,* performed here to please his mother, Girijā. He is a favourite idol of the populace, and is visited from far and near at the annual *jatrā* or fair held in his honour. The shrine is taken care of by a *panch* or committee, who pay the *gurū's* wages out of a yearly endowment of Rs. 62 per annum. The *gurū* goes there daily from Junnar.

The stair originally came up in front of the east end of the verandah: as it now stands, it is built, and closes the entrance to a cell or cistern partly under the Vihāra. The hall is 50 ft. 6 in. by 56 ft. 6 in., and 10 ft. 2 in. high, with three doors and two windows in front, and a stone seat round the three inner sides. It has seven cells on each side, and five at the back – the central one altered to make a shrine for the rat-riding god, whose large image is cut out of the rock, probably, from a Dahgoba that may originally have occupied this cell. It is smeared red, and the shrine is enclosed by wooden doors. Outside the cave is a verandah 7 ft. wide with six pillars and two demi ones, rising from a bench as in Cave III. at Nāśik, the back of this bench forming the upper part of a basement carved in the old Buddhist-rail pattern: this also resembles the general style of the Nāśik Cave just mentioned, in having animal figures over the capitals, but on the outside only, and in having a projecting frieze above, carved with rail pattern ornamentation.

Further west are two cells, noways peculiar; then a Vihāra without cells, the verandah of four columns totally gone except the bases. It had a door in the centre, another at the west end, and two windows, and measures 31 ft. 3 in. wide by 23 ft. 2 in. deep. The next is difficult of access, and of the plan of the most easterly cave, which is a very common type here.

Passing along a ledge of rock and over a small water-cistern, we come to the next, also a small Vihāra about 25 ft. wide, the front entirely gone, and with a cell at the left end and stone bed in it. Close to it is another similar to the most easterly one, – that is, a cell in the corner of a large one. Lower in the rock the next is like the last, and has a verandah with two pillars and a low screen in front, with a cistern outside at the east end.

The next is a rectangular flat-roofed Chaitya 21 ft. 10 in. deep by 12 ft. 9 in. wide and 13 ft. 8 in. high, with a Dahgoba

6 ft. 11 in. in diameter standing 3 ft. from the back wall. The cylinder is 5 ft. 7 in. high, including a base of 7 in. formed of three projecting annuli, and a cornice 12½ in. deep, of the Buddhist-rail pattern. The dome rises about 3 ft. 4 in., and the *torana* 2 ft. 4 in., and is 4 ft. 4 in. square at the top. This is connected with the roof by the stone shaft of the umbrella, for here, as in the case of several at Bhājā, the canopy of the umbrella is carved on the roof. To this cave there is a verandah 2 ft. 7 in. wide and 19 ft. 5 in. in length, which has had two pillars in front. On the left of the door outside is an inscription in two lines. (No. 3).[6]

Above this are—(1) a cell with a stone bed at the right side; (2) a small room enclosing a cell, after the common plan here; (3) another similar, but a horizontal flaw in the rock has opened the top of the inner cell and of the whole of the next cave; (4) a Vihāra, with two cells at the back, and a bench seat along each side, but the front wall is gone. Under the left front corner is a cistern, and outside is another; and (5) further along are three more cisterns. Over the first of these is an inscription in two lines (No. 4),[7] and over the second is one in three lines (No. 5), but the letters have a slant, and are not so neatly cut as most of the inscriptions here.[8]

We now come to a Vihāra 29 ft. 5 in. deep by 24 ft. 3 in. wide, the front wall much destroyed, but which was perforated by a door, and probably two windows. It has no cells, but has a stone bench round the three inner sides, and may have been a refectory or a school. Under the left corner is a well with abundance of cool water. Still westwards is a cell and cistern, then a small hall,—the front wall gone and without any cells; next, one or two more cisterns, beyond which the advance becomes more difficult, and leads to, or through, three more small caves, on the wall outside the last of which is an inscription in three lines (No. 6)[9] measuring about 2 ft. by 8 in., with the *Svastikā* to the right of it, and a curious trisular symbol at the commencement, which appears also in a modified form at the beginning of No. 2, and sometimes on other caves and on coins.

To the left of this is a recess, then two cells, and still further west are two or three others, which are almost inaccessible.

An avenue of trees said to have been planted by Amṛitrāo, the adopted son of Raghobā, runs from the Kukaḍī river to the foot of the hill in which these caves are, and which is said to be mentioned in the *Gaṇeśa Purāṇa* under the name of the Lehanādri: locally it is known as the Gaṇeśa Pahār or Sulaimān Pahār.

The Mānmodi Hill lies to the south-south-west of Junnar, about a mile west of the main road. Proceeding to the east face of the hill, I went up to the level of the most southerly group of caves. The first reached was a recess over a cell or cistern, the front fallen away; on the left side of the recess is an inscription (No. 7)[10] in one line. A little to the north of this, on the left side of a larger recess over the side of a cistern, is another inscription (No. 8)[11] in three lines, of which, however, the first letters are quite obliterated. Above a precipice to the north of this are—(1) a single cell, (2) a broken cistern, and then (3) seven cells in a line.

Returning from these and scrambling along the precipice to the south; we reach first a small Vihāra without cells, then another with two octagonal columns and two pilasters in front of the verandah, rising from a seat. The door is 5 ft. 10 in. wide and reaches to the roof of the hall, which has been frescoed. The verandah is about 2 ft. higher than the cave, and the back of the seat or low screen outside is carved with the rail ornament. The hall is 33 ft. deep and varies from 11 to 13 ft. wide, but at the back stands a mass of rock over 8 ft. wide by 5½ thick, with a squatting figure roughly sketched out on the front of it. This mass of rock is very rotten behind, and at the left side of it is a well of excellent water. The verandah is 4 ft. 7 in. wide and 19 ft. 10 in. long; the columns are of the usual Nāśik pattern but without animal figures above: over them the frieze projects considerably, and is carved in the style of Cave IV. at Nāśik,—the ends of the rafters projecting on the lower fascia, and the upper being carved with rail pattern. Over this is a recess some 2 or 3 feet deep with the Chaitya arch over it, but without any carving.

Lower down in the face of the cliff and somewhat to the north of this are some cells choked with prickly-pear and milk-bush. A few yards south of the larger cave above mentioned is a Vihāra with two pillars and pilasters in the verandah, and with three doors leading into as many cells. Still further on are one or two others almost inaccessible.

Returning from this point to the north and winding round the hill to the north-west side, we come upon another group of caves, the lower ones of easy access. Among them is an unfinished Chaitya the front of which is almost covered with inscriptions; but from their positions, and the circumstance that in most cases the surface of the rock has not been smoothed before cutting them, it may be inferred that they are only the work of visitors, and not the records of the original excavators. Three of them are given by Colonel Sykes, and others by Dr. Bird and Lieut. Brett. This Chaitya has a verandah with two columns of the Nāśik type in front, which support the entablature above the great window. Inside it is wholly unfinished: the aisles have not been commenced, for a great fault in the rock seems to have stopped operations. The capital of the Dahgoba is blocked out, and portions of a square mass from which to carve the dome. The floor is now much filled up with mud. The cave faces north by east.

At the east side of it is a cell, also deep in earth, in which is a Dahgoba, the *chhatri* or umbrella carved on the roof, but the staff has been broken,—evidently with a view to convert it into the usual Śaiva emblem. Beyond it are portions of other cells and a fragment of an inscription beside some modern steps leading up to five cells above those last mentioned. The two at the west end are converted into one by cutting away the partition. In the back wall of this apartment are two defaced figures of Buddha, and in the west wall a third sitting under foliage, with diminutive attendants or figures in the *parigara*. The *siñha* or lion is traceable on one or two of the *asanas* or seats, and a wooden framework seems to have been fitted to them, for there are holes in the stones for the wood to hold. This is now dedicated to the goddess Ambikā,—a name of Pārvatī indeed, but also the *śāsanadevī* or patron goddess of Neminātha, one of the favourite Tīrthaṅkaras of the Jains,—by whom she may have been borrowed from some Buddhist sect. Here we have Brāhmaṇs worshipping the mutilated images of Buddha as a Śaiva goddess! In the outer wall of the first of these cells there have been a standing and a sitting figure of Buddha, but these are now almost obliterated. They are the only figures of the kind I have met with in the caves here.

On the west of the Chaitya are some cells much choked up with earth, and with at least three inscriptions in them, and high up above these are a few more cells, but inaccessible. Further to the west is a cistern under a tree.

Two of the inscriptions (No. 9 an 10)[12] are in the cells on the right or west of the Chaitya; a third—one of those on the left side of the façade—is given by Dr. Bird as No. VI., but this copy is certainly wrong, at least in some of the letters.

Proceeding a considerable way round to the north-west on the slope of the hill, another unfinished Chaitya is reached, facing north-east by north, towards Junnar. This is the cave of which a very imperfect sketch by Professor Orlebar is given by Dr. Bird (plate XVI). The door is nearly the whole width of the cave; the lintel of it is broken; and the top of the aperture of the window is much lower than the arched roof of the cave. The great arch over it in the façade, however, is high, and over the window the space is divided fan-wise into seven petal-shaped compartments; in the upper or middle one is a female figure with a lotus-flower on each side; the compartments next to this have each an elephant standing on a lotus and holding up a water-jar, as frequently represented beside figures of Lakshmī or Śrī on old Vaishṇava temples. In the compartment behind each elephant stands a male figure, his hands over or in front of the head, doing *pujā* towards the central figure; and in the lowest or outer petals are two females in similar attitudes: beside each is a lotus flower and bud. Over and outside this the architrave or jamb of the great arch projects, and on each side of the finial of the arch is a figure (very unlike those n Professor Orlebar's sketch): that on the left holds a *chauri* and has wings, and some animal's head above his jaunty turban; the other holds some object in his right hand, and behind each shoulder are two snake-hoods with their tongues (?) hanging out. Right and left of these are Dahgobas in high relief but roughly formed. On the projecting frieze over all are seven Chaitya-window ornaments, with smaller ones between their finials; and two on the faces of the jambs. Inside the cave three octagonal pillars on the right side are blocked out, as is also the Dahgoba, but without the capital. There is a horizontal soft stratum in the rock, which has probably led to the work being relinquished in its present state.

Higher up the rock, on the east side of this, are four cells with neatly-carved façade, each door having a Chaitya-window arch over it, projecting about 15 in.; and between the arches are two Dahgobas with *chhatris* in half-relief, while over the shoulder of each arch is a smaller one as an ornament, and the Buddhist-rail ornament along the top. There is one plain cell west of these; and rather higher up on the east are four others. Under these latter is a Vihāra with two cells in the back and two in the left or east side, but the front is gone. It communicates by a passage with another to the west of it, nearly filled up with mud. West of the Chaitya are two small cells high up in the rock.

The Tuljā Lenā group of caves lies in a hill about a mile and a half or two miles west from Junnar, and are so named because one of them has been appropriated by the modern Brāhmaṇs to Tuljā Devī.

They face north-east, but all the façades have fallen away. Beginning from the south-east we come to (1) two sides of a cell; (2) a small Vihāra with two cells on the left side, two in the back, and one in the right side; and (3) a Chaitya of a form quite unique: it is circular, 25 ft. 6 in. across, with a Dahgoba 8 ft. 2 in. in diameter in the centre, surrounded by twelve plain octagonal shafts 11 ft. 4 in. high, supporting a lofty dome over the Dahgoba.[13] The outer aisle is arched over, from a wall line 9 ft. 1 in. from the floor, to the upper side of an architrave 7 or 8 in. deep over the pillars. The Dahgoba is plain, the cylinder being 4 ft. 4 in. high, but the capital has been hewn off to convert it into a *piṇḍa* of Śiva, and even the dome is much hacked. Before the last cave, this, and the next is a platform built by the modern votaries of Tuljā Devī. The next (4) is the back of a cell with a recess appropriated to Tuljā; then come the remains of three more cells, and a fourth on which is hung a wooden door, the cell being appropriated by the priest. The next is a plain cell, and beyond it the backs of two cells,—over the front of one of them are Chaitya-window ornaments and two or three figures; then two more plain fronts, and two with Chaitya-window heads over the doors, and smaller ones between, and the rail ornament, and quadrantal carved roll supported by slender brackets in entire relief, as at Bhājā. The last cave is a hall 23 feet wide, with one large cell at the left corner, and a seat round the three sides. In front of and considerably below the cells towards the north-west end is a tank with masonry walls on two sides. The rock is so cut away in front of the cells above, that it must have undermined the fronts of them, and aided in causing their destruction. Possibly this tank was originally a large cistern in the rock underneath the cells, and the pressure at the same time destroyed its roof and the front of the caves.

The Śivanerī hill fort lies to the west of the town, and going well along the east face of the hill towards the south, after visiting several cells in the lower scarp, we come to a cave which has had originally two columns and pilasters in front of a narrow verandah. The cave has a wide door, and inside is a large square cell with the cylindrical base of a Dahgoba—all coarsely hewn. Can the top have been of wood or other perishable or removable material? This cave faces E.N.E. On the sides of the scarp to the north of these excavations are several cisterns.

The side of the hill is peculiarly steep, and, owing to the slippery dry grass, it was ascended with difficulty. At the south end of the upper scarp a cave is reached, and in the north end of this cave is a stair leading to an upper floor. It has been a small hall, but the front is entirely gone except one pilaster at the south end. In the south wall is a small roughly hewn recess, and along the wall near the roof is an inscription (No. 11)[14] in one line of deeply incised letters, with a raised device at the commencement. The hall below this has three cells on each side and four at the back—several of them quite unfinished.

Further north and somewhat higher, beyond a recess and a cistern with two openings, is a Vihāra, the entire front of which is open, with a plain pilaster at each side having holes in them for the fastenings of the wooden front that has once screened the interior. There is a bench round the walls, and an advanced seat at the back as if for an image, or perhaps a *gurū* or teacher.

The cave has been occupied in more recent times, as evidenced by a mud wall inside. Next we come to some large cisterns of which the roof has fallen in, and over the north side of them is a large Vihāra with four cells at the back and two in the south end. In this case, again, there seems to have been originally only a wooden front; but for it has been substituted a stone one of ten courses of ashlar most carefully jointed; with a neatly carved door of the style of about the 10th century, and a well-wrought lattice stone window let into the wall. These were probably substituted by some Hindu sect not Bauddha. There is a fragment of an inscription at the north end, over a bench outside. North of this are some cells, much decayed, but which had probably all wooden fronts: holes in the rock seem to indicate this.

After a difficult and painful scramble from the last group, I reached the Bārā Koṭri group, so called from a large Vihāra with *twelve* cells. *First,* over a cistern broken in, is a Dahgoba in half-relief in front of a large cell with one stone bed, and having on the south side of the door a long inscription in five lines of varying length and in somewhat florid characters. Time did not permit my copying this, but, as the letters had all been painted, I doubt not it was copied by Dr. Bhāu Dājī's paṇḍit. *Next* come four cells, the last with a stone bed; *third,* three wells, with a small hall over the last, which once had two square pillars in front; it is reached by a stair-landing in the north end of the verandah. *Fourth,* the Bārā Koṭrī, 36 ft. 8 in. wide and 33 ft. 5 in. deep, with four cells on each side, and a bench round all four. It has two doors and two large windows, one of them measuring 9 ft. 10 in. width, with a groove in the sill for the wooden framework. Beyond this are several cells and a well, then a small Vihāra with three cells on the south side, and two at the back, with a Dahgoba in half-relief, in a recess—probably an older form than that in Cave III. at Nāśik.

The next is a fine cave; it is a lofty flat-roofed Chaitya. The front wall was probably originally pierced for two windows and the central door 6 ft. 1 in. wide, but the south window has been hewn down until it forms a door; inside the front wall is an outer cross aisle or vestibule 4 ft. 9 in. wide, separated from the inner hall by two octagonal pillars and two others just attached to the wall: these have the Nāśik or water-jar base and capitals, but the latter do not reach the cross beam above; from the capital rises a short square pillar about 2½ feet high reaching to the roof, which is perhaps 18 or 19 feet high. The inner hall is 30 ft.11 in. by 20 ft. 6 in., near the back of which stands a well-proportioned Dahgoba 10 ft. 3 in. in diameter, the cylindrical part 5 ft. 11 in. high, and surrounded on the upper margin by the rail pattern and with what are intended to represent the ends of bars projecting out below it. The umbrella is carved on the roof, and connected with the capital by a short shaft. The ceiling has been painted, and still retains large portions of the colouring: the design is in squares, each containing concentric circles in orange, brown, and white; but light was beginning to fail, and I could not be certain of the darker tints. Outside is an inscription in three lines (No. 12), first given by Colonel Sykes[15] in a not very accurate copy. Beyond this are some wells and fragments of cells.

After a four miles' walk and a steep climb the caves in a spur of a hill to the east of the Gaṇeśa Lena are reached, about 400 feet above Junnar. They face S.S.W. The Chaitya, the most easterly of the group, is a small one 8 ft. 3 in. wide inside and 22 ft. 4 in. in length, or about 15 ft. 4 in. from the door to the Dahgoba, which is 4 ft. 10 in. in diameter. The sides or jambs of the façade are carved with Chaitya-window ornaments, some having a Dahgoba inside, and others a lotus-flower, while the rail ornament is interspersed in the usual way. The face of the moulding round the window is also carved with a geometrical pattern. The walls are not straight, nor the floor level, and altogether the work seems to have been left unfinished, except perhaps the upper part of the Dahgoba, the cylinder of which is 4 ft. 10 in. high, and the total height 9 ft. 4 in. The aisle, which is never wanting in a finished Chaitya cave, has not been begun here. To the narrow ledge over the architrave of the walls is 16 ft., and to the roof 18 ft. 2 in. Next to this, but higher up and almost inaccessible, are two cells; then a well; an thirdly a small Vihāra with two windows and two cells at the back, one with a stone bed, and some rough cutting in the wall between the cell doors resembling a Dahgoba, but quite

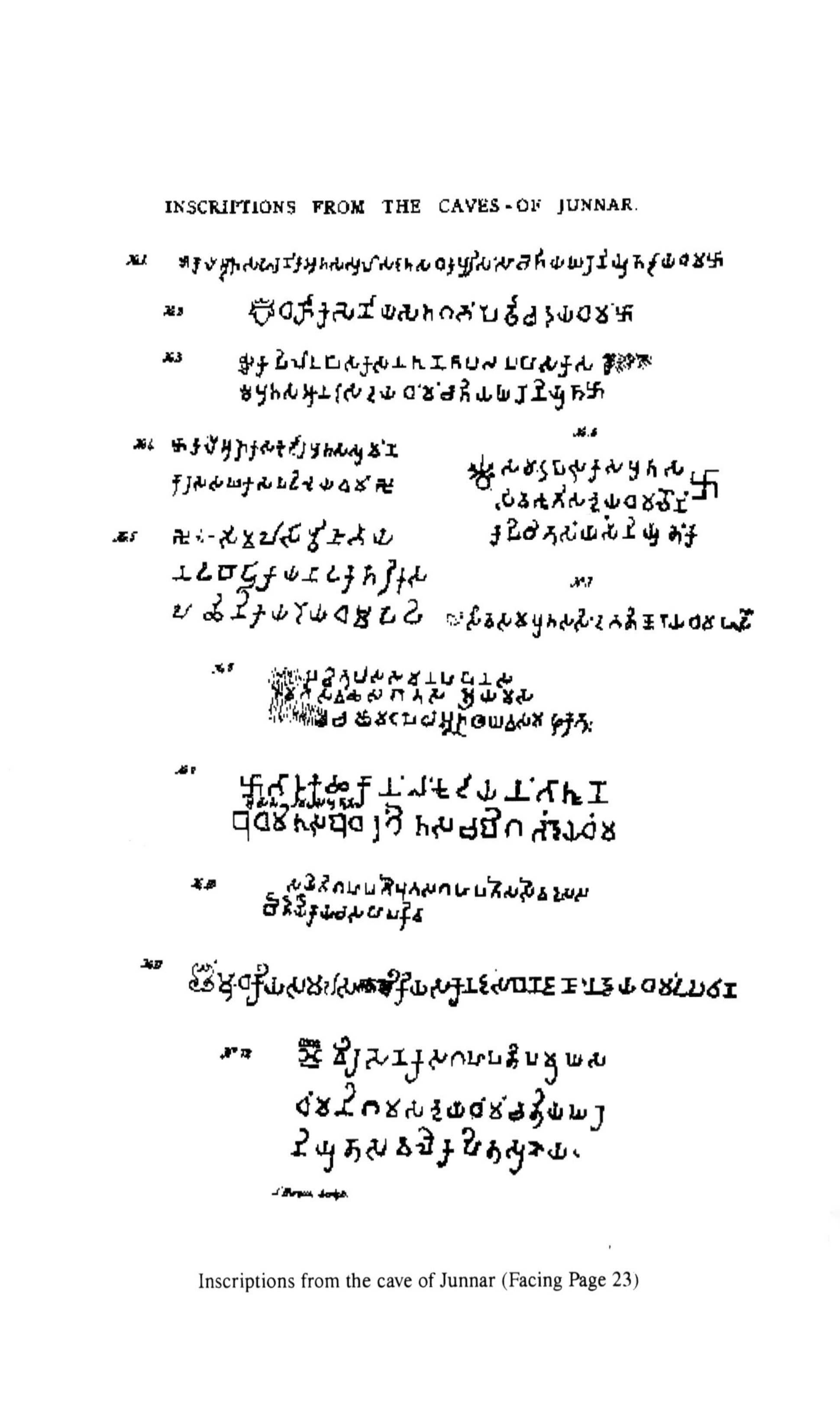

INSCRIPTIONS FROM THE CAVES OF JUNNAR.

Inscriptions from the cave of Junnar (Facing Page 23)

unfinished. It has also a cell with stone bed at the left side; outside are two more cells, and a chamber at the end of the verandah, which runs along the front both of the Vihāra and the cells. These caves, usually represented as inaccessible, from the precipice being almost perpendicular, are really difficult of access, and dangerous for any one not having a steady head or unaccustomed to climbing.

Prof. H. Kern, of Leiden, has translated a number of the inscriptions in a paper in the *Indische Studien,* XIVter Bd. S. 393–397, of which a translation is given in the next paper.

References

1. This *Memorandum* was originally prepared for Government and printed in November 1874, and is now revised for these pages. Previous to its appearance the only published accounts of the Junnar Caves were—a very short one by Dr. Bird in his *Jaina Researches,* derived from the notes of Professor Orlebar; one by Dr. J. Wilson in the *Jour. Bo. Br. R. As. Soc.* vol. III. pt. ii. (for January 1850) pp. 62-64, founded on memoranda communicated by Dr. Gibson; and that by Mr. W.F. Sinclair, C.S., in the *Indian Antiquary,* vol. II. (1874), p. 43ff. In the *Journal of the Royal Asiatic Society,* vol. IV. (1833) pp. 237-291, Colonel Sykes gave copies of a number of the inscriptions from these caves, but without any detailed account of the excavations. Dr. Stevenson attempted the translation of nearly the whole of the inscriptions from Junnar, from rough and inaccurate transcripts by Lieut Brett (*Jour. Bo. Br. R. As. Soc.* vol. V, pp. 160 *et se II*), but the result was very unsatisfactory. The translations in the following article by Dr. H. Kern will be read with interest.
2. In Dr. Bird's transcript (*Jaina Researches,* No. IX. pl. L) two letters are omitted, and others incorrectly copied: it is more correctly given by Colonel Sykes as No. 10 of his copies in the *Jour. R. As. Soc.* vol. IV. (1833), p. 290, also *Jour. As. Soc. Beng.* vol. VI. p. 1045. Conf. No. 2, *Jour. Bo. Br. R. As. Soc.* vol. V, p. 161.
3. Dr. Wilson, writing twenty-six years ago, says this Dahgoba was surmounted by an umbrella: but if so, this is not the only case among others in which the woodwork has recently disappeared from Buddhist caves of Western India. See *Jour. Bo. Br. R. As. Soc.* vol. III. pt. ii. p. 62.

4. This is No. 9 of those copied by Colonel Sykes; and p. 160: see also *Jour. As. Soc. Beng.* vol. VI. p. 1044, where Prinsep, 'correcting the second anomalous letter conjecturally,' reads it –

   "*Dhammika seṇīyaśata gabhaṁ uḍhī cha dayadhamaṁ,* which corresponds precisely with the Sanskṛit *dhārmmik-kaseniya satagarbhaṁ uḍhrīcha dayāḍharmaṁ* – 'The hundred caves and the tank of Dhārmika Senī – his act of piety and compassion.'" But for *uḍhī* we should surely read *paṭī*.

5. See *Notes on Junnar Tālukā* by W.F. Sinclair, Bo. C.S., *Indian Antiquary,* vol. II., p. 44.

6. No. 3 in Lieut. Brett's copies, *Jour. Bo. Br. R. As. Soc.* vol. p. 161.

7. This is No. 12 among Colonel Sykes's copies; No. 5 in *Jour. As. Soc. Beng.* vol. VI. p. 1046; and No. 4 of Lieut. Brett's, *Jour. Bo. Br. R. As., Soc.* vol. V., p. 161.

8. This is given by Colonel Sykes as No. 11 among his, and No. 5 among Lieut. Brett's copies.

9. This is No. 6 of Brett an Stevenson, *Jour. Bo. Br. R. As. Soc.* vol. V., p. 162; No. 13 in Colonel Sykes's copies; and No. 6 of those sent by him to Prinsep, who read it –

   Sāmaḍapasakasa putasa,

   Sivakukhīsa daya dhama dānam,

   Kapāvibhasa yase niyutakam.

   Sāmaḍapasaka putrasya Śivakukshikasya (?) dayādharmadānaṁ-kṛipāvibhasya yaśase niyuktakaṁ – 'The pious and charitable endowment of Śiva Kukhi (?), the son of Sāmarapasaka (?), redounding to the glory of this most compassionate person.' *Jour. As. Soc. Beng.* vol. VI, p. 1047.

10. No. 25 of Brett's, *Jour. Bo. Br. R. As. Soc.* vol. IV, p. 169.

11. No. 26 of Brett and Stevenson, *Jour. Bo. Br. R. As. Soc.* vol. V, p. 169.

12. Nos. 12 and 11 respectively of Brett and Stevenson, *Jour. Bo. Br. R. As. Soc.* vol. V, pp. 164, 165.

13. See Plan and Section of this cave, from the writer's drawings, in Fergusson's *History of Indian and Eastern Architecture* (1876), p. 167.

14. Not given among Lieut. Brett's transcripts, *Jour. Bo. Br. R. As. Soc.,* vol. V, pp. 160 *seqq.*

15. Conf. *ante,* p. 33, note 1 and *Jour. R. As. Soc.,* vol. IV, p. 289, No. 7; *Jour. As. Soc. Beng.* vol. VI., p. 1045, No. 3; and No. 7, *Jour. Bom. Br. R. Asiat. Soc.,* vol. V, p. 163.

5

Buddhist Symbol, &c.

E. Thomas

F.R.S., Correspondant De L'institut De France

I have lately availed myself of the opportunity of studying the collection of the Amarāvati Marbles, at present in the India Museum at South Kensington, with a view to determine the nature and bearing of the more popular symbols and devices appearing on these sculptures, so closely associated with the old homes of the Āndhras – in the hope of illustrating and explaining the parallel emblems on the series of coins, pertaining to proximate localities, recently under consideration.

My first impression, derived from a very cursory examination of these sculptures, led me to conclude, that whatever extraneous elements might have been introduced from time to time, that the Tope itself had been primarily devoted to the cause of solar worship. The dominant circular pattern indeed was obviously suggestive of such a purpose.

It need not be reiterated that the sun constituted one of the earliest objects of worship among primitive nations, as in the ordinary course it would present itself to the untutored mind, as *the* "natural selection." How many races of men intuitively adored the sun, or how many classes of the priesthood have taken "the light of the world" as the basis of their religion, it would be hard to say.

As the Greeks and Romans created many personifications of the sun-god, so the Indian Āryans recognised its leading representative deities by the various names of Śūrya, Savitṛi, Aditya and Vishṇu, besides assigning many of the attributes of the god of light in reduced gradations to several of the minor members of the Indian Olympus.

In India at large the prevalence, if not universality, in primeval times, of the worship of the sun is attested by the survival of generic names, the concurrent testimony of home tradition and inscriptions, the evidence of travellers, and the more material endorsement of sculpture.

We can roughly complete a goodly circle of geographical proof from the earliest Sauras of Saurāshṭra, by way of the Temple of the Sun at Multān, to Gayā and Orissa on the east coast, and back again to the written testimony of the Western copper-plates, and the caste-marks on the foreheads of the women in the oldest painting at Ajaṇtā.[1]

To revert of the symbols on the Amarāvati Tope.

The Wheel

The leading and most important device among the objects of worship is what it has hitherto been the custom in modern parlance, to designate as the "Buddhist wheel." To my apprehension these carvings were not designed to represent the "Wheel of the Law," or any such fanciful machine, but represent the conventional symbol of the sun, in the form of a wheel, as indicating his onward revolution. At times it is difficult to discriminate the sculptor's intention, as to whether he designed to make the wheel like the sun, or the sun like a wheel,[2] but one of the most striking examples of *the* presiding motive is afforded by the parallel figures at Bhilsa. In pl. xliii. Fig. 5, of Mr. Fergusson's work,[3] the wheel is ornamented on the outer edge of the felly with a succession of arrow points, reminding one at once of the "arrows of Apollo," or the blaze of the sun's rays,[4] an addition which, in the solid form, would have sadly impeded the roll of a mundane wheel. At Amarāvati these arrow-heads are replaced by a succession of tridents (pl. xcviii. fig. 7), and the multiplicity of the sub-divisions of the wheel itself are far more suggestive of the rays of the sun, than of useful wooden spokes. Again, in one instance of the examples of the various designs of wheels at Sanchi, we find the spokes converted into something very like flames of fire.[5]

The arrow points are still more marked and directly indicative of their purport in the numerous instances of the representations of suns on the coins, especially in the Ujjain series, whose mintage locality is determined by the insertion of the word *Ûjenini,* in Lāt characters. A large number of specimens of these pieces have been collected and figured in *Journal Asiatic Society, of Bengal,* vol. VII. plate lxi. These examples abound in the various symbols and enigmatical emblems of the sun, such as the local imagination delighted to associate with his various powers. The barbed arrow points, in these instances, start from the central wheel and project considerably beyond the felly.[6] In one case (No. 1) we have confirmatory evidence of the local reverence for the four-fold sun in the repetition of that number of smaller rings, within each of the four circles connected by the cross-lines of the standard *swastika* pattern.

We must now examine, on the other hand, what title the Buddhists can show to establish their claim to the worship of the wheel, as an essential part of their own system, except in so far as it was borrowed, in the way of an appropriation, from the earlier devisers and legitimate employers of the symbol.

A certain amount of confusion has been introduced into this enquiry by the fact that the *chakra* or 'wheel' was not only supposed to represent the sun or the wheel of the sun's chariot, but it had also a worldly significance of *'universal'* sovereignty, or the kingdom of the entire circle of the known world.[7] It is in this latter sense that Buddha himself is reported to have used the word, when he says "Bury me like a *Chakravartti Rāja*,"[8] that is as a "king," not as a saint: and, as he contemplated at the time, no worship of his mortal remains, so we may fairly infer that he did not anticipate the imaginary *wheel,* he merely claimed in virtue of his royal extraction, would be elevated into one of the symbols of the faith he taught.

Burnouf,[9] Foucaux,[10] and other early investigators were not very clear in their discrimination of the contrasted import of the term *chakra,* but later authorities altogether discard the claims of the legitimate Buddhists to any such piece of machinery as a sacred wheel.[11] Spence Hardy, while recognising the *Chakrawartti* as a universal emperor, has no such word as a "wheel" in his index.[12]

Mr. Beal, who was has consistently rejected any idea of the virtue of a wheel, as an aid to Buddhist faith, sums up the relative bearings of the question in the following emphatic terms: – "I proceed to make some reference to the scenes of the sculptures on the gates and beams at Sānchi. But before doing so, I would start the query, whether there is any proof to be gathered from the character of these sculptures, that the followers of Buddha *worshipped* either the Tree or Nāga? If they did, nothing in the world would more effectually destroy the theory of their religion. The Buddhist convert, theoretically at least, acknowledged no superior to himself in heaven or earth."[13]

M.E. Senart, who has more recently gone over the whole ground of Indian symbolical devices, in his *La Légende du Buddha,* expresses his conclusions and convictions in an equally positive way: "Quoiqu'il en puisse être, l'expression *chakraṁ pravartayituṁ* forme la partie fondamentale et vraiment significative dans notre formule. Tout nous interdit de séparer son emploi dans la légende du Buddha de son application, précédemment examinée, au Chakravartin. Dans la roue du Chakravartin nous avons sans peine reconnu le disque de Vishṇu et les images empruntées ā la roue solaire; la roue du Buddha n'a point ā l'origine d'autre sens; c'est en sa qualité de véritable Chakravartin que le Buddha la met en mouvement (*Ṛig Ved.* viii. 5, 8)."[14]

I quote M. Senart, in this instance, on account of his more comprehensive knowledge of Buddhism and Buddhist literature. I have ordinarily sought to form my own independent opinion from the Indian point of view, of questions before us.

Undue importance, I think, has been attributed in later arguments on the subject to the illustrative *label* attached to one of the scenes at Bārahāṭ; comprising the words *Bhagavato dharma chakam.* This definition of the purport of the sculpture would, undoubtedly, be of the highest importance, if we could only fix the period of its incision, or if we could pretend to determine how soon after the death of Śākya Muni, the first adaptation and appropriation of "wheel worship" was received into the Buddhist formula.[15]

If the Amarāvati Tope took anything like the three centuries to finish, which is claimed for its fellow mound at Sanchi,[16] there was room enough, in all conscience, for the growth and interchange of religious and their authorized symbols. Such an inference would, in a measure, account for the apparent variety of creeds depicted in the several groups of sculpture, and explain, in the plenitude of pilgrim's gifts of "rails and pillars," the reason for the slow progress of, what England irreverently calls, the preaching-up of a church steeple.

The 123 nominal rolls, mostly proclaiming small *danaṁs* or donations collected as a preliminary list in Genl. Cunningham's *Bhilsa Topes,*[17] sufficiently indicates the law of progress in this instance. But we have more direct and material evidence to this end, in the appropriation of a sculptured stone of ancient date by the Buddhists themselves, where they are seen to have taken advantage of the unadorned *back* of a slab of a much earlier period of art, with an original design of a tree and Vishṇu padas—to figure on the reverse in finer lines and more elaborate treatment, their conventional representation of the standing form of Śākya Muni.[18]

Vishṇu Padas

The hollowness of the Buddhist pretensions to the origination of this popular symbolic combination, was exposed some fifty years ago by a very competent judge, who examined the consistency of the faith from the point of view presented in extra-Gangetic or Siamese localities. Captain J. Low concludes his observations on the subject in these terms:—"To whatever country or people we may choose to assign the original invention of the *Phrabāt,* (foot of Buddha) it exhibits too many undoubted Hindu symbols to admit of our fixing its fabrication upon the worshippers of the latter Buddha; of whose positive dogmas it is rather subversive than otherwise, by encouraging polytheism."[19]

In somewhat the same sense, out latest commentator on these matters, Dr. Rājendralāla Mitra, freely admits that, "on the whole, the marks on the *Buddha-pad* bear a closer resemblance to Hindu than to Buddhist religion," and I am disposed to accept the authority of the inscription,[20] and to believe that the stone, though popularly called the foot of Buddha, was put up by the Hindus."[21]

In this instance, in short, the Buddhists merely acted, as other people, before and since, have had a tendency to do, *i.e.* to follow the sensible, if not inevitable, course of conciliating the local races by incorporating or assimilating the outward signs and symbols of a pre-existing faith.

We learn from the collection of Ujjain coins, arranged by Prinsep, above adverted to (*J.A.S. Beng*. vol. VII. pl. lxi), that in covering their dies with figures and forms, *dharanas* and *yantras,* the indigenous races admitted in combination many and various devices having reference to the manifest power of the *sun,* and that its emblems predominated in the general selection, if not to the exclusion, of conflicting symbols. We know what importance has been attached to caste marks in India, from the immemorial, we have seen that the *chinha* of the Jain Tīrthaṅkaras was of more consequence than the outline of the special statue itself;[22] and the question then arises, as to whether these various devices are not merely the discriminating sectarian emblems adopted from time to time, by sub-divisions of worshippers of a common object? This leads on to the consideration of the further query, as to whether all the four or five devices engraved on the soles of "the two feet" may not eminate from one and the same idea, and carry a like significance? The central wheel is many rayed and sun-like, the closeness of the spokes or rays seeming to indicate quick rotation. The *swastika*—here repeated over and over again, even unto its appearance on the toes—has already been noticed in its connection with the sun, the circle surmounted by the *triśūla* is found to be a near counterpart of the figure of *the* crude god, in the temple of Jagannāth.[23]

It forms a prominent object of devotion placed at the head of a cone, in very many of the sculptures at Amarāvati,[24] and it will be remembered that it proves to be identical in form with the ornaments which constitute the outside rays of the wheel of the sun in the same series, taking, in effect, the place of the more pronounced arrow-rays at Sānchi, but a stranger confirmation of its import and direct connexion with the sun is afforded by the so-called "Aṣoka railing," at Buddha Gayā,[25] where the lower compartment is devoted to the chariot and four horses of Sūrya himself, with his attendant archers;[26] while the upper storey of the edifice represents a covered niche or shrine in which the ball or circle with the superimposed *trisūla* object stands alone and undivided in its glory,[27] and seems to declare itself, as the direct crypto-emblem of the more definite embodiment of the god in the associate sculpture.

The fourth prominent symbol in the order of the general combination, of which there are two examples on each foot, consists of a diagram, which may be reduced into the simple alphabetical elements of र्व (*rva*) or a possible crypto वृ (*vṛi*). I fear that it would be useless at present to speculate on the meaning of the compound.

It may be the counterpart of a more Chinese-looking device, of a square pedestal or box, surmounted by a T, which figures on the leading class of Behat coins, and which General Cunningham pronounces – he does not say on what authority – to be "an emblem of the sun,"[28] a conclusion which is, to a certain extent, supported by the new evidence now adduced of the real import of the combination of the central sun and four surrounding tridents, which symbol is found occasionally to supply its place above the back of the deer.[29]

In the Assyrian system a nearly similar device constituted the ideograph of "le nom du dieu de l'onction royale," and at other times stood for the royal sign of Nebo,"[30] but it would be difficult to establish any direct connexion between the two. My own later impressions were that it was an early conventional type of the Sacred Tree, for which conclusion the appearance, in some instances, of a railing on the lower box seemed to give authority.[31]

Of the minor and subordinate devices which contribute to the filling-in of the general pattern, we may notice the insertion of four dots at the corners of the front *Swastika* near the toes, and the repetition of four flowers similar to those in the centre of the wheel towards the heels of the feet.

There are two examples of these full size ornamented patterns in the Amarāvati collection in the India Museum. The purely archaic *padas* seem to have been more simple in outline, and the ornamentation is confined to the central figure of a wheel.[32] Whereas in after times, we find the *Vaishṇavi*

Brahmans expanding the number of symbolic signs into nineteen, commencing with the half-moon, but ignoring the more potent sun, except under his typical device of the *Swastika.* The *Skanda Purāṇa* even omits the wheel[33] substituting, perhaps, the discus, but the former leading symbol is invariable in the majority of examples. The multiplication of figures on the sacred foot finally reached the extreme Siamese limit of "108, or more" objects of devotion. It is important to observe how these later adaptations of the normal outline invariably recognised the central wheel as denoting the sun, inasmuch as effect is given to the external flames in the revolving manner already noticed, so that we find Captain Low observing "according to some authorities the Hindū *chakara* was a circular mass of fire, instinct with life, darting forth flames on every side."[34]

The Horse

The coursers of Apollo find equine representatives in the mythology of the *Vedas,* but their number is, at times, increased to seven, and, at others reduced to a single steed, who is endued with many of the attributes of Sūrya himself.

"The bright red horse" avowedly symbolizes "the Sun,"[35] as in the Persian system "le soleil, souverain, coursier rapide, œil d'Ahura-Mazda; Mithra, chef des provinces," &c. embodied the same idea.[36] Professor Wilson remarks that "the hymns addressed to Dadhikrā or Dadhikrāvan, contemplate the sun under the type of a horse,[37] and Dr. Muir concurs in such an interpretation where Ushas (the Dawn) is said to bring the eye of the gods, and lead on the bright "and beautiful horse, by which the sun seems to be intended."[38] The late Prof. Goldstucker also, in commenting on the faculties of the Aświns, observed: "Their very name, it would seem, settles this point, since *aśva,* the horse, literally 'pervader,' is always the symbol of the luminous deities, especially of the sun"[39] In the *Purāṇas* "the sun in the form of a horse," is said to have appeared to Yājnavalkya, and the version of the *Vishṇu Purāṇa* goes on the state, "accordingly the sun imparted to him the texts of the *Yajus* called *Ayātayāma,* and because these were revealed by the sun, in the form of a horse, the Brāhmaṇs who study this portion of the *Yajus* are called Vājins (horses)."[40] The sacred horse is represented in the Amarāvati sculptures in various attitudes, but always guarded or over-shadowed by the conventional imperial *chhatra,* and ordinarily depicted as reverenced or worshipped by the bows and *salāms* of the surrounding attendants. In his free form, as issuing from gateways, in associate processions,[41] his mission might be taken to indicate the mere arrogance of an Aśwamedha sovereign. But when he is found to have special medallions or circular frames in the sculptures exclusively devoted to his representation, and those bosses are made to occupy the apparent place of honour, *above* the fellow-circles containing the seated figure of a saint,[42] it would seem that the intention of the artist pointed at higher things than the led-horse of an Indian Rāja. It is very possible, as has been suggested by Mr. Fergusson,[43] that the reverence of the horse was derived from the same aboriginal source, as that which has led the Gonds to retain his form in their crude worship to this day.

There is, however, one peculiarity in this re-appearance of the horse on southern soil, which has apparently escaped Mr. Fergusson. That is, that we find the animal so closely associated with the rites of the worship of the sun and the moon, as intuitively preserved among many sections of the aboriginal forest tribes.

Mr. Hislop[44] incidently alludes to "Bādu Dewa (the great god), who, in other districts, is called Budhāl Pen (the old god) * * * or Burā Pen," the chief god among the Khonds, who is identified in a note[45] with the sun-god. Some of the outside aboriginal races (the Kurs or Kuls) are described as having for the "chief objects of their adoration," the sun and the moon, "which take the outward form of wooden pillars, with horse, sun and moon set up before the houses of married people."[46]

This association of the two symbols may perhaps serve to explain the juxtaposition of the Wheel and the Horse's head in the Amarāvati sculptures, in plates xciii. and xcv. fig. 3, regarding which Mr. Fergusson remarks,[47] the horse "is introduced in mid air alongside the wheel as an object of equal reverence; and on a piece of sculpture where the wheel just above him is the especial object of worship."[48]

It is worthy of remark that the horse retained his fixed place as the symbol of the 3rd Jaina Tīrthaṅkara, and though recognised incidentally as a power in theology, he is altogether ignored in the different Paurānik lists amid the amplified nineteen authorized marks on Vishṇu's feet.[49]

P.S.—Since this note on the Horse symbol was written, General Cunningham's work in the Bārahāt Tope has been published in England.

In the new examples of old devices now contributed, it will be seen that the *Horse* takes an unusually prominent position, even to the addition of the Wings of the Pegasus of Western mythology. On the votive table, in front of the shrine of the Sun, in the lower compartment of the sculpture (Pl. xiii. *a*), may be traced the exact representation of the head of the Gond clay-horse, who was "offered in lieu of the living sacrifice," above adverted to.[50] And further, in the same dedicatory position may be traced votive flowers—pure and simple—together with clay reproductions of the symbols of the Sun under the various forms of lotus-leaves, wheels, and the marked coincidence of *Swastikas* enclosed in the simple orb circle of the aboriginal Sol.

References

1. Burgess, *Arch. Survey: Notes on Ajaṇṭa,* 1879, pls. viii, ix, x.
2. The earliest Chaldæan type of the sun was formed of a simple ring or circle, like the Indian *Sūrya-maṇḍala,* but it was speedily improved upon by the addition of crosslines within its circumference, and these again were superseded by ornamental double lines with a circular centre-boss. (Rawlinson's *Ancient Monarchies,* vol. I. p. 141). In this latter form it is figured at Bavian, in association with the half-moon and 7 planets (Layard, *Nineveh and Babylon,* 1853, p. 211). In Lajard's *Culte de Mithra* (Paris, 1847), endless varieties of the symbolic forms of the sun are collected, chiefly of more or less ornamental patterns, but in one instance (pl. xxxix. fig. 6), the sun is represented by a simple six-spoke wheel, with the worshipper in front and the half moon to the left on a similar pedestal.
3. Cunningham, *Bhilsa Topes,* pls. xxxi. 1, xxxii. 1.

4. The arrow heads are of two kinds, and are made to alternate from the rounded *cutting* point, depicted in Mr. Fergusson's Sanchi plate xxxvi, to the simple unbarbed point represented in the combats in plate xxxviii. See also arrows in the *Rig Veda,* v. i, xvi, Wilson. vol. IV. p. 26.

5. Fergusson, *Tree and Serp. Wor.,* pl. xliii. fig. 5. See also Genl. Cunningham, *Arch. Report,* vol. III, pl. xxx. B., and Col. J. Low, *Transactions Royal Asiatic Society,* vol. III. plate 3.

6. Nos. 2, 11, 16, 26, 30, &c.

7. *Dhammacahkkaṁ,* Dominion of the Law. The well known phrase *dhammachakkaṁ pavatteti* is usually rendered "to turn the wheel of the law," but that this was its original meaning I consider extremely improbable. *Pavatteti* does not mean "to turn" so much as "to set going," "to establish," &c. and *chakka* is probably used in its sense of "domain" or "dominion." It is most important to bear in mind that this famous phrase is used not of the whole period of Buddha's ministry, but *only of his first sermon* in which he "began" or "set on foot" his religion. Ajātasattu is reported to have said in reply to the priests about the contemplated general council: "It is well, venerable men, you may rely upon me, let mine be the domain of temporal authority, yours the domain of religion."—Childers' *Pali Dictionary,* 1875; *sub voce.*

8. *Journal Asiatic Soc. Bengal,* vol. VIII. p. 1005. Prinsep's *Essays,* vol. I. p. 167.

9. Burnouf, tom. II. pp. 308, 387-8, 416.

10. *Histoire de Bouddha Sakya Muni* (Paris, 1848) pp. lxii, 14 *n,* 103, &c. Le tresor de la roue divine apparaît dans la region orientale, avec mille rais, unc circonférence et un moyeu, toute d'or, non fabriquée par un charron, et de la hauteur de sept tālas (cap. iii. p. 15). Bābu Rājendralāla, in his translation of *Lalita-Vistara,* is decided in the opinion that "The Legend of the *Chakra ratna*" is no doubt an after-contrivance intended to adapt the title for a Bauddha prince," p. 28.

11. I conclude that no one has hitherto ventured to suggest the similitude of *Wheels of the Law,* to the hand-revolving Buddhist praying-cylinders, or to the larger water-power mills which call nature to aid in the performance of the religious rites of entire village communities, in making the prayer-inscribed drum, attached to the water wheel, speed their devotions to heaven. See General Cunningham's *Ladāk,* 1854, p. 375.

12. *Manual of Buddhism,* London, 1853, pp. 30, 126. See also *Eastern Monarchism* (1850), pp. 37, 82.

13. *J.R.A.S.,* (*N.S.*) vol. V. (1871) page 168. See also *The Travels of Fah-Hian,* (London, 1869) pp. 108, 127. Gen. Cunningham, in somewhat the same sense, remarks: "With respect to the title of this last work of Mr. Fergusson, *'Tree and Serpent Worship,'* I submit that it is not borne out by the illustrations; and further, that as serpent worship was antagonistic to Buddhism, such a title is not applicable to a description of the religious scenes sculptured on a Buddhist Stūpa." —*Archæological Reports,* (Simla, 1871), vol. I. page xxiv.

14. *Journal Asiatique,* 1875, vol. VI. p. 116.

15. Since this was written, my suspicions of the authenticity and good faith of these labels has been signally confirmed. The more important ones are, in many cases, obviously after-insertions, cut in at hazard in any vacant space available. Furnishing, indeed, a new proof of the cuckoo propensities of the Buddhists.

16. The author of the *Tabakāt-i-Nāśiri,* in adverting to the partial destruction of the Bhilsa Tope by Altamsh in A.H. 631, A.D. 1233, adds the information that it originally took 300 years to build, and stood at a height of 105 *gaj.*

The passage in the Persian text runs as follows (Calcutta Text, 1864, p. 176) :

وحصن وشهر بهیلسارا بگرفت وبتخانه که سیصد
سال بود تا آنرا عمارت می کردند و رفعت او بقدر صد
وپنج گز بوده خراب کرد

Major Raverty is inclined to consider that it was *the Temple* at Ujjain, that took 300 years to finish; but the text, under his own interpretation, does not sanction such an inference, even if the great elevation of the structure alluded to by the Muhammadan author, was not altogether opposed to the conclusion. *Translation of the Tabakāt-i Nāśiri* (1875), p. 621; see also Elliot's *Historians,* vol. II. p. 328.

While adverting to the Bhilsa Tope, I desire to advert to an opinion expressed by Mr. Hall of the solar indications associated with the name and the place:

"I have discovered that, in the middle ages, the sun was worshipped in Central India, under the designation of Bhāilla, —from *bha,* 'light,' and the Prakrit termination *illa,* denoting possession. There was a temple to Bhāilla at or near Bhilsa, which I take to be a corruption of bhāilla+isa, or bhāillesa." —Mr. Hall, *Vishṇu Purāṇa,* vol. II, p. 150. See also *Jour. Asiatic Soc. Bengal,* (1862), p. 112. The transcription of the name as *Bhaylesan, Mahābhalesvar,* &c. by Reinaud, quoting Albīrūnī, seems to support Mr. Hall's pronunciation. See Elliot's *Historians,* vol. I. p. 59.

17. *Bhilsa Topes,* London. 1854, —plates xvi, xvii, xviii, pp. 235, &c.

18. Fergusson, *Tree and Serp. Wor.,* p. lxxviii, figs. 2, 3, page 201; India Museum Slab, No. 56.

19. Captain J. Low, "On Buddha and the Phrabāt," *Transactions R.A.S.* vol. III. p. 64, (March 20th, 1830). See also *J.R.A.S.* (*N.S.*) vol. IX. pp. 65 and 163.

20. Sanskṛit Inscription, dated 1230 Śaka.

21. *Buddha Gayā* (1878), p. 127.

22. "The Babylonians are remarkable for the extent to which they affected symbolism in religion. In the first place, they attached to each god a special mystic number, which was used as his emblem, and may even stand for his name on an inscription.

"Further, each god seems to have had one or more emblematic signs by which he could be pictorial symbolized. The cylinders are full of such forms, which are often crowded into every vacant space where room could be found for them." —Rawlinson's *Ancient Monarchies,* vol. III. p. 467.

23. Gen. Cunningham *Bhilsa Topes,* p. 358; *J.R.A.S.* vol. VI. p. 450.

24. Fergusson, *T. and S.W.,* plates lxvii. to lxxii. page 192; *Bhilsa Topes,* pl. xxxii. figs. 4, 5, 10.

25. Rājendralāla Mitra, *Buddha Gayā,* (Calcutta, 1878), pl. 1, p. 160. I am bound to add to my interpretation of these sculptures, that the Bābū does not see anything "solar" in the leading figure in the chariot, p. 162. He does not seem to have taken any notice of the upper compartment. *J.R.A.S.* (*N.S.*) vol. III, p. 161.

26. The archers appear to be females. The bows are of the same form as those on our coins.

27. Genl. Cunningham in Vol. III. of his *Archæological Report* (1871-2) pl. xxvii, has given an engraving of the lower portion of this column. He does not however seem to have noticed the important bearing of the details of the upper portion of the pillar, p. 97. See also Kittoe, *J.A.S. Bengal,* vol. XVI. (1847), p. 337.

28. *Bhilsa Topes,* p. 354.

29. *Journal Asiatic Soc. Bengal,* vol. VII. pl. xxxii. fig. 6; and *Bhilsa Topes,* pl. xxxi. fig. 10.

30. Ménant, *Noms propres Assyriens,* p. 22.

31. *J.R.A.S.* (*N.S.*) vol. I, p. 481.

32. Fergusson, *T. and S.W.,* pl. lxxviii. fig. 2, India Museum, No. 56.

33. Rājendralāla Mitra, *Buddha Gayā,* p. 126.

34. *Transactions R.A.S.* vol. III. p. 72. The quotation is from Wilkins's *Bhagavat.* A Dallastype photograph of a very elaborate copy of the foot-print of Buddha, near Nopphbury in Siam, was published by Messrs. Trübner some time ago in their *Record.* This drawing shows the Central Sun with great distinctness. The external flames are made to curve, as in Col. Low's example, as if to indicate the rotatory motion of the luminary.

35. Max Müller's *"The Sacred Hymns of the Brahmans,"* London, 1869, p. 9, *R.V.* i. 6, 1.

36. Burnouf *Yaçna,* p. 351. The Massagetæ "worship the sun only of all the gods, and sacrifice horses to him; and this is the reason of this custom; they think it right to offer the swiftest of all animals to the swiftest of all gods." Herodotus I. 216. Compare Wilson, *Rig Veda* Vol. II. pp. 112, 121 and preface p. xii, et. seg.; Wilson's *Collected Works,* vol. IV. pp. ii. 353; and Burgess' *Arch. Reports,* vol. II. (1874-5), p. 37.

37. *Rig Veda,* vol. III. pp. x. 119.

38. *Sanskrit Texts,* vol. V. p. 157. See also *J.R.A.S.* (*N.S.*) vol. II. p. 5.

39. *Journal R.A.S.* (*N.S.*) vol. II. p. 15. and vol. IX, p. 228.

40. *Vishnu Purāṇa,* Hall's edition, vol. III. p. 57.

41. *Tree and Serpent Worship,* Pl. xxxv. p. 135; xcvi. fig. 3; xcviii; and p. 223.

42. Pls. lxxxi., lxxxii.

43. Page 203.

44. *Aboriginal Tribes of the Central Provinces.* Edited by Sir R. Temple.

45. P. 14, note †; *Calcutta Review,* vol. V. p. 55; and *Church Mission Intelligencer.*

46. P. 26, quoted Mr. Bullock.

47. *Tree and Serpent Worship,* p. 215.

48. Mr. Hislop observes, in a Note at p. 26 – "The Scythian origin of Kūrs and Gonds might perhaps be inferred from Kodo Pen and earthen horses, which are offered instead of living sacrifice."

49. Rajendralāla Mitra's *Buddha Gayā,* p. 126.

50. Note 48 above.

6

Chaityas

Narayan Aiyangar, *Shimoga*

In Bauddha works, their temples are called *Chaityas,*[1] and one of the Buddhist precepts is *Chaityam vandeta svargakāmaḥ,* i.e. he who longs for Svarga should worship the dāgaba of Buddha. No Brahmaṇical temple is called *Chaitya.* The word occurs in many places in the *Rāmāyaṇa;* and the commentators Mahêśatīrtha and Govindarāja differ as to the meaning to be attached to it, construing it in some places as *Buddhāyatana.* If this meaning is correct, it is conclusive regarding the post-Buddhist origin of the *Rāmāyaṇa.* It seems therefore necessary to examine the places in which the word occurs, to see if it anywhere really does mean a Baudda temple.

1. In II, 3, 18, Daśaratha in order to celebrate Rāma's installation orders food with *dakshiṇā* to be ready in *devāyatanas* and *chaityas.* Here the latter word has been constructed as *chatushpathas.*
2. In II, 25, 4, seeing that Rāma has decided upon going to the forest his mother blesses him, "May those (*gods*) whom you, my son, salute (*praṇamase*) in *āyatanas* and *chaityas* protect you in the forest."
3. In II, 50, 8, Rāma, on his way to the forest passed the Kosala country (Kosalān) which was studded with *chaityas* and *yūpas* (*chaitgayūpasamāvṛitan*). Here *chaitya* has been rendered as *devāyatana.*
4. In II, 71, when Bharata is brought back from his uncle's country to Ayodhya on the death of the king, he finds the *devāgāras* empty, worship not performed, in them, and that the birds (that had built their nests) in *devatāyatanas* and *chaityas* were not lively.

5. In II, 100, on seeing Bharata at Chitrakūṭa, Rāma puts to him many questions: śloka 43 says "Is the country (*under your rule*) full of hundreds of *chaityas, —chaityaśatair jushṭaḥ*) ?" The commentator says that in some copies *chityaśataih* occurs instead of *chaityaśataih,* and that in either case the word denotes the places where the *chayana* ceremony was performed at the completion of the aśvamedha-sacrifice, &c. (*aśvamedhāntamahāyajñachayana-pradeśasamūhāḥ*).

6. In V. 12, 14, Hanumat searched for Sīta in houses and *chaitya* houses (*chaityagṛihas*). Maheśatīrtha construes them as *Buddhāyatanāni,* but Govindarāja takes them to be the halls (*maṇḍapas*) at *chatushpathas.*

7. Śloka 17 also says all roads and *vedikāś chaityasamśrayāḥ* were searched. Maheśa says *chatushpathavartivṛikshādhārabhūtavedikāḥ,* Govindarāja says—*chaityavṛikshamūlapīṭhikābandhāh.*

8. In V, 15, Hanumat saw in the Aśoka forest a *chaityaprāsāda,* which had one thousand pillars and was very high. Here both the commentators take it to mean a building like a *Buddhamaṇḍira;* but the word again occurs in V. 39, where Govindarāja takes it to be a building like a *Devāyatana.*

9. In V. 22, 29 Rāvaṇa, though wearing ornaments, is described to be fearful like the *chaityas* of the burning ground,—*śmaśānachaityapratimo bhūshitopi bhayaṅkarah.*

10. The word also occurs in the *Mahābhārata.* When Bhīshma had charge of the government, the country was full of Chaityas and Yūpas—"*chaityayūpaśatāṅkitah,*" I, 109, 13. The same is stated as the case when Suhotra reigned, I, 94, 29. (I. cal. 223).

11. In the *Āraṇyaparva,* Adḥ. 12, where Arjuna reminds Kṛishṇa of his divine nature and of the several heroic deeds done by him, śloka 35 says :—

"O Achyuta, when you were seated in the middle of the *chaitya* shining with your lustre, the Ṛishis came and solicited your protection."

The word *chaitya* is derived from the root *chiñ chayane,* to collect, and the commentary on Amara called[2] the *Gurubālaprabodhika* says that it denotes a building, because it is the result of the collection or putting together of stones, &c. *chīyate pāshāṇādinā chaityam.* But it will be seen that in some of the above quotations the word is used in close connection with *yūpa,* the sacrificial post. The ceremony performed at the end of the great sacrifices is called *chayana*, i.e., the collection[3] of the sacred ashes and other relics and the grouping them into the form of a tortoise, or of the bird Garutmat as in the sacrifice called *Garuḍachayana; chita* being the sacred things thus collected, it appears that the building constructed to preserve them for the purpose of worship was called *chaitya* or *chaityā.* This place of worship, from its connection with Vedic rites, is probably of older date than the *devāyatanas.* The quotation No. 11 above shows that it was also used as a place of congregation, as our temples are where religious and caste subjects are discussed.

It is therefore clear that the *Rāmāyaṇa* alludes to the Brāhmaṇical and not to the Bauddha Chaitya. The commentators are not consistent in saying that *chaitya* means a Brāhmaṇical building when it is mentioned in connection with Rāma and his country, and a Buddhist building when mentioned in connection with the enemy's country, forgetting that Vālmīki has peopled Lankā with vedic students and sacrifices, without ever mentioning the Buddhists.

No. 7 mentions *chaitya* trees, so called probably because instead of constructing a building it was also the custom to plant trees with revetment round their stems, where the *chayana* ceremony was performed. In course of time, however, all revetted trees began to be called *chaitya* trees; and to such trees, which are generally found in all villages, Kālidāsa evidently alludes when describing the Dasārṇa country in his *Meghadūta.* Mallināthа quotes Viśva: *chaityam āyatane Buddhavandye choddeśapādape.*

The ceremony performed after the burning of dead bodies is *saṁ-chayana,* in which, after collecting the bones, a portion of the ashes is grouped into a human form, and *baśāli* or food offered to it. I take the *śmaśāna-chaitya,* alluded to in 9. to be a monumental building erected on such spot in memory of departed kings and other great personages.

It may therefore be presumed that in accordance with custom a *chaitya* was built in memory of Buddha, and that his disciples began to worship and multiply it by taking his funeral relics to different parts of the country, while the sacrificial *chaityas* of the Brāhmaṇs became scarce owing to the opposition made by the themselves having prohibited the asvamedha for the Kaliyuga.

It will be seen that the *Rāmāyaṇa* mentions temples and idolatry; but these seem to be of old date in India, though not so very prevalent as at present. Stenzler's *Gautaṁa Sūtra* 9, 66, prescribes the going round of *Devāyatana. Gṛiha-dévatās* or household gods are mentioned in 5, 13.

References

1. Properly speaking it is not the temple (*Chaityagṛiha*) but the dāgaba inside it that is called a Chaitya. In a secondary sense it is used by Jainas and Buddhists, however, to denote a temple containing a *Chaitya;* and is also applied in Buddhist books to a sacred tree as well as to a *stūpa.* –ED.
2. Hence it is closely connected in meaning with stūpa. Chaityas were known before Buddha's time (see *J. As. Soc. Beng.*, vol. VII, p. 1001), conf. Alwis, *Buddhism,* pp. 22, 23. –ED.
3. I give this description from report and cannot vouch for its correctness, though I feel sure that originally *chaitya* was connected with the Brāhmaṇical sacrifice.

7

Remarks on the Bharhut Sculptures and Inscriptions

S. Beal

To the Editor of the Indian Antiquary

Sir, – I have been much interested in the papers which Dr. Hoernle has lately contributed to the *Indian Antiquary,* and in none more than that which appears at pp. 324f of vol. X; the subject being "Readings from the Arian Pāli."

In that paper the phrase *yathiṁ aropayato* – "putting up his staff" – occurs; and Dr. Hoernle in his text invites attention to this phrase.

I think I can throw some light upon it by translating a portion of the *Vinaya Piṭaka* of the Mahāsañghika school of Buddhism, which relates to the erection of Stūpas, and providing the accessories thereof. The passage occurs in the 33rd Kiouen of the Mahāsañghika copy of the *Vinaya,* and the 15th page. The subject is "Laws respecting (the erection of) Stūpas." The passage runs thus : –

"Buddha was travelling to and fro in the Kosala country. At this time there was a Brahman ploughing his land; seeing the Lord of the world, he went in advance of him, and fixing his ox-goad staff in the ground, he fell down and paid him reverence.

The Lord having witnessed this, smiled gently, on which the Bhikshus asked Buddha the occasion of his smile[1]; "Oh ! that we might hear the reason of it," they said.

On this Buddha addressed the Bhikshus thus –

"This Brahman indeed is now worshipping two Buddhas."

The Bhikshus then asked Buddha who the two Buddhas were.

Buddha replied: "He worships me and under-neath his staff is a Stūpa belonging to Kasyapa Buddha, which he also worships."

The Bhikshus answered: "Ah! that we might be allowed to see the Stūpa of Kasyapa."

Buddha rejoined: "Request this Brahman to give you a clod of the earth (where his staff is erected)."

They did so, and having received the clod, the Lord caused to appear from the earth a seven-jewelled Stūpa of Kasyapa, in height one *yojana,* and in breadth half a *yojana.*

The Brahman having seen this Stūpa, immediately spoke to Buddha thus: Lord! my family name is Kasyapa, this then is my Stūpa (erected in honour) of Kasyapa.

Thus then the Lord in that place where the staff was put caused to be seen the dāgaba of Kasyapa.

The Bhikshus then asked – "Shall we accept this clod of earth (as a token of the Brahman's religious merit)?"

Buddha said – "Accept it!" and then he added this verse: –

"A hundred thousand fold of gold
Given in charity
Is not equal to a clod of earth
Given reverently in honour of a Tower of Buddha."

Then the Buddha himself erected (or, himself caused to appear) a Stūpa of Kasyapa Buddha, its foundation four-square, surrounded by an ornamented railing, in the middle of it a four-cornered double-staged plinth, above which rose a lofty staff with a circular ball (or, with circled rings).

Then Buddha said: "Let all Stūpas be fashioned in this way. This is the model of the old Towers of the ancient Buddhas," &c.

Then the Bhikshus said: "And may we now pay reverence to this Stūpa?"

Buddha replied in the affirmative, and added this *gātha*: –

"Though men used a 100,000 gold pieces
In charitable gifts,

This would not equal the true heart
Reverencing a Tower of Buddha."

After this follows an account of the accessories of a Stūpa, niches, lakes, railings, &c.

It would seem then that fixing the staff would be synonymous with "cutting the first sod" for the erection of a Stūpa.

I add a translation from the Chinese author I-tsing relating to Buddhist worship and other matters in India in the 7th century of our era: this may perhaps throw some light on archæological discoveries now being brought to light: –

"The land of China," he says, "from ancient times, according to traditional teaching, has only known the worship of Buddha by setting forth his names. But in the Western countries the Chaityas which stand by the roadside are reverenced (*chāityavanda*). And every afternoon or evening the assembly coming from the gates (by the convent) three times circumambulate the Stūpas with incense and flowers; and then sitting down cross-legged, they caused some skilled brother to accompany himself with music as he sings with clear voice the praises of the Great Master; and for this purpose they have hymns consisting of ten or even twenty ślokas. They then return to the temple, and having taken their seats in the usual place, they cause a preacher to mount the pulpit (lion-seat), and there to read through some short sermon (*sūtra*). The pulpit is not far from the chief Sthavira's seat, and is not so high or so large. In reading the *sūtra* (or whilst reading) they generally recite (sing) from the Saṅgita (or, *threefold collection*)[2] (*San-k'he*) which Aśvaghosha Ayusmat compiled, selecting ten ślokas or so, and as they catch the meaning of what is read, they recite the hymn of praise[3] to the three honoured names; (the preacher then) sets forth the place where the several passages occur in the true *Sūtra* spoken by Ananda.[4] The hymn or psalm being ended, they then select ten other ślokas to recite whilst they perform the usual votive procession (round the apse[5] [*hwui hiang*]). This is also composed in three parts or sections, and hence it is called *San-k'he*. All this being ended, the congregation says "*Svasti*" (Be it even so) [Amen]; this is a very favourite or choice exclamation of assent used during the recitation of the Scriptures. They also say "*Vatthu,*" which is the same as "It is well" (*saddhu*). The preacher after this descends (from his pulpit). The president then first rises and bows to the lion-throne (the pulpit), (in token of) the preparatory instruction (or the service) being finished, and afterwards he bows to the holy assembly, and then returns to his place. The second priest then bows to the two places (viz., the pulpit and the assembly), and then salutes the president, and then resumes his seat. The third priest then does likewise, and so on to the end of the assembled priests. If the number of priests is very great, then three or five, as they think proper, rise at the same time and salute as before. This done, they depart.

"This is the rule of the priesthood throughout the holy land of the East from Tamralipti to Nālanda. In the latter monastery the number of priests and disciples is so great, amounting to about five thousand, that such an assembly in one place would be difficult. This great temple has eight halls, each able to hold about three hundred at a time; in these the various congregations are assembled. The rules here are (in consequence of the numbers) somewhat different from other places. They select one singing-master (precentor), who, every evening towards sundown, goes through the various halls where the priests are assembled accompanied by a *pure brother*[6] a young man [acolyte], who precedes him, holding flowers and incense; and as they pass through the assemblies the members of the congregation bow down, and at each how with a loud voice they chant a hymn of three ślokas or five, with the sound of drums and music. At sundown, when all is just over, the precentor receives from the temple property a certain allowance as an offering (offertory), after which he again takes his place opposite an incense heap (a large censer), and singly recites with his heart (or heartily) a hymn of praise; and thus until nightfall, when after the congregation have given three complete prostrations, the assembly is broken up. This is the traditional custom of worship in the West. The old and sick occupy small seats apart.

"There were some ancient practices not exactly the same as the present Indian customs; such, for instance, as the custom of chanting a hymn when at the time of worship the distinctive marks of Buddha were recited; this was a grand chant of ten or twenty ślokas; this was the rule. Again, the "Gāthas of the Tathāgatas" and others were originally intended to be laudatory hymns in praise of the virtues of Buddha, and were in long or short verses arranged harmoniously. And because the meaning of these verses was difficult to be got at, it became customary during the religious seasons, when the congregation was assembled in the evening, to call on some distinguished member to recite 150 to 400 stanzas in praise of Buddha (and explain them) with other hymns.

"There have been certain leading men of great talent who have contributed hymns of praise for use in the worship of Buddha—such as the venerable Mātrijāta, a man of great talent. Of him it is said that his birth was predicted by Buddha when a certain parrot saluted him as he passed through a grove. Having become a convert, he first composed 400 laudatory verses and afterwards 150, arranged to the six paramitas, illustrating the most excellent qualities of the world-honoured Buddha.,

"Other hymns were composed by the Bodhisatwa Asańgha, others by Vasubandha. All who enter the ministry are supposed to learn these beforehand, whether they belong to the Great or Little Vehicle. There are also the hymns composed by Channa Bodhisatwa, by Sakyadêva of the Deer Park, and also by Nāgārjuna, who composed the work called *Sukrita.* This he left to his old patron, the king of a great southern kingdom called Sadvaha.

"We cannot pass over the special notice of the *Jātakamālā,* which is also a book of this sort. If translated it would make about ten chapters in Chinese. The origin of the book was this: Śilāditya[7] Rāja was extremely fond of literature, and on one occasion issued an order that all the chief men of the kingdom who loved poetry should assemble the next day morning at the palace, and each bring a verse on paper. In consequence five hundred assembled, and on their papers being opened the verses were put together, and this is the *Jātakamālā.*[8] Of all books of poetry known in India, this is the most refined. This islands of the Southern Sea and the ten countries all use these verses, but in China they have not yet been translated.

"Again, the venerable Aśvaghosha composed a book chants, and also the *Alaṁkāra Śāstra,* and also the Life of Buddha in verse. The whole book if translated might be included in about ten volumes. It describes the life of Tathāgata from the period of his birth in the palace, to his death between the trees. This is used also throughout India and in the Southern Sea."

With reference to Dr. Hoernle's papers (vol. X, pp. 118f, 255f) the Rev. Mr. Beal remarks that if one 'read carefully any of the many lives of Buddha he will see that "the two persons who stand by the side of the tree, and whom bad perspective has apparently placed in the air" (p. 256) are Dêvas worshipping the Tree, (or Buddha *symbolized* by the Tree) in common with the human beings below. It seems to escape the memory of many persons that Buddha was the Saviour of gods as well as men. Then, they are not "eating the berries of the Tree," but whistling with the thumb and first finger in harmony with the celestial choir. This whistling with the thumb and finger is repeatedly mentioned as a mode of praise in the Lives of Buddha (e.g. in the *Romantic Legend*).

'Then when Dr. Hoernle speaks of the Dêvas scattering the berries of the tree from baskets, (p. 256, n. 3), he overlooks the constant assertion that Suddhavara and other Dêvas poured down sandal-wood dust and other perfumes on the seat where Buddha attained wisdom (*Rom. Leg.* pp. 67, 225, 227). The ornaments or ornamental marks on the thrones in all the plates of the *Bharhut Stūpa* represent the flowers and perfumes rained down from heaven.

'Then again (p. 256), he speaks of "two persons" knocking off berries with their scarves; but they are only waving them in the air, as we might wave our handkerchiefs in token of joy or triumph. In the *Sutta Nipāta* by Fausböll (*Sacred Books,* vol. X, p. 125, § 679, 680) is an expression which illustrates this waving of their garments by the Dêvas.

'I have no doubt too that the Erāpato Nāgarāja plates (p. 258, No. 16) refer to the legend of Elāpatra and the two Nāgnīs, as I have given it in the *Romantic Legend* (p. 277), and it occurs in nearly the same form in the *Vinayapiṭaka*.' –

(*From a private letter*).

References

1. The gentle or subdued smile of Buddha is supposed to be predictive of some event; vide *Romantic Legend,* p. 12n.
2. This expression is afterwards explained to refer to the three *sections* or *divisions* of the compilation which Aśvaghosha made. It may have been in the form of a *triptych.*
3. Probably the *Saraṇāgamana,* or "glorious hymn," as Buddhaghosha terms it, in honour of the Buddha, the Law, and the Church. *Vide* Childers, *J. R. As. Soc.,* (*N.S.*) vol. IV, p. 325.
4. So at least I understand the expression *Fo-ts'in.*
5. The Chinese expression *hwui-hiang* exactly corresponds to the Greek ἄψ or ἄψ ἴενατ . The last portion of the Buddhist ritual in worship consists of the processional circuit round the spot where, in old times, the *dāgaba* or relic shrine stood, viz., in the chord of the apse. I am not suggesting that the word *apse* is derived from ἄψ , but simply pointing out the coincidence.
6. A similar expression is used by *Fā-hien* (cap. 3). The Essenes also had *pure brothers* to wait on them.
7. Śilāditya dies 550 A.D. Julien's *Mém. sur les Cont. Occid.* tom. I, p. 215.
8. This may be the copy of the *Jātakamālā* alluded to lately by Dr. Frankfürter (I think) in the *Athenœum.*

8

Notice of a Buddhist Tope in the Piṭṭāpur Zamindari

Sir Walter Elliot, *K.C.S.I.*

The recent discovery of the Stūpa at Jaggayyapêṭa, the inscriptions from which were described in the *Indian Antiquary* vol. XI, p. 156, furnishes another proof of the hold taken by the Buddhist faith in the Doab of the Kṛishṇā and Godāvarī. I desire now to place on record a similar example which fell under my observation some years ago, but which might otherwise come to be overlooked.

In 1848 the late Sir Henry Montgomery, who had been employed on special duty five years before in Rajahmundry, having told me that some curious relics had been found near Piṭṭāpur by the Zamindar, I at once applied through the Collector for information about them. In reply Mr. Forbes sent me a report by the native head of police, from which I gathered the following particulars: – In the beginning of 1848 Rāja Veṅkaṭa Sūryarāu, Zamindār of Piṭṭāpur, having occasion for some bricks in a work he was then constructing, directed them to be taken from a ruined structure near the village of Timavaram. In the course of the excavation the workmen discovered five stone vessels with covers of the same material each containing a small crystal box or casket. The latter contained each a splinter of precious stone (ruby, emerald, &c.), a small pearl, a bit of coral and a piece of gold leaf. An inventory was made of the whole, and they were sent to the Zilla Court, in conformity with the regulations for Treasure Trove. On the expiry of the prescribed period of six months they were claimed by the Rāja, who at my request presented them to the Madras Literary Society, from which they were afterwards transferred to the Government Central Museum. I intended to have published a notice of this transaction in the *Journal of the Literary Society,* and caused a lithograph to be prepared for the purpose, but having been sent to the Northern Sarkārs on special duty, where I remained five years, the matter was overlooked and the management of the *Journal,* which had been under my care, passed into other hands. The consequence was that the illustration appeared in the next number, where it stands at page 225 of Volume XIX,[1] without any explanation whatever to show what it means.[2]

References

1. The accompanying plate is a reproduction of the one in the *Journal of the Madras Lit. Society.*
2. The subject was incidently referred to, but without any particulars, in a subsequent Volume.

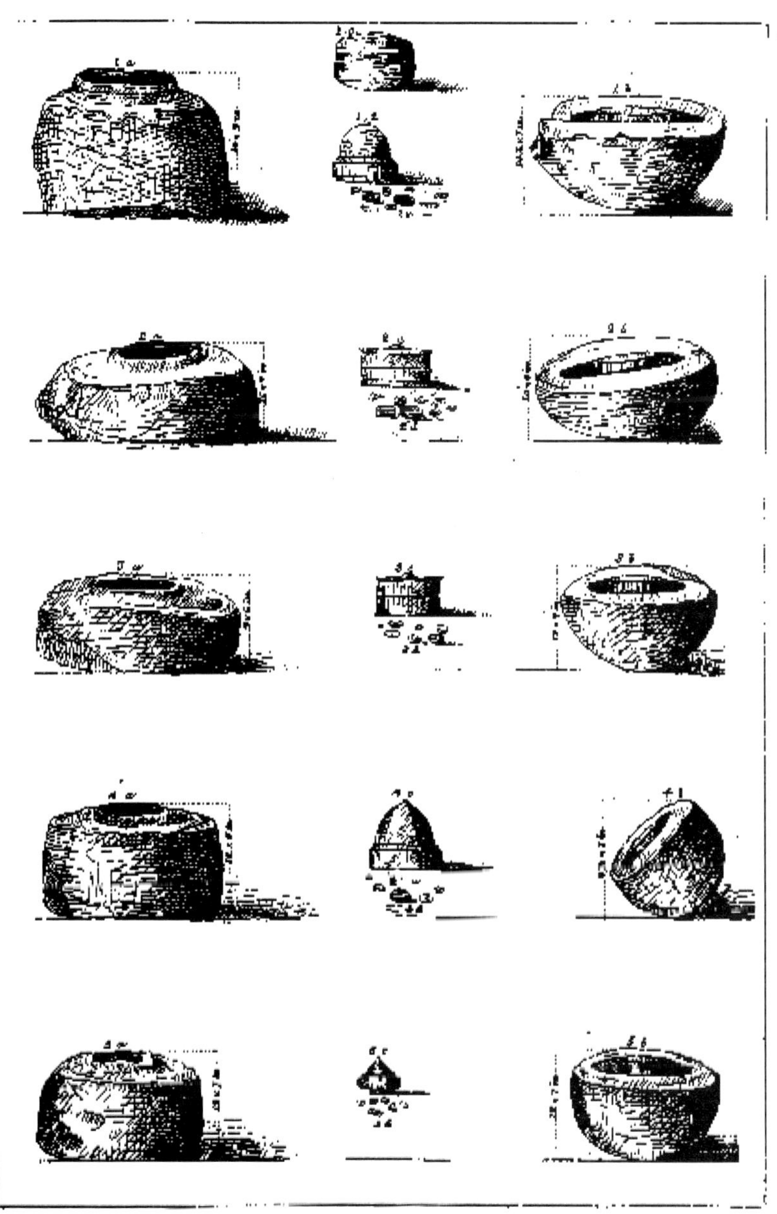

Relics from a stupa at Timavaram in the Pittapur Zamindari 1848 (Facing Page 52)

9

Nagapatam Buddhist Images

De Milloüé

Sir, – In the VIIth volume of the *Indian Antiquary* (1878), at pp. 224-227, Sir Walter Elliot has published a paper, entitled *The Edifice known as the Chinese or Jaina Pagoda at Negapatam,* in which he describes the ruined tower once in the vicinity of the Jesuit College there, and alludes to several Buddhist idols found by the Jesuit Missionaries under the roots of a Mohwā tree, which was cut down in 1856.

On reading it I have been struck by some mistakes, which, I think, it will be interesting to correct.

As regards the author's account of the tower and of the discovery of the images, I have nothing to object, the second part being the translation of a paper communicated by M. Ph. Ed. Foucaux to the *Athenée Oriental,* and by Baron Textor de Ravisi to the Academic Society of St. Quentin. But the author says, at page 226: "M. Foucaux adds that one of the idols has been retained in the college, and that the fifth had been sent to the Rev. T. Carayon in Paris, but he does not state what became of the remaining three. One of these is almost identical with that figured for our article (fig. 3), differing only in the absence of the square pedestal bearing the inscriptions, which, however, forms a separate piece from the lotus stand common to both, and in the disposition of the mantle, which is pendent from the left shoulder only and not from both as in ours. The left hand, also, is held up, instead of pointing downwards. In all other respects they are identical."

"It is probable that these three (figs. 5, 6, 7) have been deposited in the Academy of St. Quentin, and that the one retained by the Fathers is that which was given to Lord Napier."

I can supply some information about the statues. Of the five, two have been brought to the Rev. T. Carayon in Paris (and not one only) by the Baron Textor de Ravisi himself, one bronze statue and that in porcelain and clay alluded to in the article of Sir Walter Elliot. Two, those under numbers 5 and 6, were given to M. Textor de Ravisi by the Missionaries; of these he gave that numbered 5 to M. Ph. Ed. Foucaux, and it will soon be published as an illustrative plate in the new translation of the *Lalita Vistara* in the volume VI of the *Annales du Musée Guimet;* the other, the bronze standing image is still, I think, in M. de Ravisi's possession. The fifth was retained by the Fathers, as stated by Sir Walter Elliot, but it was not given to Lord Napier, for M. Textor de Ravisi says—in a note to a paper issued some years age (I don't know the date), in answer to the critics of the paper in the *Travaux* of the Academic Society of St. Quentin, entitled *Interpretations d'Antiques Idoles Bouddhiques*—"By a letter of the 7th September 1860 the Missionaries also gave me the fifth Buddha. I sent it to a relation of mine, M. Elie Pajot, landowner in Réunion Island, and Member of the Société des Arts et des Sciences of that Island."

As regards the statue numbered 7 in the plate accompanying his article, Sir Walter Elliot is entirely mistaken. First, this image was not found at Negapatam, but it was taken by a captain of Sipahis out of a shrine under the Colossal Buddha statue in the Shwé-Dagon-Prah at Rangun, after the conquest of the city by the English troops, during the Burmese war in 1824, and acquired for M. de Ravisi from the heirs of the captain by M. Alling, police inspector in Karikal, as stated in the same paper of M. Textor de Ravisi. Sir Walter Elliot has certainly been led into this error by a misunderstanding of M. Textor de Ravisi's communication before the International Oriental Congress, held in London in 1874, or perhaps he had forgotten, after some years had elapsed, that there were two different papers in the *Travaux* of the Academic Society of St. Quentin, the one relating to the idols of Negapatam, the other to the said Burmese image.

He also says at page 227: "No. 7 appears to be a female devotee of very rude workmanship." Here, also, Sir Walter

Elliot is mistaken, though, in that case, he follows the interpretations of M. Textor de Ravisi, who thinks the statue may represent Mayā-Dêvī, the mother of Gautama Buddha.[1]

It would be needless to follow the author in the discussion of the reasons he gives for considering this statue as Mayā-Dêvī; he finds them in the various parts of the figure, and refers principally to a tradition, preserved in the family of the captain of sipahis, that the idol was worshipped in Shwé-Dagon-Prah under the name of the Virgin and Mother of Buddha. Those conclusions we cannot accept, for the following reasons:—

The said statue is now in the Musée Guimet Collection, at Lyons, having been given to M. Guimet by M. Textor de Ravisi four years ago. It stands in the gallery of the first floor, first room, in the lower range of the case 3 A. The image is thus described in the new edition of the *Catalogue* at p. 63:—

"Çākya-Mouni debout, vêtu d'une grande robe et d'un manteau, la main droite étendue sur la poitrine, la gauche pendant vers la terre et tenant le bord du manteau. Marbre peint; hauteur 0.700mm. (avec le socle). Provenant de Rangoon, Birmanie."

The statue has been carefully examined by M. Guimet and myself, and by our native collaborators MM. Panditileke and Lewis da Sylva, Buddhist priests of Ceylon, M. Y. Ymāyzoumi, a scholar of the Buddhist Sīngon sect in Japan, and quite recently by M. Louis Vossiou, the present General-Consul of France at Rangun, and their unanimous opinion was that it represented the exact features of the Gautama Buddha of the Burmese.

As regards M. de Ravisi's interpretation I objected in the following terms in a letter that I wrote to him on the 5th of June 1883:—

"I cannot agree with the opinion that our statue represents the Mother of Buddha:

"1*st*. Because there is no trace anywhere of worship paid to Mayā-Dêvī, except perhaps, according to Dr. Edkins in *Religion in China*, by the Eastern Mongols, who worship the Mother of Buddha under the name of Ehe Borrhan. But such worship of a woman is quite contradictory to all Buddhist tenets, who place women in a quite inferior rank, so as to oblige them to be reborn as men before they can hope to attain to *Nirvāṇa.*

"*2nd.* Because, though the features of the face are somewhat those of a woman, they are identical, notwithstanding, with those generally given to Gaudama, as illustrated by numerous other representations of the same personage, the face being intended to represent that of a young man of about eighteen.

"*3rd.* Because the conical ornament on the top of the forehead is by no means a flame, but the *Uśnisha,* the sacred elevation of the forehead peculiar to the Buddhas when they have attained to *Bodhi.*

"*4th.* Because the equality of length in the fingers of the hands and feet is a particular characteristic of a Buddha, – one of the thirty-two external characters by which he is to be recognised as soon as born.

"*5th.* Because there is absolutely nothing in the general form of the body to allow us to conclude that it is that of a woman, the garments differing in no way from those of other images of Buddha in Burma, Siam, and Kamboja."

We, therefore, hold the said statue to be that of Śākya Muni, the Gaudama Buddha of the Burmese. Nevertheless, in order to settle entirely this question we prayed M. Louis Vossiou to try, in Rangun, to ascertain from the priests of the Shwé-Dagon-Prah whether, at any time, there was in that Pagoda an image of Mayā-Dêvī, and whether any worship was ever paid to her.

De Milloüé

Directeur du Musée Guimet ā Lyon. *Lyons,* 1883.

References

1. *Mémoire sur l'idole de la Vierge de la Pagode de Shoé-Dagon-Prah ā Rangoon,* pp. 43, 44.

10
Kukkuṭapāda-Giri and Kukkuṭa Saṅghārāma

S. Beal

Sir,—On the fourth page of vol. XV of the *Reports of the Archæological Survey of India* is this passage:—"Mr. Beal has accused me of confounding the *'Vihār'* of the Cock's foot,' which was just outside the city of Pāṭaliputra, or Pātna, with the *'Hill* of the Cock's foot,' which, according to Hwen Thsang, was 16 miles to the east of Gayā. But is Mr. Beal himself who has made a mistake, as I particularly mention in my report (vol. I, p. 16), that 'there was a monastery also of the same name (*Kukkuṭa-pāda Vihāra*), but this was *close to* Pāṭaliputra, or Pātna.' The name of Kurkihār I took to be *only* a shortened form of Kurak Vihār, which must certainly have referred to a monastery. In fact, no Buddhist establishment could have existed without a monastery, and I presume that the monastery of Kurkihār, was known as the Kukkuṭa-pāda-giri Vihāra, or 'Vihār of the Cock's-foot hill,' while the monastery at Pāṭaliputra was simply the Kukkuṭapāda, Vihāra, or Vihār of the Cock's-foot."

In reference to this extract I ask your permission to make the following remarks:—In the first place, I fail to understand what General Cunningham means when he says, I "accuse him" of so and so. In the note in my book (*Buddhist Pilgrims,* p. 132), to which reference is made, I was speaking of the confusion which exists in reference to this "hill of the Cock's-foot." First of all Fahian places it three li south of Buddha Gayā; then Stas. Julien in his Index (*Voy. des Pèl. Boud.* tome II, p. 452) refers to the "Koukkouṭārāma," and says it is the same as the convent alluded to by Hiuen Tsiang (tome I, p. 139), which was near Pātna, and yet, he adds, the correct form is "Koukkouṭapāda Saṅghārāma," and refers us to tome III, p. 6, where the allusion is to a hill of "the Cock's-foot," at least fifty miles from the convent near Pātna. Then I add that Burnouf in his *Introduction de l'hist. Ind. Bud.* (p. 366n.), has stated that the celebrated hermitage of "the Cock" was situated on the mountain called Kukkuṭapāda, near Gayā; after this I go on thus:—"To add to the confusion—the Archæological Surveyor's *Report* (1861, p. 15), identifies Kurkihār, about 16 miles to the east of Gayā, with the Kukkuṭārāma, and then adds that 'this situation agrees exactly with Fah-hian's account, excepting that there is no three-peaked hill in the neighbourhood." "I am at a loss" (the note continues) "to know to what account he refers. On the whole, I prefer to consider the hermitage and the hill as distinct localities; the former neat Pātna, the latter some 15 miles to the E. or S.E. of Gayā."

It will be seen from the above that I make no accusation, but I say that General Cunningham's account increases the confusion which exists in regard to the situation of the convent known as the Kukkuṭārāma, for he states that "the situation of Kurkihār agrees exactly with Fah-hian's account," but Fah-hian places the "Cock's hill" three li to the south of Gayā, and this does not agree with the position of Kurkihār, which is 16 miles or so to the east of that place, neither does Fa-hian say anything about a three-peaked hill, and yet General Cunningham remarks that "the situation of Kurkihār agrees exactly with Fa-hian's account, excepting that there is no three-peaked hill in the neighbourhood."

I think it will be seen that the difficulty before me at the time I wrote the note was (as indeed I state) to know to what account General Cunningham refers. But doubtless I overlooked the allusion made "to the monastery of the same name close to Pāṭaliputra" (although the names were not presumably the same, as the Surveyor General remarks in the extract given above from the XVth vol. of his *Reports*), and to that extent I would wish to modify my criticism.

But the matter has become more involved, and the confusion worse confounded, by what has been written since 1861. I hope General Cunningham will pardon me for making some further remarks on what he has written (undoubtedly by oversight, yet misleading to those less informed than himself) on this subject. In the *Ancient Geography of India,* p. 460, he says:—"According to Fah-hian's account the hill of the Cock's-foot was three *li,* or half a mile, to the south of the holy tree of Buddha-Gayā. For 3 *li* we should no doubt read 3 *yôjanas* or 21 miles, which agrees very closely with Hwen Thsang's distance of 17 miles." I had myself proposed to substitute *yojanas* for *lis* in Fa-hian's account (*Fa-hian,* p. 132n.), and I was therefore gratified to find that General Cunningham thought, in 1871, that there was "no doubt" this was the right solution (although only a partial one,—for we must also substitute *east* for *south* in the pilgrim's narrative) of the difficulty. But now all this is changed, for in the 15th vol. of his *Reports,* printed in 1882 (to which reference was first made in this letter) I find to my astonishment the following remark (p. 4, n. 2):—"Fa-hian himself has made a mistake in placing the Cock's-foot hill only 3 *li*, or half mile, to the south of Pāṭ aliputra. Mr. Beal would correct this to 3 *yôjanas,* or 21 miles. But as the actual distance is over 50 miles, I would suggest 300 *li,* or 50 miles, as the true reading."

But, where are we? Fa-hian says nothing about Pāṭaliputra; and I had thought General Cunningham was satisfied, without doubt, that three *yöjanas* must be substituted for 3 *li,* in the Chinese text. This note certainly adds to the previous confusion.

Then, again with reference to the "three-peaked hill;" in 1861 the Surveyor-General remarks that "there is no three-peaked hill in the neighbourhood of Kurkihār, but there are three bare and rugged hills which rise boldly out of the plain about half a mile to the north of the village." (*Reports,* vol. I, p. 16). These he identifies with the Cock's-foot mountain of Hiuen Thsiang. In the *Ancient Geography,* p. 460, this is repeated. But in vol XV. p. 5, we read:—"Hwen Tsiang describes the hill as lofty and scarped, with three bold peaks that spring into the air. These peaks I have already identified with the three peaks of the Murali mountain, which stands three miles to the north-north-east of the town of Kurkihār."

Are these "three peaks of the Murali mountain three miles to the N.N.E. of the town," the same as the "three bare and rugged hills about half a mile to the north of the village"? Here the confusion is as great as ever. And I am unable to find the reference to the Murali mountain. There is, indeed, allusion in the first vol. of the *Reports* to a distinct peak of the Barābar group of hills which is called Murali (p. 42), but the Barābar district is 16 miles north of Gayā. Possibly the right reference has escaped me; but yet it is confusing, for the three peaks of a mountain either half a mile to the north of the village, or three miles to the N.N.E., would seem to correspond with the description of the Cock's-foot mount given by Hiuen Tsiang, and yet we are told, "There is no *three-peaked hill* in the neighbourhood of Kurkihār." (*Ancient Geography of India,* p. 460).

But once more: General Cunningham on p. 4 of his *Reports,* vol. XV, says, that Fa-hian's account is as follows: – "The great Chia-yeh (Kāśyapa) is at present in this mountain." It is plain, therefore, that when Fa-hian wrote he was supposed to be in the Kukkuṭa-pāda-giri. He was there, as Hiuen Tsiang's account plainly says, awaiting the coming of Maitrêya Buddha, to whom he was to deliver the golden robe presented to Śākya Buddha by his aunt Prajāpatī. Accordingly Fa-hian tells us a little lower down that in a fastness within the mount, the "entire body," that is, the human body of Kāśyapa, is enshrined. But General Cunningham, quoting from a wrong translation of the Chinese text would resolve all this into "a full length image of Chia-yeh placed in a niche." Of course anyone has a right to translate a Chinese text. But I should have thought that some small acquaintance with Buddhist legend was desirable in the case of a person undertaking to translate a Buddhist book. But in any case I shall be borne out by all acquainted with the subject (and by none, I believe, more than by General Cunningham, after consideration) that the legend of Kāśyapa requires the translation I have given of his "entire, or, uncorrupted body," being still preserved in the Cock's-foot mount, awaiting the advent of Maitrêya.

This is manifest from Hiuen Tsiang's account, which General Cunningham refers to on p. 5 of the same volume. Here we are distinctly told that Kāśyapa ascended the north side of the mount, and passed to the S.W. side. There, being balked by the opposing rock, he opened a way for himself, and passed through the mount to the north-east summit; there he sat down with the robe of gold tissue in his hand; then by his spiritual power he caused the three peaks to unite as a sierra[1] over him, he being underneath the middle one. There he will await the coming of Maitrêya, who will receive from him the saintly robe, then Kāśyapa *will* ascend into the air, exhibit miracles, and his body will be consumed by self-produced fire, and thus men will be led to believe in Maitrêya.

This is the account of Hiuen Tsiang. Unfortunately Stas. Julien has missed the key to the interpretation, and translated it as though Maitrêya *had* come. But the Chinese is plain enough, and the mere fact that Kāśyapa was still supposed to be in the mountain when Fa-hian wrote his account, taken together with the fact that Maitrêya, the lord of the world, has *not* yet come, would be sufficient to show that this is the true version if there were any doubt about it; but there is none, for as I said before the Chinese is plain enough.

I have made the foregoing remarks not with any desire to find fault, much less to accuse, any one, but I have thought it right to explain myself, and to point out what I conceive to be errors of translation, and other inadvertencies, which gain authority by appearing without remark in the pages of such valuable works as the *Reports of the Archæological Survey of India. Wark, Northumberland.*

References

1. Julien gives it "*ś élévent en dôme,*" *Mém.* vol. II, p. 8.

11

Notes on Buddhist Images in Ceylon

W. Knight James, F.R.G.S., F.R.Hist.S., Colombo

I. *Buddha*—In Ceylon Wihāras or shrines, Buddha is represented in three positions: *(1)* standing; *(2)* sitting; *(3)* reclining.

1. In *standing* figures, the left arm hangs by the side of the body, the fingers are stretched out close together, slightly touching the thigh of the left leg. The right arm is placed close to the side as far as the elbow, the forearm is raised, and the hand held vertically, displaying the palm, while the thumb and index finger are joined at their tips, leaving an oval space between them. This position of the left arm is supposed to represent the inoffensiveness of Buddha, and the needlessness to the Perfect One of any temporal defence or protection. The position of the right arm indicates exhortation, and the placing together of the thumb and finger is intended to show that he covets not the smallest particle of worldly wealth.

   Sometimes the right arm to the elbow is placed by the side as above, but the under part of the fore-arm is towards the body, and the palm of the hand turned upwards with the fingers slightly inclined downwards. This position is symbolical of benevolence, open-heartedness and charity.

2. *Sitting* figures are always cross-legged, with the soles of the feet turned upwards. This is probably a device of the sculptor to show the *Maṅgalalakkhaṇas*, or auspicious marks of which Buddha was said to have had 108 on his feet.

   The hands generally rest in the lap, the back of the right hand lying in the palm of the left.[1] Sometimes the hands are separated, the right one resting on the thigh, close to the knee, and the left one placed on the sole of the right foot (the *Bhūmīsparśa mudrā*).

This position is indicative of contemplation and deep meditation (Pali, *Dhyāna*). I have never seen or heard of any sitting figure of the Buddha in Ceylon, with the feet hanging down, such as are stated by Dr. Burgess to be found in the Cave Temples of India.

3. *Reclining* figures are always on the right side, representing what is called in Pali *Sīhaseyyā*—the lion's sleep.[2] Buddha while sleeping was said to retain his consciousness. The head in this position is represented as resting on the palm of the right hand, the elbow touches the bed, and the fore-arm rests on a round pillow. The left arm is extended and rests upon the left side. The figure is always represented as stretched at full length, and the legs and feet are placed one upon the other. This position is emblematical of perfect rest (Pali, *nirodhasamāpatti*—the *nirwāṇa* to be attained in this world). Very rarely a figure of Buddha is represented as walking, but it is doubtless intended to represent the Buddha during one of the seven *satiyas* or weeks which he spent fasting, and during which time he is said to have been engaged in various exercises intended to show how thoroughly he had overcome human passions and fatigue. One of these *satiyas* was spent in walking up and down on the *Ratnachaṅkamaṇa* or walk composed of gems which was built for him by the gods.

Small images, made of gold and silver, and representing Buddha in each of the seven *satiyas,* are frequently enclosed within *dāgabas* in Ceylon. The images of the 24 Buddhas previous to Gautama, and from whom he obtained *Vivaraṇa* or approbation, are also frequently enshrined in these *dāgabas*. Sometimes in temple sculptures, but more frequently in paintings, we find these 24 figures represented with the Bôdhisattva in attendance in a reverential attitude, and occasionally he is represented as making offerings of flowers, &c., to them. There appear however to be no distinctive marks by which each of the Buddhas can be distinguished. They are usually arranged in a row, which is supposed to represent their order.

The Bôdhisattva is generally broadly distinguished:—when he appeared as a Rājā or a Cakkavatti Rājā, he is represented as wearing a kingly or imperial crown; when a Nāga Rājā as wearing a crown formed by a cobra; in Brahmanical dress when a Brāhmaṇ. He is represented as a lion when with the Buddha intended to represent Padumo, and as an ascetic wearing the *jaṭā* of matted hair, when represented as Jatilo the Bôdhisattva of Padumuttaro.

Sometimes an incident during one of the *satiyas* is represented. When Gautama was preaching rain came on, and a snake god, Muchalindo (Muchilinda) is said to have spread out its hood over his head to protect him from the storm. An image representing this, which was at one time in the Kælani Temple near Colombo is described by Totagamuwa in his *Selalihini Sandésa.*

II. *Attendants*—In Ceylon there are only two principal attendant figures, these are Sāriputta, who is always on Buddha's right, and Moggallāna, who is always represented on the left. These are the *Aggasāwaka* or chief disciples.

The posture of the attendants is generally standing with the palms of their hands together in an attitude of reverence. They are rarely represented as sitting, and never when the Buddha is standing, and we never find them represented in the reclining posture. Sometimes the disciples hold a flower (generally a lotus) in the right hand, while the left hangs by the side of the body. This is intended to represent *pūja,* or the offering of flowers to Buddha. In some temple *paintings,* with these two, and sometimes without them, is represented a large number of other disciples in various attitudes of reverence, such as kneeling, standing with bowed head, offering flowers, &c., but no distinctive names are given to any of these figures. Ānanda and Kassapa appear not to be represented in Ceylon sculptures as principal attendants.

III.*Dress, &c.*—Buddha and his disciples are always represented as wearing the ordinary saffron-coloured mendicant's robe.

In some figures both shoulders are covered, whilst in others the robe is thrown only over the left shoulder, leaving the right one bare. In Buddhist books Buddha is spoken of as wearing his robe over both shoulders when preaching, walking abroad, or in the presence of an assembly, and over one only when in the retirement of the *pansala,* but it appears doubtful whether artists have been guided by this in any way.

Although in Ceylon Buddha or his disciples are never represented as wearing ornaments or a head-dress of any kind, he is generally represented as having on his head a peculiar flame-like process which is intended to represent a sort of halo (Sin. *Siraspata*) formed by the collection of the six coloured rays of light which were said to be reflected from his body (Pali, *nīla, pīta, lôhita, odāta* and *mañjiṭṭhā*). In some paintings however this halo is represented as surrounding the whole body. Buddḥa is generally represented as having short hair arranged in the form of little curls.

IV. The figure of Buddha is invariably represented as larger than that of any of his attendants or disciples. There is among the Buddhists of Ceylon a tradition that Buddha's height was 18 cubits (27 feet) and under this notion where it is possible they make the reclining figure of this length, but at Aukana Wihara, between Dambulla and Anuradhapura, however, there has been discovered a colossal standing image of Buddha, hewn from the solid gneiss, which is said to be nearly 50 feet in height.[3] Several other colossal figures hewn from the rock and more or less defaced, have been found in the Anurādhāpura and Polonnuruwa districts.

V. *Dewas.*—In some places sculptures representing Dewas or spirits and Hindu gods as well as kings are to be found. These wear ornaments, crowns, &c., and have weapons in their hands, and are symbolical of support and protection. These figures are only occasionally to be found within the limits of the shrine, and are never represented as attendant on Buddha. They are generally placed outside the shrine, and often in a separate room or compartment.

The following are some of the gods which are found represented in temple paintings:—Vishṇu, Sumana, Śakra or

Indra, Brahmā, Māra and his attendants, Ālavaka, Kuvêra, Vibhīshana. Although Brahmā is frequently mentioned in Siṁhalese Buddhist literature, his image is not found in the Vihāras. The pictures generally are representations of Jātaka stories. The gods represented in sculpture are very few, generally Vishṇu only, who is painted black, and holds a sword and a discus. Occasionally we find Nāthadêwa, who is considered to be the Maitrêya Bôdhisattva.

Similarly a number of Siṁhalese kings are represented, *e.g.*:–

Vattagāmini Abhaya, Kīrtissri Rājasiṇha and Bhātikābhaya.

The Ceylon Pantheon appears to be remarkably small when compared with that of Buddhism in India, and although nearly all the deities of the Hindu Pantheon are referred to in Ceylon Buddhistical literature, very few are represented in the temples. There is a sameness in design and arrangement, and, as a rule, but little artistic merit.

References

1. This is the *Dhyānamudrā.*
2. Burnouf, *Lotus,* p. 342.
3. *Vide* Sir Emerson Tennant's *History of Ceylon,* vol. I, p. 604.

12

A Further Notice of the Ancient Buddhist Structure at Negapatam

Walter Elliot

Some time after I communicated the former Article[1] on the remarkable and unique edifice at Negapatam, an old friend, an officer in the Madras Army, but now an inmate of the College of St. Joseph at Negapatam, sent me, through his brother, some further information which it may be interesting to place on record. He writes as follows : – "In a pamphlet entitled *Interprétations d'Antiques Idoles Bouddhistes,* by M. Textor de Ravisi, Ancien Commandant de Karikal (Indes Orientales), being *Extraits de Travaux de* 1865 *et* 1866 *de la Société Académique de Saint Quentin,* published at Saint Quentin at the Imprimerie Jules Moureau, 7, Place de l'Hôtel-de-Ville, in 1866, I have found an account of the statuettes that Sir Walter asks after. I have not time to copy in full, but I have given above the title, author, and publisher, so that Sir Walter, who probably may have known the author in India, may get the little pamphlet if it be still in print. Textor de Ravisi says of the towers, that, when the Portuguese discovered India, they spoke in their account of Negapatam of this tower as *la tour ruinée,* and that the Dutch used it at one time as a Lighthouse. The tower, he says, was an irregular square. The materials are enormous bricks beautifully manufactured and very superior to the country manufacture of to-day. The cement is a *terre glaise* (which I take to be polished shell *chunam*), but it is stated that the cement was extremely hard and like stone.

"From those who were present at the demolition of the tower, I have learned that exteriorly there were apparently three storeys, but interiorly there were no traces of landing places or storeys, and that there were only three smooth walls, the fourth side being open all the way up. The bricks are said to have been very large; the cement as M. Textor de Ravisi describes it. The foundations were about eight feet deep, and there had apparently been an underground cellar or storey, for the middle was filled with sand, and the inner walls were covered with very hard shell *chunam* polished. No statuettes or anything else were found in the tower itself, with the exception of four little square pieces of gold, let roughly into the four corners of what appears to be the foundation stone. This stone was at the very bottom of the foundation.

"No statuettes were discovered in digging the foundations for building the dormitories that now form one side of the college quadrangle. It seems they had to cut down, and then to dig and remove, the roots of a venerable banyan tree, and among these roots several curiosities were found. Amongst others five small statuettes, some sitting, some standing, but all Buddhist, and indeed from the drawings in M. Textor de Ravisi's book, identical in shape, but miniatures of the Gaudamas so common in British Burmah. I would also draw Sir Walter's notice to a fact he may have forgotten, that shell *chunam* is very common in many of the Buddhist temples of Burmah, and this is the more remarkable as in that country it is only their temples that are built of masonry. M. Textor de Ravisi incidently mentions in another part of his pamphlet, "Ces idoles trouvées dans de tels conditions jointés ā l'existence de la tour dont la structure indique une construction bouddhiste sembleraient démontrer que ces statues remontent ā l'époque oū le culte de Bouddha fut définitivement expulsé du sud de l'Hindoustan par le triomphe de Brāhmanisme." And certainly everything that was discovered seems to speak of Buddhism, for among other things a bell was discovered in the neighbourhood of the statuettes. This bell was recast and is now the college bell. The dormitory, which now stands on the place where the statuettes were found is about 60 yards from the position occupied by the ruined tower. I subjoin or enclose some rough copies of some sketches of articles found with the statuettes. I should not forget to mention among other things a human skull that was found in a kind of small arched tomb.[2]

"With regard to the tower, one of the native Fathers now in the college, tells me that he remembers as a boy that the tower was nearly twice the height it was at the date of its final destruction, and that even then it bore the appearance of having been still higher formerly.

"I wrong the above when I was absent from the college. On my return I have consulted the *Records*, and send sketches marked A. and B., showing respectively the ground plan of the tower, and some of the ornaments dug out of the foundations of what is now one of the dormitories, and which I have already referred to above."

A

"Les briques sont énormes, sous l'une d'elles au coin de l'ouest ā l'intérieur on trouve quatre lames fines, étroites et courtes d'or. Voici le plan des fondements avec le coin oū l'on a trouvé les lames, les fondements avaient ā peu près 12 ou 13 pieds de profondeur."

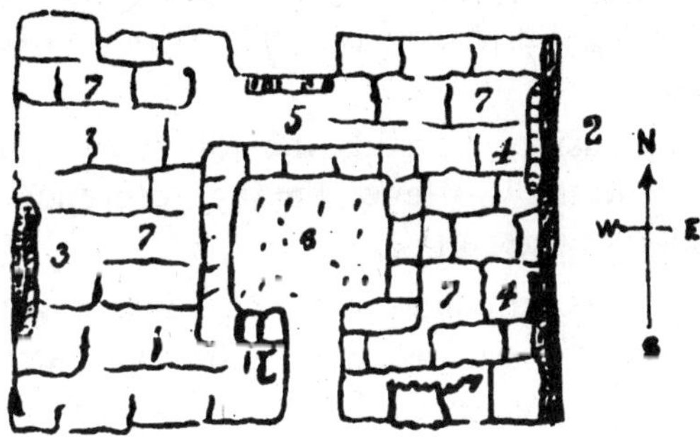

1. or
2. decombres anciens
3. mur isolement bati ā la face intérieure rellé par les coins au reste des fondements
4. idem
5. idem
6. sable marin
7. grandes briques.[3]

B

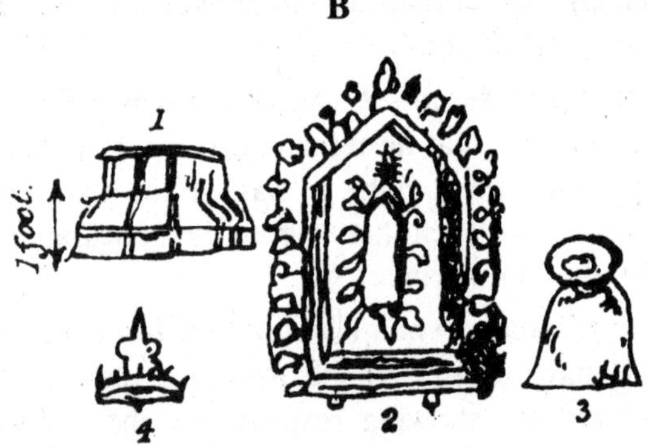

"En creusant les fondements on trouve dans la tranchée du sud-est (1) un piedestal, (2) une plaque sculptée et percée au milieu, (3) une cloche, et (4) une espèce de couronne; tout excepté la cloche en cuivre doré; dans la tranchée N.E. on trouve un crāne".[4]

"To my idea the figure No. 4 corresponds to the head pieces of the Burmese Gaudamas, and so also No. 3 to the Burmese pagoda bells. But No. 2 certainly is more like Chinese than Burmese."

In conclusion, he adds the following extract[5] from the Records of the College, having reference only to final demolition of the edifice:—

"Ā une des extremités du Collège de S. Joseph ā Negapatam l'élevait, il y a six ans, une vieille tour carrée mesurant de vingt-cinq ā trente pieds de côté. La hauteur de cette tour qui primitivement était de soixante-dix ā soixante-quinze pieds, avait été, pour prevenir les accidents, réduite de moitié. Une ouverte unique, partant de la base au sommet, donnait entrée et jour du côté du midi. L'édifice était un mur massif de briques et de terre sans aucun caractère architectural. Aux quatres côtés de la base, de profondes excavations s'étaient formées sous l'action séculaire des sels marins. Ces excavations avaient jusqu'ā huit pieds de profondeur. An sommet et sur les côtés l'on voyait une vigoureuse végétation d'arbustes.

* * * * * * * *

"Récemment, quantité d'objets, depuis long-temps enfonces, appartenant au culte bouddhique, ayant été découverts dans les environs du vieux monument, ou en conclut qu'il avait été un temple, consacré ā Bouddha. Une opinion moins accrédité en faisait un simple point de repère (*sic*) pour les navires que approchaient de la côté, et lui attribuait une origine Hollandaise, mais la croyance populaire, sans rien déterminée de son origine et de son usage, lui attachait un caractère sacré et superstitieux."

The above particulars do not add much to our previous scanty knowledge of the old building. The most interesting fact is that of the discovery made in the foundations of four pieces of gold under a large brick in the west corner, which appears analogous to the deposits of gold, coral, pearl, &c., found in the Buddhist Topes, leading to the inference of a common Buddhist origin. The discovery of the skull also tends to the same conclusion.

The only other remark I have to make is in regard to the statement that "interiorly there were no traces of landing places or storeys." With reference to that I repeat what I said in my former paper that "at the top of the lowest storey were marks in the wall showing where the floor of the second had been fixed."[5]

It may also be added that the statement of the native Father above mentioned, that "he remembered the tower twice as high as it was at the date of its final destruction," is easily explained by a reference to the plate at p. 226, fig. 2, Vol. VII. as it stood in 1846, and Mr. Middleton Rayne's sketch in 1866, fig. 1.

References

1. *ante,* Vol. VII, p. 224ff.
2. This looks like Chinese Buddhism.
3. Extracts from the Records of St. Joseph's College, Negapatam.
4. Extract from Records of St. Joseph's College, Negapatam.

5. Extract from "Des Missions Catholiques" of 17th July 1874.
6. *ante,* Vol. VII, p. 224.

13
A Dated Græco-Buddhist Sculpture

V.A. Smith, B.C.S.

The date of the interesting School of Græco-Buddhist Sculpture in the Kābul Valley has formed the subject of discussion, and is still unsettled. The paucity of inscriptions has rendered the solution of the problem especially difficult. The few which have been found are all in the Arian character.

The only published inscriptions which are directly associated with Græco-Buddhist Sculptures have been found at Jamālgarhi and Kharkai. Those at the former place consist of some masons' marks, the Hindu names of a weekday and a mouth on a pilaster, and seven characters, read as *Saphaé danamukha,* on the back of the nimbus of one of the statues supposed to be those of kings. The record from Kharkai consists merely of the three characters *a, ra* and *dê,* on the sides of a relic-chamber. Sir A. Cunningham wishes to read these as equivalent to the name of Ārya-Dêva, a Buddhist leader at the beginning of the Christian era; but this interpretation is too conjectural to command confidence. Masons' marks in Arian characters were also noticed at Kharkai.[1]

I reserve for another occasion a full discussion of the chronology of Græco-Buddhist art. My present purpose is confined to the publication of the only dated inscription which has yet been discovered, associated with an Indo-Hellenic work of art. I am indebted to the liberality of the discoverer, Mr. L. White King, B.C.S., for permission to publish this unique record.

In or about the year 1883, at Hashtnagar, the site of the capital of Peukeloaitis, in the modern district of Peshāwar, Mr.

King came across a statue of the standing Buddha, which was ignorantly worshipped by the Hindus as an orthodox deity. He could not carry away the statue, but was allowed to remove its inscribed pedestal. This pedestal, like most of the Gandhāra sculptures, is composed of blue slate, and is 14¾'' long by 8'' high. Its front is adorned by an alto-relievo, enclosed between two Indo-Corinthian pilasters, representing Buddha, seated, and attended by disciples, who seem to be presenting offerings to him. An Arian inscription, consisting of a single line of characters, deeply and cleanly cut, and in greater part excellently preserved, occupies a smooth band below the relief. This band was evidently prepared for the inscription, which must have been executed at the same time as the sculpture. The accompanying facsimile is from a rubbing taken by Sir A. Cunningham. The record is incomplete at the end, and it is probable that the lost portion contained the name of the person who dedicated the image. The extant portion was read, for Mr. King, by Sir A. Cunningham, as follows: –

Saṁ 274 emborasmasa masasa mi pañchami 5

Scale ·50

The record, as it stands, consists of a date, and nothing more. The month is stated to be intercalary, but is not further named. The numerals are distinct, and their interpretation appears to be certain; the 274 is expressed by two units, a symbol for 100, three symbols, each value 20, one symbol for 10, and one for 4; and the 5 is expressed by 1 and 4.

The main question suggested by the inscription is the identity of the era referred to. It may be the Śaka era of A.D. 78, which was probably used by Kanishka; if so, the date of the record is A.D. 351 or 352. Or the era may be that used by Gondophares in his Takht-i-Bahi inscription from the same region where this pedestal was found. The Takht-i-Bahi inscription is dated in the year 103, and numismatic evidence shows that Gondophares ruled in the first half of the first century A.D.[2] The era used by him, consequently, cannot have differed very much from that beginning in 58 B.C., which afterwards became known by the name of Vikrama. I do not, of course, mean to assert that the Vikrama era was actually used by Gondophares; I merely note the fact that he used an epoch which closely approximated to that known as the era of Vikrama. The era employed by Gondophares may have been that of the "great king Moga," in the 78th year of which the Taxila inscription of the Satrap Liako-Kusulako is dated.[3]

I hope that some one more learned in eras than I am, may solve the problems propounded by these inscriptions from the Yusufzai country. The style of the Hashtnagar relief is not very good, the figures not being undercut, as they are in the best examples of Græco-Buddhist art; and I feel more inclined to date the work in A.D. 351-52, than in or about A.D. 210-220; but I cannot say that the earlier date is impossible.

References

1. *Archæol. Surv. Ind.*, Vol. V. pp. 54, 63, Pl. xii. xvi.
2. Cunningham *Archæol. Surv. Ind.*, Vol. II. p. 60; V. pp. 59, 60; Gardner, *Catalogue of Coins of Greek and Scythic kings of Bactria and India*, p. xliv.
3. Cunningham, *Archæol. Surv. Ind.*, Vol. II. p. 132; V. 67; Gardner, p. xlix.

14

Recently Discovered Buddhist Caves at Nadsur and Nenavali in the Bhor State, Bombay Presidency

J. E. Abbott

The portion of the Bhôr State which lies in the Koṅkaṇ is, I believe, seldom visited by Europeans, and as a consequence two series of Buddhist caves have thus, till recently, remained undiscovered, in the mountains forming its eastern boundary,—the one near the village of Nāḍsūr, Lat. 18^0 34' and Long 73^0 21'; the other near the village of Nenavalī (or Kharsambḷa), Lat. 18^0 30' and Long 73^0 23'.

A study of the location of other known caves among the Western Ghauts drew my attention to the fact that they all seemed to be situated along what must have been, in ancient time, the highways from the Dekhaṇ above to the sea-port towns of the Koṅkaṇ below. These highways were doubtless then, as now, narrow foot paths, descending the upper sources of the Koṅkaṇ rivers, and following these streams to their outlets into the large creeks common along the coast. If Chaul, near the modern Rêvadaṇḍā, was the important city of ancient times it is supposed to have been, it seemed strange that the highway, along the Kuṇḍalikā River to this sea-port, should not have, somewhere along its course, the extensive Buddhist monasteries common to many of the other highways to the north and south.

Believing in the possibility of their existence, I had often inquired of the inhabitants of the Rôha Tālukā, where my missionary operations largely lie, whether they knew of any such rock caves; but it was not until about a year ago that I received any hint that my conjectures were correct. In

December 1889, I was informed that at Gômāśī, village in the Bhôr-State, there was a small rock temple dedicated to Ṛishidêva. I visited this care on the 10th December, and found it to be a plain single cell in the gorge of a hill about half a mile to the south of the village. The cell is about 15' X 7', with an image of Buddha in the *bhūmisparśa-mudrā,* placed on a platform at its farther end. I here learned that there were extensive caves a few miles further up the stream, near the village of Nenavalī, which I immediately visited. While examining these caves, I was informed of still others about six miles to the north. Availing myself of an early opportunity to verify this information, I descended the mountains near Khaṇḍāḷa, and walked southward along the foot of the Sahyādris until I reached the village of Nāḍsūr, making constant enquiries as I went along. Here my search was rewarded by the discovery of a series of twenty caves. I give below a brief description of these two Buddhist *Viḥāras.*

The Nāḍsūr Caves

The village of Nāḍsūr, belonging to the Koṅkaṇ portion of the Bhôr State, is in Lat. 18^{0} 34' and Long 73^{0} 21'; and the caves, which I first discovered on the 8th January 1890, are to be found to the east of the village about an hour and a half's climb up the mountain. The scarp of rock, in which the caves are cut, runs north and south, and the caves face the west. They are twenty in number, including a natural cave to the north. The caves are, on the whole, in good preservation, although their front portions seem to have fallen away.

The first cave of interest, commencing at the southernmost of the series, is No. III, measuring 34' X 20', and containing twelve *dāgobās.* Six of these are of solid stone, varying from 4' to 6' 6'' in diameter. Two small stone *dāgobās* are placed in niches in the walls. Four *dāgobās* are structural. Two of the solid stone *dāgobās* have their *Tees* remaining on them, one resembling in shape the *Tee* on the *dāgobā* of the Kārla *Chaitya* cave. The rail pattern appears on the base of the stone *dāgobās.* One of the niches in the wall is perfectly plain, the other is ornamented with the window façade and rail pattern resembling that found at Bêḍsa and Kārla. The structural *dāgobās* are more or less ruined, and appear to have been at some time opened with the exception of finding treasure within. One of these lies a little outside of the cave.

The next cave worthy of mention is No. VII, a large hall 48' 9'' X 39' and 11' high, with cells on the three inner sides. Between each cell is a niche in the wall. The upper part of the doorways leading into the cells, and the niches between the cells, are ornamented with the façade pattern, including the semicircular bars, almost the exact reproduction of the façades to be found at Bêḍsa and Kārla. In these façades, below the semicircular bars, and along the upper portion of the walls of nearly the entire cave, are small figures, in *bas relief,* of serpents, bulls, elephants, tigers, men and women, *dāgobās,* and the rail and façade pattern. In the centre of the roof is a figure of the lotus. On the north wall is a short inscription in two lines in the ancient cave character and in the Pāli language, which I have not been able to satisfactorily decipher, but which seem to give the name of the donor or excavator. The sculptures are in good preservation and are well executed. Separated from this hall by a thin wall is the *dāgobā* shrine, 23' by 16', with an arched roof. The base of the *dāgobā* is 9' 6'' in diameter.[1]

The only other cave worthy of mention is No. XV, a room 20' X 14' with two cells. The upper part of the east wall and the doorways of the cells have the rail and façade pattern, similar to that found in the other caves. A narrow outside verandah has at its north end a similarly ornamented niche, now partly broken, a perforated screen window, and a small figure, in bas relief, of a man and woman standing upon what looks like a fish.

No. XX is a large natural cave, but with benches running east and west. The cisterns are dry, but there is a spring of delicious water, a few rods to the south of the caves, which flows from the rainy season until about the middle of January.

These caves seem to fall into the same group as those at Bhāja, Bêḍsa and Kārla, and were probably excavated at about the same time, or about 100 B.C.

The Nenavalī Caves[2]

This Buddhist *vihāra,* which I discovered on the 10th December 1889, is situated about a mile above the village of Nenavalī, in Lat. 18^0 30' and Long 73^0 23'. The caves are cut into a scarp of rock running north and south, and face the east. They are ten in number, excluding those that are now so ruined as to be undistinguishable, and also excluding the natural cave to the south of the series. The rock in which they are cut in friable; hence the caves are all more or less injured by age. Large portions of rock, forming the roof of some, have fallen, completely running many of the caves. The rock is not suited for sculpture; there are no inscriptions; and no ornamentation of even the simplest kind.

Commencing at the most southern of the series, No. I appears at first sight to be a large cave, 56' X 28', but a restoration of its ruined walls would shew that it was formerly divided into many rooms.

No. III is the only cave of this series especially worthy of mention. It is a large hall, 67' 9'' X 52', with seventeen cells on the three inner sides. Each cell has a stone bench, and a window opening into the hall. A verandah, 9' wide, surrounds the hall, leaving a central court. Square holes in the roof of the cave, over the edge of the verandah, shew where wooden posts were once placed at frequent intervals around the central court. The roof is unsupported by pillars. The *dāgobā* shrine is placed at the north-west corner of the hall, and consists of a rectangular room, 24' X 18', with a circular roof. The *dāgobā* is 10½' high and 9' in diameter, and has lost its *Tee.*

The remaining caves have nothing of special interest. Many of them are in complete ruin. The two cisterns which I noticed are filled with debris. In many of the cells, large patches of the original plaster, in which rice husks form a large portion, still adhere to the walls, with traces of paint.

The architectural features of these caves, from which their date must be determined, and their close proximity to the Nāḍsūr caves, lead me to the belief that they belong to the same date as the Nāḍsūr caves which with Bêḍsa and Bhāja, belong to a period a little prior to the Christian era.

References

1. Since the above was first written, Mr. Cousens of the Archæological Survey has visited these caves and found another inscription on the south wall of this *Chaitya* cave, which also has not yet been deciphered – [This paper was originally received in February, 1890. It was held over, with the object of publishing plans of the caves with it. The necessary drawings, however, did not come to hand. And Mr. Cousens has since made more detailed measurements, for the publication of complete plans &c. elsewhere – Editors.]
2. Mr. Cousens, in his Government Report, has named them the Kharsambḷa Caves, from a nearer village of that name.

15

The Date of the Græco-Buddhist Pedestal from Hashtnagar

V.A. Smith

Dr. Bühler has published in the number of this Journal *ante,* Vol. XX, p. 394, an interesting note on this unique record. He does not seem to have seen M. Senart's remarks on the same subject,[1] and, I think, it will be interesting to many readers to compare the views of these two scholars.

Dr. Bühler, having before him both the facsimile rubbing and the photo-etching, reads the inscription as follows:–

"Sam II C xx xx xx x iv Pôstavadasa masasa di[va] saṁmi paṁ[cha] 5[||*]."

M. Senart, before the publication of the photo-etching, read "....proṭhavadasa masasa do[vasê] paṁchamê, 4, 1." He doubted the existence of the symbol for one hundred, and read the remaining figures as 74, not as 84. Dr. Bühler notes that the reading *poṭhavadasa* is linguistically possible, and would be good Prākṛit.

Both scholars, therefore, are agreed that the month named is the Saṅskṛit Praushṭhapada (August–September), and that Sir A. Cunningham was mistaken in reading '*êmborasmasa,*' 'intercalary.' That point may be considered as definitely settled.

Now that the photo-etching is available, M. Senart cannot well doubt the presence of the symbol for 'hundred.'[2] The date, therefore, is either 274, as read by Sir A. Cunningham and Dr. Bühler, or 284. As to this detail M. Senart observes: "Quant aux années, dont le chiffre est lu 274 par le général, il paraît certain que c'est par 84 qu'il finit (je ne puis faire aucune difference entre le troizième et le quatrième chiffre des dizaines)."

The difference between the third and fourth symbols for the tens (or rather the twenties) does, however, exist, though it is very slight. The fourth symbol is somewhat more slender and less curved than any of the three preceding ones. I prefer, consequently, to accept 274 as the correct reading.

As to the era used, Dr. Bühler, considers as very improbable the suggestion that the Śaka era may be that referred to. My only reason for making the suggestion was the inferior style of the sculpture. But M. Senart has pointed out that the workmanship of pedestals is generally much inferior to that of statues. The inscription under discussion is on a pedestal adorned with a relief, and nothing is known of the artistic merits of the statue which stood on the pedestal. Very likely, it was executed in a much better style. I, therefore, give up the suggestion that the Śaka era is referred to in the inscription.

M. Senart is a firm believer in the early extinction of the Arian or Kharôshṭrī alphabet, and remarks that "l'ère de Gondophares est done seule en cause, parmi celles qui nous sont actuellement connues." The exact date of Gondophares is not known, but he lived somewhere about the middle of the first century B.C. The probable date of the inscription is therefore approximately 284-50=A.D. 234, or 274-50=A.D. 224. By a slip of the pen M. Senart gives the date of Gondophares as "environ 50 après J.C."

I have sent to the Asiatic Society of Bengal a fuller notice of M. Senart's paper.

7th February, 1892.

References

1. *Notes d'Epigraphie Indienne, extrait du Journal Asiatique, III.*, Paris, Imprimerie Nationale, MDCCCXC.
2. But, in his recently published work '*Coins of Ancient India*' (Quaritch, 1891), Sir A. Cunningham (page 37) refers to the Hashtnagar Inscription as being dated 84 only.

16

The Buddhist Origin of Naugaza Tombs

D. G. B. in* P. N. and Q. *1883

See Cunningham, *Archæological Survey of India,* 1872-73, pp. 98 ff., 130-1. The suggestion that they are of Buddhist origin is due to Mr. W. Simpson, *J.R.A.S.* Vol. XIII, p. 205. It is difficult, however, to see how figures of Buddha could have come to be regarded as the tombs of Patriarchs and Muhammadan heroes. Such tombs are not likely to present signs of antiquity, as they are always kept in repair.

17

A New Inscribed Græco-Buddhist Pedestal[1]

G. Bühler, Ph. D., LL.D., C.I.E.

Some weeks ago Dr. M.A. Stein kindly sent me two photographs of a lately found Græco-Buddhist pedestal, which is now in the Lahore Museum, and bears the number 1194. According to his remarks it was discovered in the Charsada mound, belonging to the ruins of Hashtnagar, which mark the site of the ancient town of Pushkalāvatī, the Peukelaotis or Peukelaitis of the Greeks, and once the capital of Western Gandhāra.

The front of the apparently hexagonal stone shews in a niche, which occupies nearly its whole breadth, in high relievo, five male figures, a seated in the centre and two standing ones on either side. The standing figures are easily recognised as Buddhist monks by their shaven heads and arrangement of the dress, which leaves the right arm free. The pair of them on the proper left and the one on the proper right, who stands nearest to the central figure, join their hands (*kṛitañjali*) in adoration, and the second holds, it would seem, a garland. All four turn their faces towards the seated person. The latter, who sits cross-legged on a square stone slab, apparently covered with a cushion, raises the right hand in the manner usual with teaching or speaking persons. This posture as well as his *ushṇīsha* and the rather full dress characterise him as a teaching Buddha. Two feet, which belonged apparently to a statue of very large size, are attached to the top slab of the pedestal. What makes the sculpture particularly valuable is an inscription in Karoshṭ hī characters, engraved below the five figures. In the centre and on the proper left there appears[2] to be one line only, while on the proper right two lines are visible. With the help of some very good paper-impressions, which I owe likewise to Dr. Stein, I read it is follows:

(1) on the proper left—*Arog* . . . .

(2) in the centre—*Saṁghamitrasa Sham* (?) . . . *sa danamukhe Bu*

(3) on the proper right, I. 2, *dho tu* . *sa* . .

I. 1, *Arog* . . *me* . . .

The line in the centre and the first letter of line 2 on the proper right no doubt belong together and form one sentence which means: "A Buddha, the excellent gift[3] of Saṁgnamitra Sham . . ." The explanation of the remainder of the letters on the proper right is more difficult. Possibly it began with the wish, frequently expressed in votive inscriptions: *Arog[iyaṁ]me [bhava]tu,* "may I obtain health." But in order to make the reading certain, a larger photograph is required. The mutilated signs on the proper left—*arog* . . . indicate that the same formula was repeated there. The portion of the inscription which can be explained with certainty, shews first, that the pedestal bore a statue of Buddha. Secondly, the type of the characters leaves no doubt that the inscription belongs to the time of one of the three well-known Kushana kings, Kanishka, Huvishka, Vāsushka or Vāsudeva. For the palæographically characteristic signs *da, bu* and *mu* exhibit the strangely cursive forms of the Kharoshṭhī of the Maṇikyāla, Zeda and Suê Bihār inscriptions as well as of that of the Wardak Vase.

The antiquity of the so-called Græco-Buddhist sculptures has been for many years a matter of dispute. Of late Mr. V.A. Smith[4] and Prof. Grünwedel[5] have expressed the opinion that they belong, one and all, to the first three centuries of our era, and they have supported this view with very strong and convincing arguments drawn from the style which these sculptures exhibit. The only other known inscribed piece, the Hashtnagar Pedestal, of which Mr. Smith has published an excellent photo-etching in the Journal of the Asiatic Society of Bengal (*loc. cit.* Plate x), furnishes no clear and certain indications as to its age. Its inscription, a revised reading of which was first given by M. Senart[6] and later by myself,[7] is dated in the year 274 or 284[8] of an unnamed era, and its letters are, as it happens, such as possess no characteristic palæographic peculiarities. The new inscription makes it certain, that the Charsada pedestal belongs to the second century A.D. Hence the determination of the age of the sculptures from Gandhāra, made in accordance with the principles of archæology, is supported, in this case, by palæographical considerations.

References

1. This note appeared first in German, in the *Anzeiger der philosophisch-historischen Classes der Wiener Akademie der Wiss.* 1896, No. xiv. The date of the Hashtnagar Pedestal inscription has been given there by a *lapsus calami,* as 276 or 286.
2. Above the middle of the central line the photograph and the impressions shew a number of strokes, which appear to me to be merely ornamental lines, not letters or numeral figures.
3. The word *danamukhe* has first been explained by M. Senart. Its Pali equivalent *dānamukha* occurs in Jātaka No. 524, Vol. V, p. 163, II. 8 and 25.
4. "Græco-Roman Influence on the Civilisation of Ancient India," *Jour. As. Soc. Bengal,* Vol. 58, p. 108 ff.
5. *Buddhistische Kunst in India,* Berlin, 1893, p. 79 f.
6. *Notes d'Ēpigraphie Indienne,* III. p. 16 f.
7. *Indian Antiquary,* Vol. XX, p. 394. I regret that, when writing this note, I had overlooked M. Senart's remarks on this inscription. He certainly first recognised that Sir A Cunningham's *emborasmasa masasa* is erroneous and that the month is the Indian Praushṭhapada.
8. With Sir A. Cunningham and Mr. Smith I read the figure for 200 with certainty on the photo-etching, and I think that 70 is more probably 80.

18

Deposit of Sutras in Stupas

V.A. Smith, *M.A. I.C.S.* (*Retd.*)

When Dr. Hoey and I described the find of inscribed bricks, as yet unique, at Gōpālpur in the Gōrakhpur District (*Proc. A.S.B.* 1896, p. 100) we failed to understand the nature of the ruined building in which they were enshrined. The bricks were inscribed with the *sūtra* of the 'Twelve Nidānas,' or the 'Chain of Causation,' and had been deposited on a brick stand or platform in "a small chamber, about eight feet square and about eight feet below the surface, which was built of huge bricks, about a foot and a half long, and some three inches thick . . . On a ledge in the chamber Dr. Hoey himself found a small earthenware saucer containing eleven copper coins, which had evidently been undisturbed since they were deposited." Ten of the coins belonged to the Kushān kings, Kadphises II (Hima), Kanishka, and Huvishka, while one was a specimen of the 'Cock and Bull' series of Ajodhya, with the name Ayu, or, as Mr. Rapson reads it, Ayya (for Ārya), Mitra.

Apparently, therefore, the deposit was made in the reign of Huvishka, the latest of the four kings represented. Possibly the number of coins, eleven, may be intended to signify the years of his reign. If so, the date, according to my chronology, with assumes the Kushān inscriptions to be dated in the Laukika era, would be A.D. 164. Even if my theory of the early use of the Laukika era should not be sustained, and it should be proved that the great Kushān kings employed a special 'era of Kanishka,' the date named would still, I am convinced, be approximately correct. The reasons for placing both Kanishka and Huvishka in the second century A.D. seem to me to be overwhelming.

A passage in I-tsing's work, *Records of the Buddhist Religion* (transl. Takakusu, p. 160), proves clearly that the chamber at Gōpālpur opened by Dr. Hoey was the relic-chamber of a stūpa. "The priests and the laymen in India," I-tsing observes, "make *chaityas* or images with earth, or impress the Buddha's image on silk or paper, and worship it with offerings wherever they go. Sometimes they build *stūpas* of the Buddha by making a pile and surrounding it with bricks. They sometimes form these *stūpas* in lonely fields, and leave them to fall in ruins. Anyone may thus employ himself in making the objects for worship. Again, when the people make images and *chaityas* which consist of gold, silver, copper, iron, earth, lacquer, bricks, and stone, or when they heap up the snowy sand (*lit.*, sand-snow), they put in the images or *chaityas* two kinds of śarīras [relics]: (1) the relics of the Great Teacher; (2) the Gāthā of the Chain of Causation. The Gāthā is as follows:–

'All things (*Dharmas*) arise from a cause.
The Tathāgata has explained the cause.
This cause of things has been finally destroyed.
Such is the teaching of the Great Śramaṇa (the Buddha).'

If we put these two in the images or *chaityas,* the blessings derived from them are abundant."

In a note Mr. Takakusu cites Professor Oldenberg and Rhys Davids as remarking that this famous stanza, the so-called 'Buddhist creed,' doubtless alludes to the formula of the twelve Nidānas, which explains the origination and cessation of what are called here '*dhammahêtuppa bhava.*' Instances may be quoted of this stanza having been either enshrined in a *stūpa,* or incised upon the building, but as yet the full sūtra of the twelve Nidānas has not been found in any stūpa, except that at Gōpālpur.[1]

I may add that Dr. Hoernle has for long entertained the intention of publishing a complete edition of the Gōpālpur inscribed bricks, but has not yet found an opportunity of doing so. A small scale photograph of one side of one of them is given in Prof. Rhys David's latest book, *Buddhist India* (p. 123, fig. 27). The fact is also worth noting that bricks of huge dimensions were still used as late as the second century A.D.; but it is possible that they were taken from an earlier building. Bricks of such size are commonly associated with buildings of greater antiquity.

References

1. Compare the late Mr. Carlleyle's discoveries in the great mound near Kasiā in the Gōrakhpur District, which was for a long time erroneously believed to be the site of Kuśinagara. He writes: – "This sitting figure of Buddha . . . was actually found inside and in the centre of the base of a small brick votive *stūpa.*" In clearing away another similar, but ruinous, little *stūpa,* he found in the centre of its base a fragment of sculpture exhibiting a female figure, apparently broken off from a group. "This placing of religious sculptures, or small statues," Mr. Carlleyle observes, "inside small brick votive *stūpas* was something new to me; and I thought this circumstance to be very curious and worthy of record." In a deep excavation in front of the temple of the Dying Buddha, he obtained a small plate of copper, about four and a half inches in length by an inch in width, inscribed with the usual Gāthā, *Yé dharma,* &c. The script was judged to be of the fifth century A.D. I have no doubt that this plate also had been used as the sanctifying deposit placed inside either an image or votive *stūpa.* (Cunningham, *Reports,* XVIII. 70).

19

The Peregrinations of Indian Buddhists in Burma and in the Sunda Islands

Dr. E. Muller-*Hess of Bern*

Translated from the German by

G.K. Nariman, *Rangoon*

The sources, which are at our command for the ancient history of Burma, are the holy scriptures of southern Buddhists composed in Pāli. These were written in India and touch on the history of further India and Burma only cursorily and as a disgression. Besides they cannot claim implicit reliance; but implicit reliance cannot at all be placed in Oriental annalists since a simple straight narrative without ornamentation of their own imagining has been always foreign to them.

According to the concordant testimony of all the histories, the Burmans came from the Ganges Valley and their kings were relatives to the Princes of Kośala and Kapilavastu. Of this tradition only this much is true, namely, that the Burmans emigrated no doubt, from the north and possibly in the course of their migration touched the valley of the Ganges. But there can be no possibility about their being related to the Aryans of India: that would be in conflict with their racial peculiarities as well as their language, which, no doubt, belongs to the monosyllabic group. The whole theory of the descent of the Burmans from India was first invented, after the conversion of the country to Buddhism, by court historians, who thereby flattered the reigning kings, inventing for them a kinship with the clan from which the Buddha had sprung.

In another instance the Burmese tradition comes in contact with the history of India, namely, as regards prince Daśaratha.

He, too, was a descendant of the Śākya dynasty of Kapilavastu to which Gotama belonged, and wandered after renouncing the throne eastwards to Burma, where he founded the so called second Tagaung Dynasty.

From these repeated attempts of the historians to connect the history of Burma with that of India and especially with Kapilavastu, it follows that at an early date a regular intercourse must have been established between the two countries. Thus, we read in the sacred books of merchants from Ukkalā or Suvarṇabhūmi (these are the ancient names of Burma) who carried on business in Central India. Two of these merchants came in direct contact with the Buddha himself, as is reported to us in one of the oldest texts. (*Mahāvagga,* Book I, Chapter 4). The account is naturally somewhat fantastically embellished, still I assume with certainty that a historical kernel underlies it. It is stated there that the Tathāgatas was seated at the foot of the Rājāyatana tree sunk in deep meditation, when there came up to him two men named Tapussa and Bhallika from Ukkalā bringing to the Buddha rice cakes and honey, offering the same to him as a present from themselves. The Buddha thought that "the Tathāgata do not take any food in their hands; how then shall I receive these rice cakes and honey?" Upon this the four Mahārājas of the four directions produced before him four stone utensils, in which the Buddha received the offered rice cakes and honey. These two merchants thus became the first lay disciples of the Buddha. This account in the *Mahāvagga* is confirmed by the inscription of the Shwe Dagon Pagoda at Rangoon, which dates from the year 1485 during the reign of king Dhammacheti. This king sent out eleven monks to Ceylon to enable them to receive their Upasampadā consecration at the celebrated Mahāvihāra, since their own ordination had become null, as they had not observed the prescriptions of the *Vinaya.* The pagoda of Shwe Dagon itself is said to have been built in the life time of Gotama; though, of course, this is mere legend. This inscription repeats the account as given in the *Mahāvagga* and adds that both the merchants received eight hairs from Gotama, which they took back to their country and enshrined in their pagoda on the summit of the Tamagatta Mount, east of the city of Asitanjanagara.

Both these accounts differ only in one essential point. For while in the *Mahāvagga,* the two merchants came from Ukkalā overland, the Shwe Dagon inscription states that this journey was made by ship. From this it appears that the compiler of the *Mahāvagga* understood Ukkalā to be Orissa, which is a province of India, from where one could journey overland to the Rājāyatana tree. Dhammaceti, on the other hand, the author of the inscription on the Shwe Dagon, understood by Ukkalā the territory at the foot of the Shew Dagon Hill stretching up to the Irāvadi, where a number of colonists from further India must have settled at an early date. Hence he makes the two merchants voyage in a ship.

When we look into the later Buddhist Literature we find the history of Tapussa and Bhallika also in the commentary of Buddhaghosha to the *Vinaya* and to the *Anguttaranikāya,* which is a production of the 5th Christian century. There also the city from where they came and where they erected the pagoda on their return is called Asitanjananagara, just as in the inscription on the Shwe Dagon. Accordingly, there seems to be no doubt that Buddhaghosha, too, the most celebrated of the later Buddhist theologians, had in his mind Burma and not Orissa, and that the Shwe Dagon Pagoda was actually built on the spot, where the two merchants buried the hair relics presented to them by Gotama. The name Dagon can be traced to an old Tikumbha "the three alms bowls", and with this is linked the legend that Gotama and his two favourite disciples, Sāriputta and Moggallāna had buried their alms bowls at that place. The name came into use first in the 16th century, while before that time the pagoda was called Singuttaracheti. Buddhaghosha's testimony is, therefore, of special value, in as much as he composed the greater number of his *Commentaries* in Burma, after he had spent some time in Ceylon with a view to study the sacred scriptures at the latter place. The Burmese historians even assert that he was born in their country. But this is contradicted by the evidence of the Mahāvansa, which alleges his birth place to be in the vicinity of the holy Bodhi Tree, and, therefore, is not to be accepted as a historical fact. The identity of Ukkalā and Burma, as asserted by Buddhaghosha, is no doubt, (as Kern indicates), in conflict with the statement of the *Lalita-Vistāra,* which places the home of the two merchants in a country to the north of the Deccan, and it likewise is not in accord with the information of the Chinese Pilgrim Hiuan-Thsang, who makes the merchants come from Baktria. But the *Lalita-Vistara* has proved itself in may cases to be an unreliable source and the expression "northern country" is so vague that it might indicate almost any country. As regards Hiuan-Thsang he is a great authority for Northern Buddhism; but, he has little knowledge of Southern Buddhism, and when his evidence is in conflict with that of Buddhaghosha, we must explicitly give precedence to the latter.

We assume, therefore, that the first two lay disciples of Gotama originally came from Burma; but that is not the same thing as to say that Buddhism had already been introduced into Burma by that time. That event took place after the Council of Pāṭaliputra, which was held under the patronage of king Aśoka. At this Council, at the suggestion of Tissa Moggaliputta, it was resolved to send out missionaries to various directions with a view to proselytise the surrounding countries to Buddhism. Both the children of king Aśoka, Mahinda and Sanghamittā, went over to Ceylon; to Burma went the apostles Sona and Uttara. These two arrived there after a long journey, because the country was at that time in the possession of a sea monster who was working havoc there. The apostles succeeded in destroying the monster and naturally gained unexpected success in their mission of proselytisation. Two-thousand-five-hundred men and one-thousand-five-hundred women forthwith accepted monkhood, and the kings of the country thence-forward bore the name of Sonuttara.

The port where Sona and Uttara landed in Burma was called Golanagara or Golamattikā-nagara, and lay some twenty mile north-west of the capital, Thatôn. The late Doctor Forchhammer, who rendered considerable service to the archeology of Burma, discovered there tolerably extensive ruins which go to prove an old settlement at the place. The name of the city in an inscription at Kalyāni belonging to the 15th century is explained so as to suggest that it consisted of earthen houses after the style of those constructed by the Gaula or Gola in India. It was also probably an old Indian colony from pre-Christian times similar to the one mentioned above at the foot of the Shwe Dagon Hill. In the 16th Century the city was called Takkala, and at present it is named Ayetthima. Forchhammer attempted to identify this Golanagara with the territory called Kalah mentioned by Arab geographers, and accordingly propounded quite a new hypothesis with reference to a question which had already been taken up by Sir Emerson Tennent and others. The Arabs speak about a kingdom, which bore the name of Zabedj and extended in the 8th and 9th Centuries over the Islands to the south and east of Malacca, and consequently to Java, Borneo, Sumatra, etc. To this kingdom belonged likewise the southern extremity of India and also the country in question called Kalaḥ. This place was the centre of commerce in aloes, camphor, sandlewood, ivory, and lead. The ships coming from the east, China, and from the west, Persia, met at Kalaḥ and exchanged their respective commodities. This Kalaḥ therefore, must have been situated somewhere in the Indian Ocean and the supposition of Sir Emerson Tennent that it would be Point-de-Galle in Ceylon has nothing improbable about it. Even this day Ceylon constitute the Centre of Commerce and the meeting point of passengers in the Indian Ocean, and if Point-de-Galle has been replaced as a port in course of centuries by Colombo, it was because the port of Point-de-Galle is in the first place unsafe, and secondly, because, it was the government which directed the intercourse towards the capital Colombo. In the accounts of the Arab geographers we come across a group of islands which must have existed in the vicinity of this ancient Kalah, and this has probably placed us on the right track. Sir Emerson Tennent thinks in this connection of the Maldive Islands but that is scarcely probable, because, the Maldive Islands lie two and a half days' journey west of Point-de-Galle, a situation which must have proved one of great distance for the then commercial circumstances. Perhaps we would be nearer the mark if we understood by Kalah the north-west coast of Ceylon, for, as a matter of fact there does exist a group of islands in close proximity, which constitutes what is called the Adams Bridge, and which was even a connecting link with the main land in pre-historic times. In the immediate neighbourhood of Kalah lived according to Cosmas Indicopleustes the king who had the hyacinth (ὁ εις εχων τὸν ὑακινθον) which is an attempt at transcribing the precious stone district in Ceylon at present called Sabara Gamuva, and with it was connected the land where the pepper goods *i.e.* the district between Puttalam and Adams Peak which is known in modern times by the name of Maha Oya. The Arab geographer Abu Zayid further narrates that the country in his time was subject to two kings. . . . the one was the Sultan of Zabej whose domination extended over Malacca, the Sunda Islands, and Travancore, the other was a Singhalese king who lived as a dependent on the Sultan.

Of another opinion is the author of the anonymous work on Ceylon which appeared in 1876 in London under the title, "Ceylon, a general description of the Island, historical, physical, and statistical". He is of the view that the vessels which plied between China and Persia must have sailed from Cape Comorin straight over the Gulf of Bengal to the Nicobar Islands; they must have touched at the port of Kalah which must have been in that case one of the islands or peninsulas belonging to Hinter India, possibly, the modern Kedah near Penang. There is nothing more to adduce in support of this hypothesis except the more or less questionable similarity of pronunciation between Kedah and Kalah. This hypothesis, however, has more of probability in it than that of Forch-hammer, because, the vessels must have sailed past Kedah, while in order to call a halt at Golanagara, they would have to make a long detour towards the north. I therefore, remain an adherent of the view of Sir Emerson Tennent concerning the situation of Kalah; only for Point-de-Galle I would substitute the north-west coast of the Island of Ceylon.[1]

We will now leave Burma and the question connected with it and cast a glance at the Sunda Islands. The date of the first colonisation is here also a matter of doubt, though the place whence the colonists immigrated was in all probability Kalinga, the district to the north of the mouth of the Godavary. The name Kalinga or Kaling, which is the designation bestowed by the Chinese on the Javanese, is no strong proof of this, for, the Chinese so call all the Indians who crossed over the ocean to the Celestial Empire. But it is very likely that they originally came from there, because it was also the provenance of the Singhalese. The Chinese Pilgrim Fa-Hian, who landed at Java about the year 413 on his return voyage from India to China, and sojourned there for a time, found an Indian civilisation in full growth. Brahmans and the so called heretics, as Fa-Hian calls all Shaivites, were in large numbers, while there were few or no Buddhists at all. This is confirmed by Sanskrit inscriptions in western Java and east Borneo, which to judge by the formation of the alphabet must be at the latest as old as the 5th Century, From these inscriptions, which are of the Vaishnavite character, we can conclude that both Java and the east coast of Borneo were hinduised prior to the 5th Century. Moreover, we learn from a Chinese report that in the year 435 there reigned in Java a prince, whose name was the pure Indian Dhāravarman and his title Śrīpāla. We possess documents belonging to Java and composed in its native language, the *Kavi* from 9th Century. From this it follows that about that time the country was completely Hinduised and that there were traces of Buddhism in the Mahāyāna form. Probably, the Buddhists had immigrated to Sumatra and Malacca in the 5th Century soon after Fa Hian's visit. This is supported by the Sanskrit inscriptions of Kedah and province Wellesley, as well as of the celebrated temple of Boro Bodor, the most extensive Buddhist structure in existence. According to the opinion of Fergusson and Burgess, the temple was completed in the 7th Century and its construction must have taken somewhere about a hundred years so that its building was probably commenced in the 6th Century.

We find Indian influence equally in Sumatra, although not in such a high degree as in Java and Bali. The alphabet which is used in Sumatra can be traced to an Indian origin, and the language has adopted a number of Sanskrit words. There are tolerably numerous names of places of Sanskrit origin. Buddhism must have flourished there from the 10th to the 14th

Centuries, as can be inferred from several inscriptions and ancient buildings. Of all the islands of the Archipelago. Java alone seems to have admitted the division into castes according to the Hindu model, and this is an indication of Brahmanical and not Buddhist influence, for the Buddhist strove to do away with caste. The most prominent Brahmanical sect in Java was the Shaivite. Shaivism and Buddhism were the two officially recognised religions in Java, just as they are in Nepal of to-day where the King and the ruling classes are Shaivites, whereas the mass of the people do homage to the Buddha. We even find a kind of syncretism of both the religions in Java, in as much as the Buddha is regarded and adored as younger brother of Śiva. At great festivals like that of Pañchavalikrama, it so happens that four Shaivite and one Buddhistic priests officiate in co-operation. The Buddhist priest turns his face towards the south, three of the Shaivites facing the three remaining cardinal points and the fourth sitting in the centre. We see from this that the Buddhists of the Sunda Islands were far from fanatics and allowed the adherents of other faiths to live there undisturbed. The situation was probably similar to that obtaining in Ceylon though in an inverted order, for the Buddhists were the first to occupy Ceylon, Hinduism having crept into the island only at a subsequent period along with Tamil immigrants. There, too, we meet with, as at Dondra on the southern coast, in one and the same temple images of the Buddha, of Vishṇu, of Gaṇeśa, and the holy Bull from Tanjore, all of them being installed there without mutual disturbance or error in the prayer offered by the faithful of these various creeds.

References

1. There is much more to be said for Kalah=Kedah than the author seems to be aware of.—ED.

20

Bauddha Vestiges in Kanchipura

T.A. Gopinatha Rao, M.A.; *Trivandrum*

Kāñchīpura (Conjeevaram) is one of the seven most ancient and famous cities of India; it is mentioned in the *Mahābhāshya* of Patañjali, whose age is placed by scholars somewhere about the middle of the 4th century before the Christian era. Besides being remarkable s a beautiful city, Kāñchīpura was always a great seat of learning. In it dwelt men of various religious persuasions and schools of different systems of philosophies. The Vêdic professors lived side by side with the professors of non-Vêdic philosophies, such as the Jaina and the Bauddha. That all these religions were equally treated by the ancient kings may be inferred from the fact that the early Pallava rulers of the Toṇḍai-maṇḍalam assumed such names as Buddhavarman, Skandaverman and Paramêśvaravarman – names which perhaps indicated the sects to which they individually belonged. We are at present concerned with the period of Bauddha dominancy at Kāñchīpura, and therefore let us confine our attention to Buddhism and the Bauddha vestiges found in and around Kāñchīpura.

Yuan Chwang states that, when he visited Kan-chi-pu-lo (Kāñchīpura), it was about thirty *li* in circuit. "The region had a rich fertile soil; it abounded in fruits and flowers and yielded precious substances. The people were courageous, thoroughly trustworthy, and public-spirited, and they esteemed great learning; in their written and spoken language they differed from 'Mid-India'. There were more than 100 Buddhist monasteries with above 10,000 Brethren all of the Sthavira School. The Dêva Temples were 80, and the majority belonged to the Digambaras. This country had been frequently visited by the Buddha, and king Aśôka had erected topes at the various spots where the Buddha had preached and admitted members into his order. The capital [Kāñchīpura, of the Ta-lo-pi-tu or Drāviḍa country] was the birth-place of Dharmapāla Pūsa[1], who was the eldest son of the high official of the city . . . . . Not far from the south of the capital was a large monastery which was a rendezvous for the most eminent men of the country. It had an Aśôka tope above 100 feet high, where the Buddha had once defeated Tīrthakas by preaching, and had received many into his communion. Near it were traces of a sitting-place and exercise-walk of the four Past Buddhas."[2] Thus we gather from the testimony of this eye-witness that Kāñchīpura not only had a large Buddha population but many places of public worship in the 7th century A.D.

The statements of the Chinese pilgrim are borne out by the descriptions we meet with in the *Maṇimêkhalai,* one of the five famous epic poems of the Tamil Classic Period. We are here told that the heroine Maṇimêkhalai was advised by her grandfather to assume the form of a young monk and to seek instruction in their respective philosophies from the learned in the Vaidīka, Śaiva, Vaishṇava, Ājīvaka, Nirgrantha, Sāṅkhya, Vaiśêshika and Lôkāyatika religions at Kāñchīpura, and to embrace that one which satisfied her best. While there, she visited the Buddhist Chaitya erected by Kiḷḷi, a Chôḷa prince. On her arrival being made known to the then reigning king of Kāñchi, he paid a visit to her with all his ministers and showed her the grove and tank which he had caused to be made in imitation of those in the island of Maṇipallavam; and at her request the king erected a seat for Buddha and temples for the goddesses Dīpa-tilakai and Maṇimêkhalai.

That the Bauddhas were in existence at Kāñchi in the days of the Śaiva saint Tirujñāna-sambandha, that is, in the middle of the seventh century A.D. appears to the certain; for he refers to them by the names *Bôdhiyār* (the worshippers of the *bôdhi* tree) *Thêras,* as also by the description of their monks as the wearers of mats for their garments.

Then again there is the tradition that Śaṅkarāchārya, the great Vêdāntic teacher, vanquished the Bauddhas in a religious

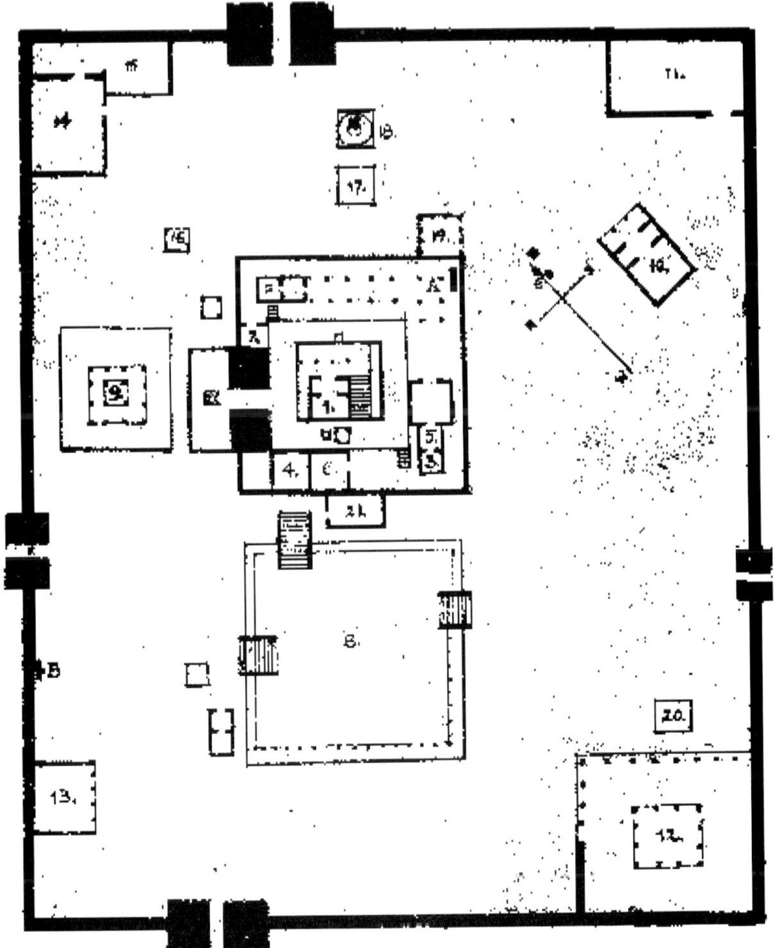

Sketch Plan of the Temple of Kamakshidevi at Conjeeveram (Facing Page 106)

1. Central Shrine of the Kamakshi Temple, **2.** Shrine of the Utsava-Vigraha, **3.** Bhangaru-Kamakshi Shrine, **4.** Sankaracharya Shrine, **5.** Saravati Shrine, **6.** Store-room, **7.** Palliyarai (Bed-room), **8.** Tank, **9.** Sculptured Mandapa, **10.** Siva Shrine, **11.** Kitchen, **12.** Navaratri-mandapa, **13.** Kottay-mandapa **14.** Temple Office, **15.** Garden, **16.** Well, **17.** Flag-Staff, **18.** Bali-pitha, **19.** Dhvajarohanamandapa, **20.** Kuttu-mandapa, **21.** Vishnu Shrine in three storeys

Image of Buddha, Conjeevaram, Fig. 1: Found in the innermost *prakara* of the Kamakshidevi Temple Height 7' 10''

Image of Buddha, Conjeevaram, Fig. 2: Found in the second *Prakara* of the Kamakshidevi Temple, Height about 3' 6''

Image of Buddha, Conjeevaram, Fig. 3: Found in the garden adjoining the Kamakshidevi Temple, Height about 5' 6''

Image of Buddha, Conjeevaram, Fig. 4: Found in the Karukkil-amarnda-amman Temple, Height about 3' 9''

Image of Buddha, Conjeevaram, Fig. 5: Found in the Karukkil-amarnda-amman Temple, Height about 2' 6''

wrangle and drove them out of Kāñchi. A similar tradition exists in connection with the Jaina priest Akaḷaṅka, who is said to have challenged before king Himasītala of Kāñchi the Bauddhas residing in that city to a religious dispute, and to have won a complete victory over them. Thus a large number of accounts, both historical and legendary, exists in proof of the predominance of the Bauddha influence and the existence of Bauddha places and objects of worship in Kāñchīpura, even so late as the 9th century A.D.

The question thus naturally arises, that while the Jaina temples are still in existence, what became of the places and objects of worship of the Bauddhas ? Modern scholars, who have written on the antiquities of Kāñchīpura, the Pallava supremacy in Kāñchi, and on other similar subjects, have all uniformly deplored the paucity of sculptural and architectural materials to corroborate the truth of the statements made by Yuan Chwang and others concerning the Bauddha occupation of Conjeevaram. It may be stated without fear of contradiction that most of these authors have done little or nothing in the direction of tracing vestiges of Buddhism in Kāñchīpura. Unfortunately the official archæologists do not also appear to have paid that amount of attention which this most interesting place deserves. In the course of a twelve hours active search, I came upon no less than five images of Buddha within a radius of half a mile from the famous temple of Kāmākshidêvī. I was also told that two other megalithic images of Buddha lie buried in a garden adjoining the same temple. I give below a short description of the images and the places where they are found.

The first and the most remarkable of these five figures is a standing image of Buddha Fig. I. It is found in the first *prākāra* of the Kāmākshidêvī's temple, at the place marked A on the ground plan of that temple, a sketch of which is separately given. The total height of the image, including the pedestal, is 7 feet 10 inches, and the detailed measurement are as follows: –

Height of the images without the pedestal 7 feet.

Height of the pedestal alone .... 10 inches.

Width across the shoulders, ... 2 feet.

Length of the face, ... 9 inches.[3]

Breadth of the face, ... 8 inches.

Height of the neck, ... 2½ inches.

Its two hands are broken; wherefore it is not possible to state definitely what they carried; presumably the right hand was held in the *abhaya* pose and the left carried an alms-bowl. The nose of the images is much worn; otherwise the image is in an excellent state of preservation. The long flowing robes descending from the left hand and the folds of the same over the right thing are exquisitely worked out. The present position of the image with respect to the temple of Kāmākshī can be explained by two plausible hypotheses, namely, (1) that the image did certainly occupy some important place in the very temple itself; or (2) that it was brought in there by some one for safe custody. Let us consider the second hypothesis first, for, if its untenability is proved the possibility of the first becomes patent. If it is to be believed that the huge stone image was deposited in its present position by some well-intentioned man, the questions which remain to be answered are (1) where could it have lain before it was brought into the temple? and (2) a man of what religious persuasion could have brought it in? It may have been lying at some distance from the temple, or near it, or within its compound. In the first two cases, it must indeed have been a herculean task to have carried the image, weighing some tons, over a long distance and lifted it to a height of about seven feet in order to deposit it in its present position. In its transit into the temple no less than two or three gateways have to be crossed. And why, after all, should it have been taken in? If it was for preservation, it could have been set up in a well-illuminated place in, say , the outermost *prākāra,* which would not have involved so much trouble and labour as carrying it to the innermost place of the temple. On the other hand, it is easier to believe that the image was in some place very near its present position and was removed from its original seat and just set down where it is at present.

Again, who was the person who took the trouble to put the image into the innermost *prākāra* of the temple, a Hindu or a Buddhist? If it was a Hindu who removed it into the temple and was so considerate towards this image, why did he not extend his sympathy also towards the other images lying near the temple? It is quite unlikely that a Hindu would have taken all the trouble to have brought the image for safe custody in a Hindu temple. On the other hand, he could have easily removed it from some important place occupied by it in the same temple and placed it in its present position. If, on the other hand, it is to be said that a Buddhist brought it from outside and deposited it in the Hindu temple, that would be a patent absurdity, for no Hindu would allow a Buddhist to place a Bauddha image in safe custody in his temple. Thus then it is impossible that the image was lying outside the Hindu temple of Kāmākshī and brought into it for safe custody; rather, the probability is the the temple itself or at least a portion of it was a Buddhistic one. The temple of Kāmākshī was, in all probability, originally a temple of Tārādêvī and, as with many other temples of alien faith, converted into a Hindu temple in later times.

The second image, whose head is broken and lost, is found in the second *prākāra*. It was covered with debris and with some trouble the image was unearthed for photographing. Its position is marked B on the ground plan of the temple. Both the hands of the image lie on its iap in the *yôga-mudrā* pose. See Fig. 2.

The third image is to be found in a garden situated near the temple of Kāmākshīdêvī. It is also seated in the *yôga* attitude, with the hands in the *yôga-mudrā* pose. The *jvālā* on the head, thc upper cloth and other minor features declare it to be an image of Buddha. I heard that in the same gardcn there are lying buried two more very large seated images of Buddha. It would be interesting if these could be excavated and exposed by the Archæological Department. See Fig. 3.

The fourth and the fifth images are kept in safe custody in the Karūkkil-amarndaamman temple on the way to Vishṇu-Kāñchi. I was told that a pious man collected all stone images lying round this goddess's temple and set them up in their present position. It is worshipped now by the Hindus who visit the temple. One of these has its right hand in the *bhūsparśa-mudrā,* while the two hands of the other are in the *yôga-mudrā,* attitude. See Figs. 4 and 5.

I am inclined to believe that if a vigourous and earnest search for more Bauddha vestiges is made, many more pieces of sculpture and architecture are likely to be discovered. It is to be hoped that the enthusiastic and energetic Archæologist with the Government of Madras will turn his attention to this interesting field of investigation.

References

1. He was a Hīnayānist monk, who appears to have been converted to Mahāyānism when he went to N. India. He was a professor in the famous University of Nālanda at the time Yuan Chwang visited that place.
2. Watter's *Translation,* Vol. II, p. 226.
3. Hence it is evident that the images is made according to the *uttama-daśa-tāla* measure. See Appendix B, in my "Elements of Hindu Iconography," Vol. I.

21

Alleged Buddhist Influence in the Sun Temple at Konarak

Guru Das Sarkar, M.A.; Calcutta

It was Raja Rajendra Lala Mitra who seems to have first suggested in his *Antiquities of Orissa* that like Darpan, the place of Ganesha, Konarak, the place of the Sun, "may fairly be suggested to have been Buddhist" (*Ant. Orissa,* Vol. II, p. 148). In his much earlier work Stirling—the first western worker in the field of Orissa History—makes no mention of such a theory in the chapter dealing with the great temple of the Sun, though he expatiates at some length on the architectural remains and the beauties of the door-frame carved in black chlorite.

Dr. Mitra apparently based his theory on the existence of a car-festival in Konarak. Popular belief and the accounts in the existing religious works like *Kapila Saṁhitā* seem to indicate that this extinct festival was one of some importance. It appears to have been once a sort of article of faith in these parts—that the person who witnessed the car-festival held in this sea-side shrine had the privilege of seeing the Sun God in a corporeal existence (*Śārīri Rūpa*). "Maitreyākshye vane puṇye rathayātrā-mahotsavam je paśyanti narā bhaktyā te paśyanti tanu raveḥ" (*Kapila Saṁhita,* Chap. VI).

The presence of an Aśoka inscription at Dhauli not far from Bhūbaneswar—the city of numerous temples—and the mention in Yuan Chwang's work of about a dozen *stūpas* built by the Emperor Aśoka in the Oḍra tract was regarded in Dr. Mitra's times as a sufficient basis for holding many of the principal shrines in Orissa as primarily of Buddhist origin.

In the passage referred to above (quoted by Dr. Mitra from the translation of Stanislaus Julien) there is a reference to the extraordinary prodigies exhibited, at some of these *stūpas,* and to the scholastic activities of some ten thousand monks who studied 'the great vehicle' in some hundred local monasteries where heretics and men of the faith lived 'pell mell'. It seemed to have been argued that as Buddhism was once in such a flourishing condition in two province of Orissa, it was quite reasonable to suppose that other shrines within 3 or 4 days journey from Dhauli would still contain lingering traces of their Buddhist origin either in ceremonials or in the architecture and sculpture. Dr. Mitra also lays considerable stress on a passage from the *Foe-ku-ki,* of which an English translation from the French rendering by MM. Remusat, Klaproth and Landresse seems to have been available in Calcutta at least 27 years before Dr. Mitra published his great pioneer work. The passage in question refers to the observance in ancient Pāṭaliputra of a car-festival, a close analogue of which the Chinese Pilgrim saw in a festival in Buddhist Khotan on his way to India. The description of the ceremony seems to have made a deep impression on the Indian Orientalist and the car-festival *per se* seems to have been regarded as a special feature of the Buddhist faith.

The Khaṇḍagiri caves lying within a few hours journey from Dhauli–once regarded as the habitation of Buddhist monks–have now been proved to be of Jaina origin from the *Hāthigumphā* inscription of King Khāravela supposed by Bhagwānlāl Indraji to be the 2nd century B.C. (Actes du sixième congrès des Orientalistes, Vol. III, pp. 174-177, and Mr. K.P. Jayaswal's paper in *JBORS,* December, 1917) and the following three minor inscriptions : (1) the inscription referring to the Jaina Monk Śubha-chandra (in Navamuni Gumphā), (2) the inscription of the Chief Queen of Khāravela (in the Manchapuri cave), and the (3) Udyota Keśari inscription in the Lalatendra Keśari Gumphā supposed on epigraphical grounds to date from the 10th century A.D. (*Ep. Ind.,* Vol. XIII, pp. 160, 165-166).

The emperor Aśoka flourished in the 3rd century B.C. If only after the lapse of a century or two, Jainism could leave such lasting evidence of its long continuance in the Kumāra and

Kumāri Hills in close proximity to Dhauli,[1] it is difficult to understand why Buddhism should be dragged in to account for the existence of a thirteenth century Solar Temple which copper-plates of Ganga Kings (Narasiṁha Deva II and IV, *JASB,* 1906 and 1905) agree in attributing to Narasiṁha Deva I (Langulya Narasiṁha or Narasiṁha of the tail), a king whose name is also mentioned in this connection in Abul Fazal's *Ain-i-Akbari.*

Mr. M.M. Chakravarty has, after very minute and careful calculations, ascertained the periods of reign of the respective kings of the Ganga dynasty in Orissa and there cannot be the least hesitation in accepting (1238-64) as the period of first Narasiṁha's reign–(*JASB.,* part. I, 1903). Mr. V.A. Smith also agrees in holding that the Konarak temple was built in the 13th century though he assigns the period between A.D. 1240 to 1280. The only inscription found at Konarak on the pedestal of an image since removed to the Indian Museum, though undated, may safely be assigned on paleographic and other grounds to the third quarter of the 13th century as has been done by Mr. M.M. Chakravarty in his note in the *JBORS,* Vol. III, part II, p. 283.

Though the palm-leaf record at Puri ascribes the erection of the temple to a mythical king of the Keśari dynasty–one of the so-called Caesars of Orissa as Dr. Rājendra Lāla Mitra was pleased to style them–there are in the remains at Konarak no trace of any earlier structure which might reasonably lead to the presumption that the present foundations were laid on the ruins of an earlier shrine.

The late Dr. Fleet, in his paper on the Somavaṃśī Kings of Katak, rightly disbelieves the temple-chronicles and puts forth convincing arguments in favour of the supposition that except the two Somavaṃśī kings[2] of the 11th century–Yayāti Keśarī or Mahāśiva Gupta and Janmejaya Mahābhava Gupta–the other Keśarīs styled Kūrma, Varāha, &c., are mere figments of the chronicler's imagination (*Ep. Ind.,* Vol. III, pp. 324, 336 *et. seq.*). Except the inscription of Udyota Keśarī mentioned above no other inscription or Copper-plate has been found of any other Keśarī king. In Sandhyākara Nandī's *Rāmacarita* (*Asiatic Society Memoirs,* Vol. I, p. 146, and p. 36 *ṭīkā* of śloka 5),[3] there is mention of one Karṇa Keśarī. But of this king also no inscription or any other reliable epigraphic evidence has yet been discovered. If Purandara Keśarī, referred to in the Palm-leaf record, had really existed and been the builder of this important temple, Choḍa Ganga's descendants would hardly have tried to filch the honour from him and in all likelihood some of the inscriptions of these monarchs would have set forth details about the earlier origin of the temple. It may be argued that as the Keśarī kings were staunch Hindus according to tradition and popular belief, their connection with the temple, even if proved to be a historical fact, would not be of much help to the supporters of the theory of Buddhist origin. But even in this regard there seems to be a divergence of opinion. Some architectural ornaments on the temple such as Gaja-Siṃha or elephants surmounted by lions or leogriffs, have been explained in a manner more clever than convincing—as the symbols of the triumph of the Hindu Keśarī kings, represented by the lions, over Buddhistic faith—of which elephant representations are said to be the special symbols. It is thus suggested, inspite of reliable evidence to the contrary, that the mythical Keśarī transformed or built up anew in parts a shrine originally Buddhist, and in token of his dominance put up these huge figures on the pyramidal roof of the temple as prominent sculptural decorations. The assertion that lions were the symbols (*Lāñchhana*) of the Keśarī kings, still remains to be proved.[4] The seal of the Murañjamura copper-plate of Yayāti Keśarī (*JBORS.*, March, 1916) is a figure of *Śrī* or *Kamalātmikā* and that on the copper-plate of Janamejaya (described in *Ep. Indi.*, Vol. XI, p. 95, *et. seq.*) is the representation of a man in a squatting posture. It would thus appear that no evidence is forthcoming at present to connect the temples with any line of kings anterior to Ganga Dynasty. The Udytoa Keśarī Jaina inscription at Khaṇḍagiri further proves that during the reign of this king with the Keśarī title (of about the 10th century A.D.), no intolerant persecution of heretical sects had taken place. In India it is hardly safe to theorize about the creed of the builders of a sacred shrine merely from the way the temple is fashioned or from its architectural or sculptural remains. Like Buddhist *stūpas,* Jaina *Stūpas* have also been discovered, and Hindu curvilinear temples like those of the Jainas are by no means uncommon. It has therefore been rightly held by modern authorities like Mr. V. Smith tht works of art and architecture should be classified with regard to their age and geographical position only, and arbitrary divisions formerly favoured by specialists like the late Mr. Fergusson according to the so-called religious styles have now been abandoned. We have so far been able to show that there is nothing in the geographical position of Konarak or in the age or style of the temple which would lead to a reasonable inference as to any Buddhist influence. We shall now examine to so-called Buddhist indications which are said to be still lingering in the name of the place, the traditions regarding past ceremonies, the peculiar style of architecture and the subject of some of the principal decorative sculptures.

As regard traditions, as to the so-called Buddhist ceremonies, much has been made of the car-festival or Ratha Yātrā, as already alluded to. Whatever may be the origin of this festival there is no doubt about the fact that the system of perambulation in cars and other conveyances appear to have been early adopted as an integral part of some of the Hindu observances.

In the *Agni-Purāna,* we find, even in connection with such a rather unimportant affair as the consecration of hand-written books or manuscripts that after the Pratisṭhā ceremony the book is to be perambulated (apparently round the city or town) in cars or elephants *'Rathena hastinā vāpi bhramayet pustakaṃ naraiḥ'* (Vol. I, p. 186, chap. 63, v. 16, *Biblioth. Indic.*). Thus it would appear that mere perambulation or carrying to and fro in cars of an image or simulacrum cannot always be taken as a Buddhist observance—specially in a period when Buddhism had no longer any hold on the province.

In his otherwise excellent monograph on Konarak published under the authority of Government Mr. Bishan Swarup tries to make out a strong case in favour of the "Buddhistic" theory. The name Kona Kone or Kona Kona occurs in certain verses in the copper-plates of Narasiṁha Deva II (*JASB,* 1896, p. 251, and of Nṛisiṁha Deva IV, (*JASB,* 1895) referred to above (Koṇā

Koṇe Kutir Kamachikara Dushṇa rashme) कोणा कोण कुठिर कमश्चिकर दूष्ण रश्मे। The common-sense inference from this is that the place was known at the time as Kona Kone or Kona and the word Konaraka means only the Arka or Sun God at Kona. This explanation (simple as it is) has met with the approval of so careful a scholar as Mr. V.A. Smith (*History of Fine Art in India and Ceylon,* p. 28, foot-note). Mr. Bishan Swarup, however, makes bold to assert that Konakona is an abbreviated or corrupted form of Koṇā Kamana or Koṇā Gamana, the name of one of the previous Buddhas (*Konarka,* p. 85). Whether phonetic decay can account for this change seems to be very much open to doubt, but when the ingenious author of *Konarka* proceeds to account for the last two syllables in Konaraka by bringing forward from the Sanskrit dictionary, *Amarakosha* (1, 1, 15), the word Arka Bandhu as one of the appellations of Buddha—one though convinced of the ingenuity of the explanation can hardly accept it as a correct or scientific statement of actual facts.

Then as regards the form, the temple looks like a huge car furnished with wheels—beautifully sculptured in the plinth. There are still some remains of big stone horses, which Mr. Havell regards as splendid specimens of Indian sculpture. Any one acquainted with Indian iconography would admit that the Sun God is represented as being drawn by seven horses in a car driven by his charioteer Aruṇa. Though there is nothing to show that the number of these horses at Konarak were increased at any subsequent date, Mr. Bishan Swarup supposes—I do not know on what authority—that the number of horses in this car pagoda was originally four and was increased to seven at some late date (*Konarka,* p. 89). He was apparently thinking of some sculpture at Bodh-gayā, reference to which will be made in a subsequent part of the paper, wherein Apollo is said to be represented as being drawn in a car with a team of four horses.

The key-stone of the Buddhistic theory appears to be the subject represented in some of the sculptures in the temple and it is necessary to consider them *seriatim.*

Much has been made of the abundance of elephant figures not only in the various friezes of the temple, but also in the elaborately sculptured altar or Ratna-Vedī.

In Konarak there are not only elephant friezes, but goose friezes as well, and there are cornices containing rows of processions of horsemen and infantry. While it must be admitted that elephant figures are met with in some of the oldest Buddhist remains such as the Aśokan cave known as the *Lomasa Ṛishi Guhā* in the Barabar Hills, similar sculptures are also to be found in structures almost contemporaneous with Konarak temple such as the temple of Hoysaleswar, an undisputed Hindu shrine supposed to have been built between A.D. 1117 and 1288. In the Hoysaleswara temple in Southern India there are amongst the animals depicted, figures of horses, elephants and Śārdūlas (lions) and the last were believed by some to be the symbols of Hoysala Ballalas, even as the lions or leogriffs in Konarak sculptures were taken to be the emblems of the Keśarīs. Architectural ornaments of this description are also not quite uncommon in Ellora Caves. M. Langlés says in describing the Ādināthа Sabhā in Ellora (Tome II, p. 79), "on a aussi pratiqué de petites retraitês (Nos. 8, 9, 10, 11, 12, 14, 15, 16, 17, 18) couvertes d'une multitude innombrable de sculptures. L'exterior est orné, d'elephants de lions et autres animaux." A careful study of these with reference to Sanskrit works has convinced the modern scholars of the prevalence of "a *canonical scheme of decoration*" of which such frieze-borne figures formed a part. (*History of Fine Art in Indian and Ceylon,* by V. Smith, p. 42, foot-note 2).

The Khajuraho group of temples are believed to have been erected between the 4th and 8th century of the Christian era and in the precincts of one of them—the temple of Viśvanātha—there is a colossal elephant carved out of stone. Elephant figures are also to be met with in the Ellora Caves. The huge stone-elephants at Konarak considered by connoisseurs to be not less vigorous in execution than the much-belauded horses of Sun cannot therefore be regarded as something singular or exceptional. The picture of a boy and elephant in the Konarak altar reminds Mr. Bishan Swarup of the Jātaka story which describes how the mother of the future Buddha saw in a prophetic dream that a white elephant was entering into her womb by piercing one of her sides. Mr. Swarup further mentions that Buddha himself was born as an elephant-keeper or driver in one of his incarnations (*Konarka,* p. 88). On this slender foundation is based the identification of the sculpure as illustrative of the Jātaka story. Mr. Swarup identifies another part of this very altar as depicting the meeting of Śāmba—the son of Kṛishna—and the Sun God, after the former had been cured by the special favour of the latter—of the dread disease of leprosy—the result of paternal curse for a thoughtless indiscretion. If the boy and elephant had merely been illustrative of a Jātaka story, it is only natural to suppose that the continuity of the subject should be maintained in the adjoining panels as well—as is said to be the case in regard to some of the far-famed sculptures at Boro Budur, but to identify at the same breath two such neighbouring sculptures, formed component parts of a single altar piece, as depicting the Buddhist Jātaka and Hindu Pauranic legends, can hardly be regarded as a satisfactory way of reconciling facts with theory. The prevalence of so-called Buddhist ornaments like the goose-frieze, the elephant-frieze and the *Baṛājhānjī* ornament consisting of reproductions of a water-weed on the pilasters,[5] the scroll work of Nāgas and Nāgakanyās, and the figure of Lakshmī on the lintel, seem only to indicate that like that of Makara in Hindu ornaments, in Toraṇas (gateways) and water-spouts (*Annual Report of Archæological Survey of India,* 1903-4, p. 227), the use of these architectural devices extended far back into the Buddhist age. In the mediæval period these conventional ornaments and decorations seem to have been adopted by architects in southern and south-eastern part of India. Similarly in some Buddhist *stūpas* miniature productions of these sacred structures are found in the ornamental pilasters. It would be as safe to ascribe the existence of a temple to Buddhist influence because of the existence of the *Baṛājhānji* decoration, goose-friezes or elephant friezes as it would be to attempt to lay at the door of Buddhism the type of Śaiva temple of the Bengal School[6] (of 17th century) which are still to be found in some parts of Nadia and other Bengal districts – simply because the pilasters of these buildings contain reproductions of temples in miniature.

The sculptural representation of trees found in the plinth have been taken to stand for the sacred *Bodhi-Tree* of the Buddhists. In the Jaina caves at Khaṇḍagiri, trees enclosed in railing are also found carved in relief. Tree-worship is prevalent among the Hindus to this very day. Kalpadruma, the legendary Tree of Desire described in sacred literature, the model of which used to be constructed in gold and given away as *Mahā-dāna,* may also have some influence in determining the *motif* of such architectural ornaments. That a Kalpadruma existed at Konarak like the *Vateśvara* at Puri appears clear from the *Kapila Saṃhitā* from which the following translation of an extract is given in Dr. Mitra's work. "There exists an all-granting tree named Arka-Vaṭa adorned by numerous birds and at its foot dwell many saints and whoever goes to the salvation-giving *banian* tree becomes, for certain indestructible. For the good of animated beings Sūryya himself has become the tree and those who recite the excellent *mantras* of Sūryya under its shade in three fortnights attain perfection." (*Ant. Orissa,* Vol. I, p. 147). Under the circumstance these trees, should, I think, be taken as conventional decorations only. As regards the semi-ophide *Nāga* and *Nāginī* figures represented singly and in couples, usually forming part of the beautiful scroll work and said to be an evidence of Buddhist Architecture (*Konarka,* p. 86), Mr. M. Ganguly in his work on Orissa has pointed out (Ganguly's *Orissa,* p. 177-78), that in the *Mahābhārata Ādiparba,* mention is made of the thousand Nāgas, the offsprings of Kaśyapa. Even to this day when performing *pūjā* of the Serpent Goddess Manasā, the name of the principal eight Nāgas – Vasukī, Padma, Mahāpadma, Takshaka, Kulira, Karkaṭ a, Śankha, &c. – are duly recited. Mr. Ganguly holds – I think with the majority of Hindu opinion in his favour – that these demigod-like Nāgas were probably borrowed by Buddhism from Hindu sources. At any rate there is no reason to suppose that every Nāga representation found in Hindu temple should be the outcome of Buddhist cult, simply because there is mention of Nāgas in Buddhist sacred books, this does not in any way militate against the generally accepted opinion that a certain amount of resembles is noticed among the Buddhist Nāga figures as represented on the *topes* of Sanchi and Bharhut, and the Nāga representations of the later Brahminical period as found in the south-eastern (Orissa) temples.

The Indian sculptors of old never carved their names underneath the works of art coming from their chisels nor described the subject which they represented in the various sculptures. Hindu iconography as a science is still of recent origin. To this may be ascribed the conflict of opinion which is so often noticed in regard to the identification of sculptures by different scholars and sometimes ludicrous mistakes are made because of the partiality or bias towards a particular theory.

Instances of such clashing opinions are by no means uncommon in regard to the Konarak sculptures. The well-known "Teaching Scene" has been taken by Mr. Swarup to represent Buddha in the act of delivering a sermon or imparting religious teaching to some of his disciples (*op. cit.,* p. 86). Dr. A.K. Coomaraswamy, a scholar well learned in Hindu and Buddhistic lore, describes this in his *Viśvakarma,* Part VII, plate 72, as Vaishṇava Guru. Any one who has the opportunity of examining this picture carved in chlorite or the beautiful reproduction of it as given by Dr. Coomaraswamy will admit that there is nothing in it peculiarly Buddhistic, which may confirm Mr. Swarup's identification.

There is another representation, known as the "Archery Scene," which Mr. Swarup considers to be the illustration of an incident from *Śarabhaṅga Jātaka* (*op. cit.,* p. 87). Buddha, though he was without any previous training, is said to have defeated all his competitors in an archery competition. Among the local people this sculpture is said to illustrate the shooting of arrows by Paraśurāma. In the Hindu sacred books there is mention of an incident referring to Paraśurāma's reclaiming land from the sea-bed by shooting arrows. Whether the mound or projection in the sculpture which the arrows are represented as piercing through is meant for a sea-side cliff or is due merely to a wrong idea of perspective is more than what can be asserted with confidence. As instances are not wanting of representations of purely secular incidents—such as hunting scenes—among the Konarak sculptures there need be no objection in taking this at least as a secular feat in archery. Among these sculptures some have been identified as pictures of *Pauranic* incidents such as marriage of Sita and killing of Mahishāśura and accepted as such without cavil even by Mr. Bishan Swarup. A number of images of Hindu deities such as Bishnu, Sūrya, Gangā, Bālagopala and Bṛihaspati, &c., have also been discovered among the ruins. It does not seem therefore probable that among Hindu *Pauranic* sculptures of this description, illustrations of Buddhist Jātaka stories would also find a place in a scattered disconnected sort of way. Mr. Bishan Swarup identified one of these stone-carved pictures as Buddha with Muchalinda the Serpent God (*op. cit.,* p. 87) and the two small female figures standing on two sides were declared to be Sujātā the wife of the rich *Śresṭhī,* who brought the Enlightened One food after his prolonged abstinence, and her maid-servant Punna. Mr. Swarup's objection to the group being a Hindu Vaishnavite image lies in the fact that ordinarily Vishṇu is depicted as lying on the Ocean of Milk with the serpent Śesha or Ananta spreading its hoods over his head.

In the catalogue of exhibits published on the occasion of the centenary of the Indian Museum, 1913, there is a description of an authentic Buddha and *Muchalinda* image (No. 6290 of the Catalogue). It is noticeable that in this sculpture Buddha is represented as seated on the head of the Serpent God. Serpent hoods are found also on the head of the image of the Jaina Tīrthaṅkara Pārśvanātha. It does not seem quite safe, therefore, to classify an image as Buddhistic merely from the accompanying serpent symbol. In his comprehensive work on Hindu Iconography, Mr. T.A. Gopinatha Rao describes a Vishṇu image of the *Bhogasthānaka* order, in which the god is shown in a standing posture with the serpent's hood over his head, flanked on two sides by the figures of Lakshmī (Goddess of Wealth) and Pṛithvi (The Earth Goddess). In a silver statuette of Vishṇu discovered in the village of Churāi in Bengal (given in plate No. 24, of Mr. R.D. Banerji's *History of Bengal*) the god is shown as standing upright and has over his head a sort of arch which seems to be made of hoods of serpents. While there may be still some doubt as to the definite classification of this so called Muchalinda sculpture, the statement that it is an image of Buddha cannot be held to have been established. On the lintel of the beautifully carved chlorite door-way of the temple well-known as a memorable production of Orissa art, is depicted the image of *Śrī* or *Mahā Lakshmī,* a fact which is sought to be made one of the strongest proofs of the theory of the Buddhist origin of Konarak ruins. The goddess *Śrī* has been described in the *Matsya Purāna* in the chapter dealing with Sun God and other minor gods and goddesses (Chap. 26, Slokas 40 to 46) and it mainly agrees with the noticeable features of the deity ordinarily depicted in the sculptures.[7] As Mr. B.C. Majumdar has shown in one of his learned articles in the Bengali magazine, *Sāhitya* (*Sāhitya* 1312 B.S., p. 131-138), these *Śrī* images are identical with Kamalātmikā, one of the Daśamahāvidyās of the Hindu Pantheon. It will appear from Mr. M. Chakravarty's learned notes on Dhauli and the caves of Udayagiri and Khaṇḍagiri (Calcutta, 1903), that the images of *Śrī, Gaja-Lakshmī* or *Mahālakshmī* and pictures of trees, &c., are common alike in Hindus, Buddhists and Jainas. Even to this day trees, are represented in Jaina place of worship and Kalpadruma of the sacred lore[8] has by no means fallen into oblivion. *Śrīmūrtis* are not peculiar only to Buddhist *stūpas* at Sanchi, but reproductions of these figures are met with in Orissa as in the Lakshmī temple in Jagannātha enclosure, Puri.

Mr. D.R. Bhandarkar, in the *Annual Report of the Archæological Survey, Western Circle,* 1904, gives an interesting account of the Hindu temple of Narasiṁha Nātha situated in another part of the province of Orissa. The temple which he ascribes to 9th century or to an earlier period has got a chlorite door-frame somewhat resembling the one at Konarak and in the lintel is depicted the image of Lākshmi and two female attendants bearing flyskips and over the head of the goddess are represented two elephants holding aloft two water-jugs in their trunks. Professor Bhandarkar referring to plate No. 1, and p. 71, of Fergusson and Burgess's *Cave-Temples of India,* observes: "It is no wonder that Lakshmī image should be found on the lintel of the temple—as these are met with alike in the ancient caves of Katak and the temples of Southern Orissa". Like the *Svāstika, Śrī* or *Kamalātmikā* figure seems to have been looked upon as a beneficient symbol and as such came to be adopted as a sort of conventional decoration by Hindu architects, especially in connection with sacred places of worship.

The erotic sculptures at Konarak—the likes of which are also found in other Orissa temples—have also been brought into requisition in the attempt to establish the Buddhist claims. These pairs of human figures in various attitudes (*bandhas*) are taken to be due to the influence of the *Tāntriks* of the *Left Path School.* The Pro-Buddhist arguers assert that the union of these erotic pairs is a crude way of representing the union of Buddha and *Prajñā* (wisdom) (*Konarka,* p. 63). In direct contradiction to this theory it has been stated by a writer in a vernacular journal that the object of these carvings was to prevent the austere devotees of Buddhism from approaching the neighbourhood of the temple. This view may be dismissed without much comment as under some of its degraded *Tāntrik* forms, a good deal of license seems to have been allowed to followers of the faith. Sir J.G. Woodroffe in his preface to Mr. M. Ganguly's book on Orissa, has referred to Dr. Maeterlink's mention of the occasional existence of a type of erotic representation on the walls of Gothic cathedrals. It has been justly held that mere sentimental or spiritual explanation of these sculptures do not explain away their bearing as a natural land-mark in the evolution of human faith and morality, and one is reminded of Kraft Ebbing's well-known dictum that "sexual feeling is really the root of all ethics and no doubt of aestheticism and religion" (*Psycho. Sex,* p. 2). Messrs. Stephen and Catherwood in the course of their explorations in Central America discovered ruins of huge edifices in the cornices of which were found depicted symbols of an erotic character 'membra conjuncta in coitu' (Squier's *Serpent Symbols,* p. 48). Mr. Westropp, mentions having met with the symbol in temples and public buildings at Panuco (*Primitive Symbolism,* p. 33). It is interesting to observe that like the sculptors illustrating the descriptions in *Kāmāśāstra* on the steps of *Mahāmāyā* or *Rāmchaṇḍī* temple, and on the porch of the Sun Temple at Konarak, he explains these pictures as representing in various manners the union of two sexes. Another remarkable feature of similarity in religions so diverse as Mexican and East Indian is the worship of the Sun God in Mexico, which appears to have been interconnected with the worship of the Phallic symbol. Representations similar to those which Dulaure found carved or painted at Panuco were observed by Bertram on the sacred edifices at Tlascalla, where among the local creek tribe heliolatry was strongly in evidence. No connection has yet been established between the religious cults of India and Mexico and what appears to have been stage in the natural evolution of human faith or as it has been called—a 'cosmic process,' should not be hastily ascribed to a degraded form of any particular religion. One is therefore inclined to hold that these erotic figures by no means establish the Buddhist origin which is claimed for Konarak. It may be stated in this connection that according to Hindu works like *Utkalakhaṇḍa* (Chap. XI) sculptures of this description are carved with a view to prevent the buildings being struck by lightning (*Vajrāpātādi-bhītyādi-vāraṇārtham,* वज्रपातदिभीत्यादि वारणार्थे। &c.). Mr. V. Smith whose attention seems to have been drawn to such Sanskrit texts has also remarked that "such sculptures are said to be a protection against evil spirits and so serve the purpose of lightning-conductors" (*History of Fine Art in India and Ceylon,* p. 190, foot-note). In the *Agnipurāṇa* also, we find directions regarding the representations of these human couples in certain parts of sacred buildings (*Agni.* Vol. I, p. 356, Ed. *Biblioth. Indic.* Ch. 104-30. *Mithunai pādavarṇābhi Śākhāśesham vibhūshāyet* मिथुनैः पादवर्णाभिः शाखा शेषं विभूषयेत।). It has also been asserted that according to the *Śilpa Śāstras,* it was customary to depict on the temple buildings scenes portraying the nine principal sentiments (*Rasa*) and the erotic passion or *Śringāra Rasa* being the first in the category, has naturally come to occupy a more prominent place. These explanations coming as they do from Hindu sources, certainly go to show that carvings of this kind were not the hall-mark of any particular creed. Not content with the so-called indirect evidence of once prevailing Buddhism, an attempt has been made to silence all dissentients by making a bold assertion to the effect that there is an image of Buddha at Puri which can be traced to Konarak. The image of Sun in the Sun Temple at Puri is said to have been removed from the Konarak temple and there is also a tradition recorded in the Palm-Leaf Temple annals (*Mādlā Pañjī*) which lend support to this. In the Sun Temple there is another partly mutilated image which the *Pāṇḍās* or the custodians of the temple declare to be that of Indra, the Hindu Jupiter Pluvius. Mr. Swarup declares this image to be that of Buddha (*Konarka,* p. 84), an identification which would naturally lend a strong support to his own theory. Mr. Swarup's opinion in this matter cannot, however, be accepted as final as we find that a very different view has been put forth by an independent scholar, after a minute and careful personal inspection. In an article in the *Modern World,* July 1913, Mr. Himangshu Sekhar Banerji, B.L., who took careful measurements of the altar at Konarak and the pedestal of the images in the Puri Sun-Temple, has described the similarity of the so-called Buddha, with that of the Moon-god, in the Navagraha frieze at Konarak and in view of the tradition that the Moon was also worshipped there along with the Sun, he is inclined to hold that the image in question is that of the Moon. If there had been anything peculiary Buddhistic about the image which was likely to lead to a satisfactory identification, the fact would hardly have escaped the attention of modern researchers. Mr. M. Ganguly, whose work on Orissa is probably the latest of its kind from the pen of an Indian scholar, has also been careful not to hazard such a guess. Mr. Swarup's identification can therefore only be regarded as 'proven' under the circumstance.

Some of the Indian writers are so much obsessed with 'Buddhist' theories that we find in a vernacular work on Puri Shrines (*Purī Tīrtha*) by Mr. Nagendra Nath Mitra, a statement to the effect that there are big images of Buddha on the pyramidal roof of the Konarak porch or Jagmohan. We had an opportunity of inspecting these images at close quarters, having risked a climb to the roof with the help of the local *chowkidar.* Being four-headed they are popularly believed to be representations of Brahman Mr. Swarup with Mr. Longhurst of the Archæological Survey (*Arch. Survey Report, E. Circle,* 1906), so far differs from the popular identification as to take these images for representation of Śiva or Maheśvara, the matted locks being considered a fifth head on the strength of certain passages quoted from Hindu Texts. The author of "Konarka" monograph seems to be under no illusion that these images were made to represent the founder of Buddhism in any of the varying attitudes (*Mudrā*), but Mr. N. Mitra seems to go a step further even than other theorists of this school. Mr. Swarup, in view of his own peculiar views, seems to be anxious to relegate the Solar cult to a very subordinate position, and enunciates the view that it could never make a stand as a distinct or separate creed having subsequently become absorbed in the Saivite faith—the Sun God coming to be regarded as one of the eight forms of Śiva or Rudra. To an unsophisticated person the obvious object of this assertion would appear to be that if Sun-worship were reduced to a mere 'subsidiary cult,' it would be easier to attribute the building of this famous lane to a once flourishing and widely prevalent faith like Buddhism. Heliolatry seems to have once been fairly established in this land—from the temple of Martand[9] in Kashmir in the far north to that of Konarak in the southern shore. In Punjab, Multan (Mulasthn) on the Chenab (Chandrabhāgā) was an ancient seat of Sun-worship. (Cunningham's *The Ancient Geography of India,* p. 232). Mr. N.N. Vasu quotes *Varāha Purāṇa* (178, 49-55) to show that Sun images were consecrated by Śambu, the Pauranic founder of the cult at Muttra, Multan, and Ujjain (Introd. to *Vraja Parikramā*), and in *Vabishya Purāṇa* also there is mention of Multan and Chandrabhāgā in connection with heliolatrous rites (*Viaṣṇavism, Śaivism, &c.,* by Sir R. G. Bhandarkar, p. 153). In Central India the shrines of the Sun God were not quite a negligible factor (*Report Arch. Survey, W. India,* Vol. IX, pp. 73-74, one of the interesting remains of early heliolatry in the Gwalior inscription of Mihirakula, now *in situ* in the Indian

Museum, Calcutta, which records the erection of a Sun temple by this blood-thirsty son of the White Hun Toramana, is the 15th year of his reign, *i.e.,* about A.D. 530. (Fleet No. 37). Mr. D.R. Bhandarkar in his interesting progress report of the *Archæological Survey, W. Circle,* 1905-06, pp. 51-52, describes a 7th century Sun temple at Basantgaḍh in Sirohi, and a 8th century one at Osiah in Jodhpur State, both of which are rich in artistic sculptures. M. Langlés describes a Sun God in the peristyle or verandah of the cave at Ellora Djenouassa (Jānwāsā)—a Śaiva cave which may be ascribed to 8th or 9th century (Le toit du verandah ou peristyle sur les murailles du quel on a sculptê . . . Souria (le soleil) tranée dans son char par sept chevaux, p. 89, Tome II).

There is an old Sun Temple at Gaya to the north of the Vishṇupāda Temple, the sacred fane which contains according to Hindu belief the foot-print of Vishṇu.[10] The Sun in this temple is as usual shown as being drawn in a seven-horse car. The image is important in the sense that the sculptor has followed the description of the God as given in the Hindu scriptures instead of taking for his model the standing figure with two archer companions said to be an adoption of Greek Apollo found on an Aśoka railing in Bodh-Gaya, to which reference has already been made.

If the Apollo model has no influence in determining the nature of the image at Gaya itself, it is not likely that it would have any influence on the 13th century artists at Konarak. Gaya is not the only place in Bihar containing traces of Solar worship. In an open courtyard inside the temple of goddess Pattaneśvarī, the guardian deity, according to the local Hindus of the city of Patna, was found a big image of the Sun God.[11]

A twelfth century chlorite Sun image found at Rajmahal on the border of Bengal, has been thought deserving of a notice in Mr. V. Smith's *History of Fine Art and Sculpture.* In Bengal itself instances are not unknown of the Sun God being worshipped under a totally different name as the result of forgetfulness or misconception on the part of local inhabitants.[12] Mr. Brajendra Nath Banerji in the *Journal of the Sāhitya Parishad,* describes the so-called image of Shasṭhī (the guardian goddess of infants) worshipped at Chinsurah which is in reality an image of the Sun God with the usual top-boots and lotuses in both hands (*Journal of the Bangiya Sāhitya Parishad,* Vol. XVIII, p. 193). Mr. Nikhil Nath Roy in his history of Murshidabad, describes an image of a Sun God seated on a horse known as *Gangāditya,* which is still worshipped in the village Amarakuṇḍu, lying not far from Berhampore, the headquarters of the Murshidabad district. In the Kandi subdivision in the same district the Sun God is regularly worshipped at Jemo Rajbati, and also at Gokarṇa, Pātāndā, under the name of Kuśaditya (*Journal of the Sahitya Parishad,* Vol. XIV, p. 144). Not long ago the late Dr. Bloch discovered at Maldah the image of the Sun God of the Āditya class. Some of the Sen Kings of Bengal—who flourished before the Mahomedan conquest—were Sun-worshippers and Keśava Sena in the Edilpur Grant (*JASB.,* Vol. X, 1914, p. 103), describes himself as *Parama Saura.* The Solar cult which was once so wide-spread and has left such important archæological evidence of its influence cannot be called a 'subsidiary' one, and there appears to be no proper foundation for the idea that at Konarak the Sun worship had flourished like a parasite on the ruins of a once popular Buddhist place of worship.

It is not the place to discuss the relative merits of the theories as to whether the Sun worship ultimately got merged or incorporated in Narayanic or Vaishnavic cult or in the Saivaic one, though certain facts are certainly in favour of the former supposition. It is worthy of note that at Vrindaban, one of the principal seats of modern Vaishnavism, Sun is even now worshipped in a temple on the *tīlā* of twelve Adityas, and at Muttra another sacred place of Vaishnavite pilgrimage there is a Sun temple on the Surya Ghāt or Surya tirtha where according to Hindu belief Balī, the lord of the Pātāla regions, obtained from the Sun God the jewel Chintāmanī as a reward of the austerities practised by him. In the Copper-plate grants of Keśava Sena, and Visvarūpa Sena (*JASB*, Vol. LXV, Pt. I, p. 9), after the opening words *Namo Nārāyaṇāya* नमो नारायणाय (Salutation to Nārāyaṇa) occurs the *śloka* (*vande Arabindabana-vāndhabam = andhakāra-*

kārānibaddhabhubanatrayamuktihelum) वन्दे अरविन्दवन बान्धवमन्धकार कारानिवद्धभुवनत्रयमुक्तिहेतुम्। Salutations to Thee Thou friend of the lotus plants and deliverer of the three worlds from the prison of darkness, &c. That the stanza is to be taken as referring only to the Sun God hardly requires any comment. In reference to the Martand temple is also mentioned 'the local name of Vishṇu as the Sun God'. In popular parlance the Sun God is even to this day referred to in Bengal as Sūrya Nārāyaṇa. A carved stone in the Indian Museum—known as Sūrya Nārāyaṇa Śilā—on the top of which is sculptured the lotus symbol of the Sun seems to bear convincing testimony to the union of the two tenets. At any rate, so far as Konarak is concerned, there seems to have been no such clashing of rival Hindu sects and the claims now rashly advanced on behalf of Buddhism restricts the discussion to the actual influence, if any, exercised in this part of Orissa by the Buddhist faith alone. In the *Arch. Survey* reports there is no mention of any Buddhist remains found at Konarak. Nowhere on the temple do we find any representation of the characteristic Buddhist symbol of *Tṛi-ratna*. Messrs. Vincent Smith and Havell in their well-known works on Indian Art and Sculpture have made no observations on this point. Mr. R.D. Banerji, now Superintendent, Archæological Survey, Western Circle, who had on more than one occasion studied the Konarak remains on the spot declared to me that nothing Buddhistic has yet been found on the site in the course of excavations made by the officers of the Archæological Survey. Mr. M. Ganguly also maintains a discreet silence and does not commit himself to the views enunciated by Mr. Bishan Swarup.

As we have shown above the so-called evidence adduced in support of the pro-Buddhist theory is exceedingly unsatisfactory, as Dr. Rājendra Lāla Mitra himself admits,[13] and so long as no new results of archæological or epigraphical discoveries are forthcoming to corroborate such statements no accurate or scientific writer should speak of Buddhism or Buddhistic influence in connection with the Konarak ruins.

References

1. Mr. Jayaswal says in his paper on the Hāthigumphā inscription of the emperor Khāravela (*JBORS.*, December, 1917, p. 448), that before the time of Khāravela there were temples of the Arhats on the Udayagiri Hills as they are mentioned in the inscription as institutions which had been previously in existence.
2. Mr. B.C. Majumdar is on opinion that these kings had their *raj* at Sambalpore although their territories extended to Chandwar or Cuttack in Orissa (*Ep. Ind.*, Vol. XI, p. 102).
3. Siṃha iti Daṇḍabhūktībhūpatīradbhūtaprabhavākarak-arakamalamūkula – tulitotkaleśakarṇa – keśarī saritvallabha-kumbhasamvabo Jayasiṃhaḥ.
4. The stone image of an elephant surmounted by a lion is also met with in the Doumar Layna (grotto), one of the Hindu Śaiva caves in Ellora (*Monuments de L'Hindusthan* par M. Langlés, Tome II, plate *contra*, p. 87). Mr. B.C. Majumdar has kindly suggested to me that the fabulous strength of the king of beasts could best be indicated by a design in which he is shown as tearing open the skull of huge elephants. In Sanskrit literature the capacity of lions to strike down the huge pachyderms of forest seem to be emphasisd in passages such as *bhinatti nityaṃ kari-rāja kumbham.*
5. The goose-frieze is found in the Aśokan pillars, *e.g.*, the pillar at the entrance of the Indian Museum, and *Baṛājhānjī* decorations are met with in the remains at Bodh-Gaya. There is a prominent goose-frieze in he semi-circular moonstone at Anuradhapura, which is over-topped by a mixed frieze of lions, horses, elephants and bullocks (Plate 90, *Viśvakarma,* pt. VII, published by Dr. A.K. Coomaraswamy).
6. Mr. R.K. Mukerji, referring to this class of temples in the chapter on "Building and Carving" in his *Foundation of Indian Economics,* observes: "In the older brick temples the spaces between the curved lines and roof-base and on the sides are covered with carvings.......there are also mixed panels of rosettes or geometrical patterns and in some instances miniature temples are piled one above the other along the arched openings" (p. 247). A temple of this kind has been described by the present writer in his writer in his article on the remains at Śrinagar (Nadia) in the *Journal of the Śāhitya-Parishad* (Vol. XIII, p. 259).

7. श्रियं देवी प्रवक्ष्यामि नवे वयसि संस्थिताम्।
सुयौवनां पीनगण्डां रक्तोष्ठिं कुचितभ्रुवम्॥ ४० ॥
पार्श्वे तस्याः स्त्रियः कार्य्याश्चामर व्यग्रपाणयः।
पद्मासनीपविष्ठा तु पद्मसिंहासनस्थिता॥ ४५ ॥
करिम्यां स्नाप्यमाना सौ भृङ्गाराम्यांमनेकशः
प्रक्षालयन्तौ करिणौ भृङ्गाराभ्यां तथापरौ॥ ४६ ॥
मत्स्यपुराणे प्रतिमालक्षणं नामैकषष्ठयधिकद्विशाततमोऽध्याये

8. In Khāravela's inscription there is mention of a Kalpa Tree (in gold) given away by the Emperor with leaves on (*JBORS.*, December 1917, p. 463). Mr. K.P. Jayaswal refers to Hemādri's *Chaturvarga Chintāmaṇī* for description of this *Mahādāna* (*Dānakhaṇḍa* 5), a fact which seems to show that ceremonies of this kind like the conception of the tree itself were essentially Hinduistic in character.

9. Built by king Lalitāditya in the 8th century between A.D. 24 to 760.

10. The shrine evidently belongs to Buddhist times and proves that Sun-worship as a distinct cult was even then in vigorous existence. Inside the temple is an inscription in the era of Buddha's *Nirvānā,* year 1813. (*List of Ancient Monuments of Bengal,* p. 280. Above Vol. X, p. 341).

11. The image is no longer worshipped and was lying neglected when the writer of this note visited the shrine with some delegates to the last Bengali Literary Conference held at Bankipur.

12. It is interesting to note that lingering traces of heliofatrous rites are still to be observed in the *Chhat* (Sansk, *Chhata*?] festival of Bihari and up-country women.

13. "The evidence available is certainly exceedingly meagre and unsatisfactory, but without the assumption of previous sanctity and celebrity it becomes difficult to account for the selection of a sea-beach for the dedication of so costly and magnificent a temple as the Black Pagoda" (*Ant. Orissa,* Vol. II, p. 148). As regards the inaccessibility or loneliness of some of the wellknown sacred places of the Hindus, one is tempted to quote from the beautiful lay-sermon of Sir Rabindranath Tagore "What is Art?" (*Personality,* p. 28-29 & 32), in justification of the selection of such beautiful sites).

22

The Great *Stūpa* at Nāgārjunakoṇḍa in Southern India

A.H. Longhurst

Nāgārjunakoṇḍa, or Nāgārjuna's hill, is the name of a big rocky flat-topped hill on the right bank of the Krishna river in the Palnād taluk of the Guntur district of the Madras Presidency, and 15 miles west by north of Macherla railway station, the terminus of the new line from Guntur opened in 1931. The hill stands in a valley completely shut in by a ring of hills, an offshoot of the Nallamalais (Black Hills) of the adjoining Kurnool district, on three sides, with the Krishna river on the fourth or north-western side, where it forms the boundary between the part of the Madras Presidency and the Nizam's Dominions. The annexed site plan (Plate I) shows the geographical features of the area and the positions of the monuments discovered.

Nāgārjunakoṇḍa is about 60 miles distant from Amarāvatī as the crow flies, but considerably further by river. It is a wild and desolate spot, and being shut in by the surrounding rocky hills is usually very hot during most months of the year. There is a rough cart track from Macherla to Nāgulavaram, a distance of 10 miles, but the remaining 5 miles over the hills and through the valley to Nāgārjunakoṇḍa has to be performed on foot, as no cart traffic is possible.

The hill was once fortified, and remains of brick and stone fortifications still remain all along the rugged cliffs surrounding the plateau on its summit, showing that it was once used as a citadel; but no ruined buildings of interest were discovered on the hill. At the eastern foot of the hill and scattered throughout the valley are a number of ruined *stūpas* of all sizes, from little structure 8 feet in diameter to large onces like the Great *stūpa,* 106 feet in diameter. There are also many ruined monasteries and apsidal Buddhist temples, showing that, at one time, there existed here a large flourishing Buddhist settlement, far larger in fact than the one at Amarāvatī lower down the river. A number of important inscriptions in Prakrit and in Brāhmī characters of about the second century A.D. were discovered in connection with the Great *Stūpa* and two apsidal temples. Professor Vogel of Leiden University has published an account of these old records in the *Epigraphia Indica,* volume XX, 1931. Besides a number of inscriptions and ruined buildings, many lead coins of the Āndhra period, gold and silver reliquaries, pottery, statues and over four hundred magnificent bas-relief sculptures similar to those from Amarāvatī, were recovered during the excavations which I conducted at Nāgārjunakoṇḍa during the cold seasons of 1928 to 1931, when I completed the explorations. A brief account of these discoveries appears in the *Annual Reports* of the Archæological Survey of India for those years, but a fully illustrated account of the remarkable discoveries made would fill a large volume, and has yet to be written.

The historical information furnished by the inscriptions is somewhat meagre, and the careless manner in which some of them were engraved adds to the difficulty of interpreting the precise meaning of certain words and sentences. The records belong to the Southern Ikhāku dynasty, who were ruling in this part of India between the second and third centuries A.D. It is clear from these inscriptions that they were kings of considerable importance, as they formed matrimonial alliances not only with the rulers of Vanavāsa (North Kanara), but also with the kings of Ujjayini in Central India. A curious fact about these Southern Ikhākus revealed by the inscriptions, is that while the rulers were followers of Brahmanism and performed Vedic sacrifices, their consorts were devotees of the Buddha and erected buildings for the Buddhists settled at Nāgārjunakoṇḍa and made pious donations to the *stūpas*. Most of these buildings owed their existence to the piety of certain queens and princesses belonging to the royal house of Ikhāku,

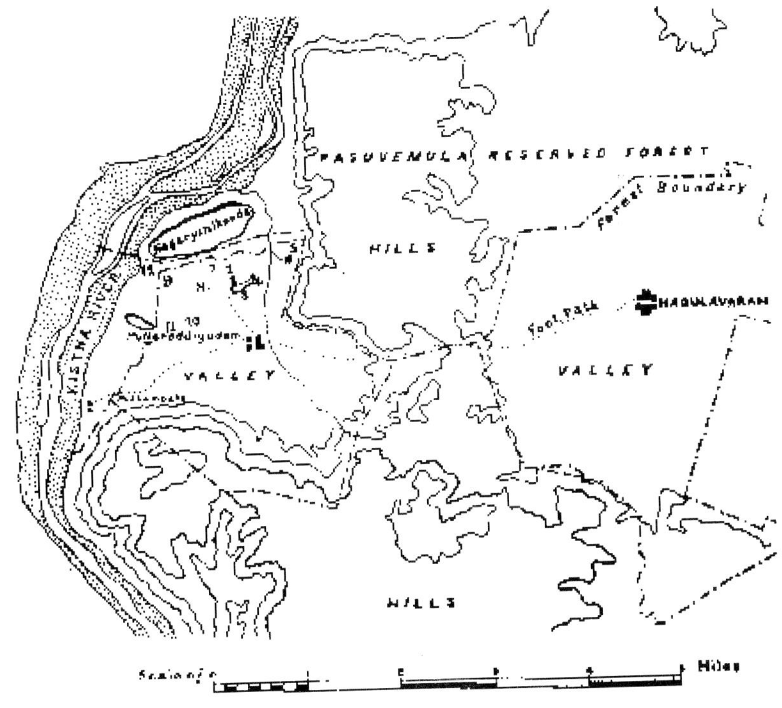

Plate 1: Showing Positions of Monuments discovered at Nāgārjunakoṇḍa, Palnād Tāluk, Guntur District. (Facing Page 134)

References to Numbers

1. Great *Stūpa* No. 1, **2.** Chaitya No. 1 and Monastery No. 1, **3.** Chaitya No. 2 and Monastery No. 2, **4.** Chaitya No. 3 and 4, Monastery No. 3 and *Stūpa* No. 4, **5.** *Stūpa* No. 2, **6.** *Stūpa* No. 3, **7.** Monastery No. 4 and *Stūpa* No. 5, **8.** *Stūpa* No. 6, **9.** Monastery No. 5 and *Stūpa* Nos. 7 and 8, **10.** Palace Site, **11.** *Stūpa* No. 9, **12.** Wharf.

Plate 2: Fig. 1: The Great *Stūpa*, Nāgārjunakoṇḍa, after excavations. (Dotted line shows original height of *Stūpa*).

Fig. 2: The Great *Stūpa*, Nāgārjunakoṇḍa (restored).

Plate 3: Fig. 1: Chamber in the Great *Stūpa* at Nāgārjunakoṇḍa which contained the relics. (Find spot marked X).

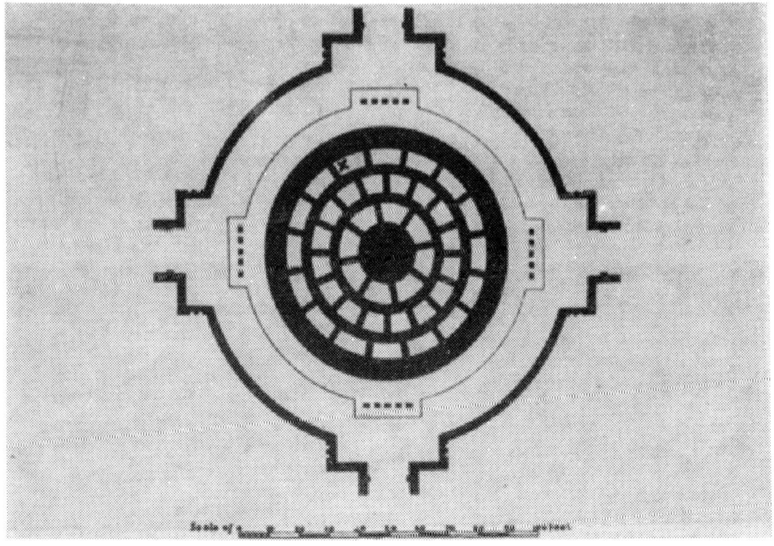

Fig. 2: Plan of the Great *Stūpa* at Nāgārjunakoṇḍa. (X marks spot where the relics were found).

Plate 4: Fig. 1: Remains of the broken pot containing the relics found in the Great *Stūpa* at Nāgārjunakonda.

Fig. 2: The Buddha relics from the Great *Stūpa* at Nāgārjunakoṇḍa. The bone relic and gold reliquary are marked 1 and 2 respectively (actual size).

the principal founder being a princess named Chāmtisiri, who is praised for her munificence in many of the inscriptions belonging to the Great *Stūpa,* or *Māhāchetiya,* as it is called in the pillar inscriptions belonging to it, and which was founded, or perhaps rebuilt, when the pillars were added, by the lady in question in the sixth year of the reign of king Siri-Virapurisadata between the second and third centuries A.D. The same royal lady built a monastery and an apsidal temple close to the eastern gate of the Great *Stūpa,* the ruins of which remain. Another important inscription was found engraved on the stone floor of an apsidal temple situated on a rocky hill about two furlongs to the east of the Great *Stūpa,* and known locally as Nāharāḷḷabôḍu. This temple and a monastery standing alongside of it were built by a lady named Bodhisiri and dedicated to the fraternities of Ceylonese monks settled at Nāgārjunakoṇḍa. The inscription relates that these Ceylonese Buddhists had converted the people of Kashmīr, Gandhāra, China, Ceylon, Bengal, Kanara, and other places in India. The latter part of the inscription mentions other pious works by Bodhisiri, including a pillared hall or *maṇḍapa* at Kantakasela, which, as Dr. Vogel points out in his account of these inscriptions, must be identical with "the emporium Kantikossula" mentioned by Ptolemy as being situated "after the mouths of the Maisôlos (Krishna)." The *Periplus* speaks of "the region of Masalia" stretching a long way along the coast," and adds, "a great quantity of muslins is made here." The ancient name by which the Krishna delta was known to the Greeks is preserved in that of the seaport of Masulipatam.

In the same inscription (F of Dr. Vogel's list), the name of the ancient city that once existed in the Nāgārjunakoṇḍa valley is given as Vijayapurī, and the hill now known as Nāharāḷḷabôḍu, on which Bodhisiri erected the temple and monastery for the Ceylonese monks, is called the Lesser Dhammagiri situated on Śrīparvata. The hill in question is an offshoot of the surrounding Nallamalais of the adjoining Kurnool district. These hills extend in a south-westerly direction all along the river into the Kurnool district, where, on the top of a wooded hill some 50 miles south-west of Nāgārjunakoṇḍa and facing the river, stands the famous Śrīśailam temple sacred to Śiva and a great place of pilgrimage in the spring, when a big annual festival is held there. It thus seems from this inscription that in early times the Nallamalais were known as Śrīparvata. This is an interesting point, because there is an ancient tradition preserved in Tibet that the famous Buddhist divine Nāgārjuna ended his days in a monastery on Śrīparvata in Southern India. If this monastery is the same as the ruined one on the Lesser Dhammagiri, it would follow that the association of Nāgārjuna with this locality has been preserved up to the present day in the name Nāgārjunakoṇḍa (Nāgārjuna's Hill).

The fact that a monastery and a temple were built specially for the benefit of Ceylonese monks shows that very cordial relations must have existed between the Āndhra Buddhists and their co-religionists in Ceylon at that period. The existence of such relations can be readily accounted for by the sea-borne trade which was carried on between the ports of Ceylon and the great emporium Kantakasela of the Krishna delta. It was no doubt this trade which was mainly responsible for the flourishing state of Buddhism in this part of Southern India, which enabled the Buddhist merchants and their royal masters to raise monuments of such magnificence as those at Nāgārjunakoṇḍa and Amarāvatī. As Dr. Vogel mentions, the decline of Buddhism in the lower Krishna valley may have had other causes besides the general wane of that religion all over India, there may have been economic factors at work, such as the decline of the sea-borne trade with the West, which had caused vast quantities of Roman gold to pour into Southern India. There was also the conquest of the South by the Gupta Emperor Samudra Gupta and the rise of powerful dynasties devoted to Brahmanism, like the Pallava dynasty in the South and the Chālukya in the West.

The ruined buildings discovered, represent the remains of *stūpas,* monasteries, apsidal temples and a palace. They were all built of large bricks measuring 20"X10"X3", the same dimensions as the bricks recently found at Bulandībāgh near Paṭnā in Bihār, the ancient site of Pāṭaliputra. It is stranger that at two sites so far distant both should yield large bricks of the same dimensions. The pillars, floors, statues and important sculptures were executed in white or grey limestone resembling marble. No other stone was used, and it was brought to the site by means of the river and landed at a stone-built wharf that still remains (see Plate I, 12). The wharf is about 250 feet in length, 50 feet wide and 6 feet in height along the river front and at both ends. Three rows of broken stone pillars extending from end to end show that it was originally provided with a wooden roof, probably thatched. It seems to have served as a kind of Customs House, with a row of shops or godowns on either side. Here, the Krishna is more than half a mile wide, with numerous sandbanks and huge rocks in its bed, but during the rains it is a very large river and navigable for country craft right down to the sea.

On plan and in construction, the Āndhra *stūpas* differ from those found in the North. They are built in the form of a wheel with hub, spokes and tire all complete and executed in brickwork (see plan of *stūpa* on Plate III). The open spaces between the radiating walls were filled up with earth, and he dome or brick casing built over the structure. As no traces of structural stone *tees* have been discovered in Southern India, we may presume that they were built of brick and plaster and decorated with the rail ornament in the latter material. The *stūpas* were covered with *chunam,* or fine shell-lime plaster, from top to bottom, and the moulding and other ornamentation was usually executed in stucco or plaster. The dome rested on a circular platform or drum from 2 to 5 feet in height according to the size of the monument. On top of the drum was a narrow path encircling the foot of the dome, and on each of the four sides, facing the cardinal points, was a rectangular platform resembling an altar and the same height as the drum. In the inscriptions these platforms are described as *ayaka*-platforms, because they usually supported a group of five stone pillars, called *ayaka-khambhas* (*ayaka*-pillars). The precise meaning of the word *ayaka* is not known, but it is used much as we use the word 'altar'. From the bas-relief representations of *stūpas* recovered from the Nāgārjunakoṇḍa and Amarāvatī *stūpas,* the *ayaka*-platform appears as an altar, on which pious donors are portrayed depositing their offerings of fruit and flowers. All Āndhra *stūpas* had these platforms, but only those belonging to large and important monuments were provided with pillars. As each group consisted of five pillars, the total number of pillars for each *stūpa* so decorated was twenty. The inscriptions show that these pillars represent gifts made to the *stūpa* in honour of the Buddha and to the merit of the pious donors who provided the money for the work; but no information is given as to the meaning or symbolism of the pillars.

The chief scenes portrayed in the sculptures recovered from these Āndhra *stūpas* represent the five great 'miracles,' or chief events in the life of the Buddha, namely, the Nativity, Renunciation, *Sambodhi,* First Sermon, and the Buddha's Death. These five incidents are portrayed over and over again, either as beautifully executed bas-relief scenes, or else as mere conventional symbols, such as a tree, wheel and *stūpa*. In this form they are found engraved on some of the bases of the *ayaka*-pillars belonging to the Amarāvati *Stūpa* now in the Madras Museum; and I discovered at Nāgārjunakoṇḍa four bases of *ayaka*-pillars each ornamented with a bas-relief representation of the 'First Sermon'. The presence of these symbols carved on the bases of the pillars seems to indicate that they were set up to commemorate the five great miracles; just as we know Aśoka erected pillars to mark the sacred spots where these events are said to have occurred in Nepāl and Bihār. As it was impossible for those living in the Krishna district to erect the pillars on the actual spots in Northern India, they seem to have hit upon the idea of conventionalising the pillars into groups of five for the sake of convenience, so that the events could be commemorated locally, and also, perhaps, with a view to adding to the splendour and importance of the *stūpas,* as in the case of the Amarāvatī *Stūpa,* where the stone casing to the dome, the *ayaka*-platforms and pillars, and the stone railing, were all added to the monument in the second or third century A.D. This we know from the inscriptions belonging to that monument. In earlier times the *ayaka*-pillars were unknown, and they only occur in the Ānanda *stūpas* of that period.

The platforms and pillars vary in size and height according to the dimensions of the *stūpa* to which they belong. The pillars vary from 10 to 30 feet in height, with square bases and octagonal shafts. The tops are round, showing that they could not have supported capitals or any other kind of ornaments. In some of the bas-relief pictures of *stūpas,* the pillars are shown crowned with *triśūla* ornaments, the centre pillar often with a miniature *stūpa* as a capital. This is incorrect and purely decorative, as they never supported anything and could not do so as the tops were round, so that any ornament placed there would fall immediately to the ground. In this case the ornaments merely indicate that the pillars were dedicated to the Buddha, and the inscriptions confirm this.

In the sculptures two kinds of *stūpas* are depicted—one a plain brick and plaster structure like the *stūpas* of the Aśokan age; and the other is similar in all respects, except that the brick surface is faced with richly carved stone slabs embedded in mortar. This stone casing was applied only to the face of the drum, *ayaka*-platforms and lower portion of the dome. The upper portion of the domes of all Āndhra *stūpas* was executed in brick and plaster and decorated with a characteristic garland ornament encircling the dome. This ornament always appears in the bas-relief representations of *stūpas,* and is in the form of a broad festoon decorated with big lotus medallions executed in plaster.

The stone casing was applied only to the base of the dome, as it is obvious that flat stone slabs could not be fixed to the curved surface of the upper portion of the dome. In order to do this, each stone would have to be specially cut with a convex front and a concave back, and even then it would be very difficult to keep the stones in position, so this part of the *stūpas* was always in plaster. These decorated *stūpas* were faced partly with stone slabs and partly with plaster ornamentation, the two materials being used together, and when the work was completed the *stūpa* was given a coating of shell-lime plaster from top to bottom, to hide any defects or inequalities in the work. For this purpose, the white limestone used for this work was specially suitable, as it was of the right colour and takes whitewash or plaster readily, being very absorbent. It was no doubt these considerations and the fact that it is soft and easy to work when freshly quarried, that led to its general use on the Krishna valley. From the remains of slate-stone bas-reliefs and plaster ornament recovered from the ruined *stūpas* of Gandhāra, it seems that they were decorated in the same manner as those erected by the Āndhras. The inscriptions show that there was considerable intercourse between the Buddhists of Gandhāra and their co-religionists in the South, and in all probability the Āndhras adopted the custom from the Gandhāra builders in the second century A.D., or thereabouts. Gandhāra influence is also strongly marked in many of the Āndhra bas-reliefs and statues in the round. Traces of Roman influence are also manifest in a few of the sculptures and in two small gold medallions recovered from Nāgārjunakoṇḍa. This is not surprising, as we know that in the second and third centuries of our era there was considerable sea-borne trade between Rome and this part of Southern India.

When complete, the Great *Stūpa* at Nāgārjunakoṇḍa must have been a perfect example of a plain Āndhra *stūpa* (Plate II, fig. 2). It is built of large bricks measuring 20"X10"X3", and in the usual form of a wheel (Plate III, fig. 2). It was covered with plaster from top to bottom, the dome being decorated with the usual garland ornament, and the drum with a few simple mouldings executed in plaster. No stone was used in its construction, the *ayaka*-pillars alone being of that material, and, as at Amarāvatī, they probably represent a late addition to the *stūpa*. They were gifts, as their inscriptions show, and were erected between the second and third centuries A.D. The diameter of the *stūpa* including the drum is 106 feet. The drum is raised 5 feet above the ground level, and the total height of the monument, excluding the *tee,* must have been about 70 to 80 feet. On top of the drum is a narrow path, 7 feet wide, extending all round the base of the dome. No traces of steps up to this path were found, but it is possible that they may have existed. No steps are depicted in the bas-relief representations of *stūpas,* so perhaps there were none to any of these monuments. The *ayaka*-platforms are 22 feet in length and 5 feet in width, and the bases of the five stone pillars were securely built into the brickwork. In the stone-faced *stūpas,* the *ayaka*-platforms were the most highly decorated features of the *stūpa.* Here the Āndhra sculptor exhibited his best works of art, partly because these platforms were regarded as very holy structures resembling altars on which votive offerings were placed, and mainly perhaps, because they faced the four open gateways of the *stūpa,* so that they were the first objects seen by anyone entering the sacred precinct around the *stūpa.* The *stūpa* was surrounded by a processional path 13 feet in width, and enclosed by a wooden railing standing on brick foundations, which still remain. The gateways were formed by extending the railing outwards, so as to form a screen on each side of the entrance, but there were apparently no transoms spanning the entrance, like those of the Sāñchī *toraṇas.* No traces of stone rails or *toraṇas* were found at Nāgārjunakoṇḍa, and it is quite clear that none existed there.

As a rule, the rails and gates were constructed of carved woodwork, no doubt resting on brick foundations, to protect them from damp and the ravages of white ants. It was only in very special cases that they were ever executed in stone, and then they were merely stone models of carved wooden originals.

When first discovered, the Great *Stūpa* at Nāgārjunakoṇḍa was a large mound of earth and broken brick overgrown with grass and jungle, with two *ayaka*-pillar standing erect, the remaining eighteen pillars having fallen. As the whole of the dome of the *stūpa* had been demolished, the *ayaka*-pillars and platforms thrown down and broken by treasure seekers, the chances of finding any relics in the edifice appeared very remote indeed. The first thing was to remove the debris and trace out the plan of the structure and recover the broken pillars. When this work was finished and the excavations completed, the appearance of the Great *Stūpa* may be gathered from Plate II, fig. 1.

Fortunately, instead of placing the relics in the centre of the Great *Stūpa,* they were deposited in one of the outer chambers on the north-western side of the *stūpa,* where they escaped the notice of the treasure seekers who wrecked the monument (Plate III, fig. 1). As the *stūpa* contained 40 chambers, all of which had to be excavated down to the natural ground level, the excavation of this monument was a very laborious task that took a month to complete. At last, when we had given up all hopes of finding anything of interest, one of the coolies noticed a small broken pot in the north-western corner of the chamber marked with a cross on the plan (Plate III, fig. 2). The pot had been crushed when the chamber was filled with earth by the Buddhists, and all that remained is shown in Plate IV, fig. 1. On the surface were a few white crystal beads and a tiny gold box. After carefully sifting the contents of the pot the following objects were found:—a fragment of bone placed in a small round gold reliquary three-quarters of an inch in diameter. This was placed in a little silver casket, shaped like a miniature *stūpa,* 2½ inches in height, together with a few gold flowers, pearls, garnets and crystals. The three large crystal beads and the round ear-ornament were placed in the pot and not in the casket. The latter unfortunately was very corroded and broken, but a replica was made, which appears in the photograph showing the finds recovered from the tomb (Plate IV, fig. 2). The earthenware pot containing the casket and reliquary was placed originally in the corner of the chamber, which was filled up with earth as soon as the consecration ceremony was over. The brick dome was then built over the remains, and the plastering the decoration of the *stūpa* completed. No traces of ornamental plaster were found in the debris round the monument, except portions of simple mouldings that once decorated the plinth and cornice of the drum. It must have been a perfectly plain structure like those of the Aśokan age before the *ayaka*-pillars were added in the second century A.D. (Plate II, fig. 2).

In the inscriptions belonging to the Great *Stūpa,* the monument is called the "*Mahāchetiya* of the Lord, the Supreme Buddha," clearly showing that the tomb was consecrated to the Great Teacher and to nobody else. The discovery of the *dhātu,* or bone relic, proves that the monument was a *dhātugarbha,* or 'tomb containing a relic,' and that it was not a mere 'dedicatory' *stūpa.* The latter were memorial *stūpas,* which contained no relics, and, like Aśoka's pillars, were erected on celebrated sites sacred to the Buddha, such as his birth-place, and so on. It is, therefore, obvious that the Great *Stūpa* did not belong to this class of memorial monument. The inscriptions do not definitely state why the *stūpa* was built; they merely state that the *ayaka*-pillars were dedicated to the Buddha, and that they were set up by the princess Chāmtisiri and other royal ladies of the same house. Supposing the *stūpa* to have been already in existence prior to the erection of the pillars, it would have been necessary first to enlarge the drum and build the *ayaka*-platforms to accommodate the pillars, and then replaster and decorate the *stūpa* from top to bottom to complete the work. In fact, it would have meant rebuilding the whole of the exterior of the monument. Dr. Vogel is of opinion that the inscriptions show that the *Mahāchetiya* was "founded" by Chāmtisiri, but it is by no means clear whether she built, rebuilt, or merely contributed to the structure. If she did build the *stūpa,* then it was she who enshrined the relic found in the chamber; but it is impossible to believe that so great an event as this could have occurred without the fact being recorded in at least one of the many inscriptions referring to the *stūpa.* We know that the monument was consecrated to the Buddha, as the inscriptions are quite clear on this point. Therefore, it is reasonable to assume that the relic recovered from the tomb represents a *dhātu,* or corporeal relic of the Great Teacher, otherwise there could be no possible reason for calling the tomb the *"Mahāchetiya* of the Lord, the Supreme Buddha." That the *Mahāchetiya* was regarded as a particularly holy shrine is obvious from the tone and wording of the inscriptions found at the site. Again, the size of the tomb, the number of pious donations made by ladies of royal blood, and the fact that pilgrims came from all over India and Ceylon to reverence it, afford testimony of this.

Unfortunately, the meaning of some of the words and phrases met with in the inscriptions is very obscure. Commenting upon this, Dr. Vogel says—"A considerable difficulty in the way of interpreting the Nāgārjunikoṇḍa inscriptions is the want of precision of which they show ample evidence. Considering that these inscriptions were meant to be perpetual records of pious donations made by ladies of royal blood, the careless manner in which they have been recorded is astonishing. Not only single syllables but whole words have been omitted." Dr. Hīrānanda Sāstrī, Epigraphist to the Government of India, who has also made a study of these inscriptions, found the same difficulty, and, as might be expected in the circumstances, his interpretation of the precise meaning of certain words differs from Dr. Vogel's. The records belonging to the *Mahāchetiya* open with an invocation to the Buddha, who is extolled in a long string of laudatory epithets. Dr. Hīrānanda Sāstrī is of opinion that the style and wording of the invocation shows that the *Mahāchetiya* has been specified in these inscriptions as "protected by the corporeal remains of the Buddha" and that the genitive case is used here to discriminate this *stūpa* from others not similarly consecrated. Nine ruined *stūpas* were discovered at Nāgārjunakoṇḍa, four of them highly decorated with stone bas-reliefs similar to those recovered from Amarāvatī, but the *Mahācheitya* is the only one bearing inscriptions indicating that it was consecrated to the Buddha.

The discovery of the relic and the fact that inscription B. 2 of Dr. Vogel's List, definitely gives the name of the monument as the *Mahāchetiya* of the Buddha, seem conclusive evidence that the monument was originally built to enshrine some corporeal remains of the Buddha, as Dr. Hīrānanda Sāstrī maintains. The *stūpa* was probably built long before Chāmtisiri set up the pillars and rebuilt the structure in the second century A.D., or thereabouts, which would explain why the inscriptions give no information about the consecration or how the relic was obtained. If the *Mahāchetiya* did exist prior to the second century A.D., the fact that it contained corporeal remains of the Great Teacher would have been known throughout India and Ceylon, thus making it unnecessary to record this information in inscriptions added to the monument in later times.

We know from the inscriptions recovered from Śāñchī, Sārnāth and Amarāvatī that the great *stūpas* that existed at these three famous sites were all rebuilt in later times. These inscriptions give the names of some of the pious donors who found the money for the additions to these monuments, but, like the Nāgārjunakoṇḍa inscriptions, they give no information concerning the purpose for which the *stūpas* were built, or when they were erected, just the very points which we should so much like to know. The Amarāvatī inscriptions show that the stone casing, *ayaka*-pillars and stone railing were added to the Great *Stūpa* at that place in the second or third century A.D., that is, at the same period as that in which Chāmtisiri set up the pillars and rebuilt the *Mahāchetiya* at Nāgārjunakoṇḍa. Originally, the Amarāvatī *Stūpa* seems to have been a plain brick and plaster *stūpa* similar to the *Mahāchetiya,* and it must have been a particularly holy shrine, else it would never have been enlarged and decorated in so costly a fashion. Perhaps when Chāmtisiri learned what was taking place at Amarāvatī, she felt it incumbent upon herself, as the leading devotee of the Buddha at Nāgārjunakoṇḍa, to redecorate and improve the *Mahāchetiya*.

Personally, like Dr. Hīrānanda Sāstrī, I do not think there can be any doubt that the *Mahāchetiya* was originally built to enshrine some corporeal remains of the Buddha, and that the fragment of bone found in the gold reliquary represents a genuine *dhātu,* or relic, of the Great Teacher. There is no reason why such a relic could not have been obtained from Northern India long before the days of Chāmtisiri.

Note: The copyright of the photographs reproduced to illustrate this article is reserved by the Archæological Survey of India.

23

Prof. H. Kern's Dissertation on the Era of Buddha and the Aśoka Inscriptions[1]

J. Muir, D.C.L., LL.D., Ph.D., Edinburgh

The writer begins by remarking that the year 543 B.C., adopted by the Southern Buddhists that of the Nirvāṇa or death of Buddha, has, ever since Turnour argued in favour of its correctness, in the Introduction to his edition and translation of the *Mahāvanso* (Ceylon, 1837), been pretty generally accepted by scholars as the real date of that event. And yet the first maintainers of this view, as Turnour and Lassen, admit that in this calculation there is an error of 60 years in reference to King Chandragupta, the Sandrakoptos of the Greeks, whose date we know with certainty from classical sources. How any value could be attached to a calculation which is thus shown to be erroneous as regards the end of the 4th century B.C. would be inexplicable, were it not that the dates adopted by the other Buddhists (the Tibetans, Chinese, and Japanese) were less probable. The Cingalese chronology stands favourably contrasted with their more extravagant estimates. But, as Dr. Kern remarks, there is a great difference between relative or comparative value and absolute credibility. And even this comparative value of the Cingalese chronology must undergo some deduction, as, though the later Buddhists of the North place Buddha far too early, yet their older books contain other data, consisting of a determination of the time of the first two councils and the Aśoka's reign. And the question is, whether, with the help of these data, the age of Buddha may not be fixed with more probability than it can be by following the Cingalese books. This problem can only be completely solved when the entire literature of the Northern Buddhists shall have become accessible to us in the original languages.

Prof. Kern thinks that in so far as the books of the Northern and Southern Buddhists are yet known to us, the latter are in many respect undoubtedly the more trustworthy. But, as we have already seen, by the miscalculation of 60 years, they are not to be implicitly depended upon. Anything, therefore, that they contain which is improbable in itself and is not confirmed from other quarters, may reasonably be regarded as open to doubt. One of these doubtful points is the account which they give of the three Councils, one of which is unknown to the Northern Buddhists. According to the Cingalese, the first council was held immediately after the Master's (Buddha's) death; the second exactly 100 years later, under a king called Kāla-Aśoka; and the third 118, or 135, years after the second, under King Aśoka or Dhārma-Aśoka. Here we have (1) the improbability of two successive councils being held by kings of the same name; (2) neither the Buddhistic nor the non-Buddhistic books of the North know anything of two Aśokas; (3) the name Kāla-Aśoka, the chronological Aśoka, is suspicious; (4) the *Mahāvanso* is at variance with itself, for in chapter V. 218 years are said to have elapsed between the *Nirvāṇa* and the inauguration of Aśoka, which took place four years after his accession; whilst at the end of the same chapter we are told that the third council took place in the 17th year of Aśoka's reign. The third council would thus, according to the *Mahāvanso,* have been held in the 235th year after the *Nirvāṇa,* though on p. 22 of the same work it is said to have occurred 218 years after that event, which is, indeed, the ordinary assumption.

The Northern Buddhists know only of two councils down to Aśoka's time, one immediately after Buddha's death, and the second 110 years later, under Aśoka. A third council is placed by them under Kanishkā, more than 400 years after the *Nirvāṇa.* In this chronology Dr. Kern finds nothing improbable or suspicious: on the contrary, the correct determination of the distance in time between Aśoka and Kanishkā forms a strong argument in favour of the credibility of this particular Northern tradition. In order to justify its rejection, an extraordinary degree of credibility must be assigned to the Cingalese books, to which they cannot justly lay claim. For in addition to the specimen already given, as Dr. Kern goes on to say, almost every page of the *Mahāvanso* offers evidence that it is not a pure source of information for the earlier history of Buddhism. He then proceeds to adduce various instances of this untrustworthiness, in the shape of exaggerated numbers, miscalculation, contradictory, improbable and absurd statements, and concludes that a work of which the chronology abounds with inconsistencies, and which contains a loosely connected narrative mixed up with all sorts of absurdities, must be undeserving of reliance. The chronology of the Southern Buddhists, where we can control it, is unsatisfactory. To assume that it is correct, where we have no means of controlling it, can only be the result of extraordinary prejudice.

After introducing some remarks on the Pāli language (to which I shall return), and other matters (pp. 12 ff.,). Dr. Kern returns (in p. 25) to the question of the Cingalese chronology, and combats Mr. Turnour's arguments in favour of the correctness of the date assumed by the Southern Buddhist as that of their great teacher's death. He urges—in reply to Turnour's assertion that "there is a chain of uninterrupted evidence in the historical annals of Ceylon from B.C. 161 to the present day, all tending to the confirmation of the date assigned" to the *Nirvāṇa*—that even if a book written 460-470 A.D. could be good evidence of what occurred in the interval between 161 B.C. and 460 A.D., as Turnour assumes, it could afford no proof regarding events which occurred before 161 B.C., and then proceeds to remark that Mr. Turnour's reasoning in favour of the date 543, if he understands it rightly, appears to resolve itself into this: the chronology of the Cingalese, in almost all the points where we are able to control it, is faulty and falsified; but we cannot show that the date assigned to the *Nirvāṇa* is false: therefore it is true. Dr. Kern himself prefers to reason otherwise, and say that our inability to disprove this date is a result of the want under which we labour, of contemporary dates; that the date of the *Nirvāṇa* is inseparabely connected with those which follow, and must stand or fall therewith. And further that the upholders of the date 543 must at the same time show, or make it probable, that the *Nirvāṇa* is not to be placed 218 years before Aśoka, but 260 years or more. As we cannot, Dr. Kern proceeds, accept any date on the ground of tradition alone, we must choose between the divergent suppositions, and must hold that to be the most probable which is least in conflict with facts and dates that are historically ascertained. It must, at the same time, be admitted that the most probable date may some time or other be disproved by the discovery of sources of information at present inaccessible.

Prof. Kern proceeds as follows to determine the date of the *Nirvāṇa* which, in the present state of our knowledge, appears to him to be the most probable. He places the beginning of Chandragupta's reign in 322 B.C. He reigned 24 years, and his son 28, making together 52 years. Thus Aśoka, who came next, became Emperor in 270 B.C. From the names of the Grecian kings who are mentioned in Aśoka's inscriptions, and from the dates when they ruled, as well as from the date assigned for Aśoka's conversion to Buddhism, it is to be concluded that these inscriptions must date from 258 B.C., or not long after. And as it is independently established that Aśoka began to reign in 270 B.C., we may, from the concurrence of the two calculations, safely infer that Chandragupta's reign commenced in 322 B.C., and his grandson Aśoka's in 270 B.C., and that Lassen's calculation or conjecture is wrong. According to the *Vāyu Purāṇa* Aśoka reigned 36 years, and 37 according to the *Mahāvanso*. His death is consequently to be placed in 234 or 233 B.C. If we assume, with the *Aśoka-avadāna* (see Burnouf's *Introduction, &c.* p. 370) that Buddha's *Nirvāṇa* took place 100 years before Aśoka's accession, we obtain 380 B.C. as the date of the former event.[2] This date, Dr. Kern remarks, approaches so near to the year in which the Jina Vardhamāna, or Mahāvīra, is said to have died, that it is difficult to think that the coincidence can be accidental. The Buddhists and Jains seem originally to have formed one sect. Notwithstanding the notable difference between the legends of Jina Śākyamuni and Jina Mahāvīra, there are also, as others have pointed out, striking points of resemblance. The Jina Mahāvira is said to have died in 388 B.C. As, further, it appears, for the reasons stated above, that the assumption of the Southern Buddhists regarding a council of which the Northern Buddhists know nothing, and which is stated to have been held by the chronological Aśoka, rests on a mistake, or on invention, we must deduct 100 years, on account of the period between the *Nirvāṇa* and this supposed additional council, from the 218 years, which are said by the Cingalese to have elapsed between the *Nirvāṇa* and Aśoka. According, therefore, to the oldest, uncorrupted Cingalese tradition, the *Nirvāṇa* must have taken place only 118 (not 218) years before Aśoka's accession and coronation. Adding this 118 to the 270 B.C. (the year of Aśoka's accession) we obtain 388, exactly the same date as is assigned to the *Nirvāṇa* of Mahāvīra.

Professor Kern does not think that the discrepancies between the chronological traditions of the different Buddhist schools of the North at all affect the justice of his conclusion, as he attaches no credit to those traditions in general, but only to such of them as present the appearance of credibility. Nor is the unanimity of the southern Buddhists any proof of the correctness of their chronology, as, if it were, we should, on the same ground, have to admit the Chinese and Japanese date, which differs from the Cingalese. But he thinks that in Ceylon there must originally have been divergent traditions, which are afterwards harmonized, as well as this could be managed. We conjecture that the earlier existence of these divergencies may even yet be recognized. According to one tradition, he thinks Aśokā's reign was considered to have begun 100 years, and according to a second 118 years, after the *Nirvāṇa*. Instead of choosing between the two, the Cingalese writers have adopted both. But the same Aśoka could not have begun to reign both 100 and 118 years after Buddha's death. There must therefore, they concluded, have been two Aśokas, one who came to the throne 100 years after the *Nirvāṇa,* and a second who became king 118 years after the first.

I now return to Dr. Kern's remarks on the Pāli (pp. 12 ff.). It appears, he says, from various sources, that the Buddhists laboured to make out their religious doctrine to be older than it really was. A result of this disposition was that they were led to represent their sacred language, the so-called Pāli, as identical with the Māgadhī, an as the source of all languages. In the grammar ascribed to Kachchāyana a verse occurs stating that the Pāli is the Māgadhī spoken by men, &c. at the commencement of the creation. (See, however, my *Sanskrit Texts,* ii. 54, note 991, where it is stated, on the authority of

Mr. Childers, that the verse in question is not found in Kachchāyana). This claim put forward on behalf of the Pāli, to be the oldest of the languages, Dr. Kern sets aside as absurd. (See *Sanskrit Texts,* ii. 65 ff.). He also denies that the Pāli is the same as the Māgadhī. This he says, is proved by the Inscription of Aśoka, which show that Pāli differs from Māgadhī more than it does from the other Prākṛits. Māgadhī, the dialect of the province of Magadha, of which Pātaliputra was the capital, was employed by Aśoka in various inscriptions found in the east and centre of India. In the northern and north-western parts of the country he made use, for the same purpose, of the dialects there prevailing. The Pāli has none of the linguistic peculiarities of real Māgadhī, as found in the inscriptions, but, on the contrary, approaches nearest to the Śaurasenī of the dramas, although it has forms belonging to all sorts of dialects, excepting only such as characterize the Māgadhī. The Pāli, in Dr. Kern's opinion, is shown by its phonetic system to be of later date than the language of any of the Inscriptions, and has a striking resemblance to the corrupt Sanskṛit found in the books of the Northern Buddhists, the principal elements in both being drawn from an actually existing language, in the one case the Sanskṛit, and in the other some one of the Prākṛits (excepting Māgadhī). But neither the corrupt Sanskṛit nor the Pāli were living tongues for those who employed them, but artificial languages which were no longer under the whole-some control of the current forms of speech. This alone explains how both contain so many absurd and incongruous words and forms, displaying mistakes of a kind which only scholars could commit, but which never occur even in the most barbarous popular dialect. Some examples of these blunders of the Pāli grammarians are then given, such as *vīṁānsā* from *mīmānsā, appābādhatā* instead of *apābādhatā, atrajo* instead of *attajo* from *ātmaja*. Prof. Kern considers that, with the imperfect data which we possess, it would be rash to try to decide from what popular dialect if there were not more than one from which it has been drawn, the principal elements of the Pāli were derived. One thing, however, is clear, viz. that Pāli is not Māgadhī, and that it is decidedly later than any dialect of the third century before our era. In tracing the origin of the Pāli we encounter the same difficulties as we meet with in our enquiries into the original dialect of the *Gāthās* in the books of the Northern Buddhists, such as the *Lalita Vistara* and *Saddharma Puṇḍarīka*. From beneath the varnish of Sanskṛit with which these *Gūthās* are overlaid, the original Prākṛit shines clearly through, though it is only as an exception that we can make out which of the Prākṛits it is. The prose parts of the works in question, written in a corrupt Saṅskṛit, are, as Prof. Kern considers, nothing but paraphrases of the metrical *Gāthās,* and of later date than they. This subject is further treated and illustrated in an appendix (pp. 108 ff.).

The rest of the Dissertation (pp. 31-107), forming its larger portion, is devoted to a series of critical and grammatical remarks on the text of the rock or pillar Inscriptions of Edicts of Aśoka, to an endeavour to present them in a correcter text, to revised translations (into Saṅskṛit and Dutch) of their contents, and to a statement of the facts and conclusions which may be derived or deduced from these contents.

Our acquaintance with the purport of these inscriptions is still, Dr. Kern observes, extremely imperfect, owing to different circumstances, but especially to the wretched state in which we possess the texts, arising first from the carelessness of the masons who hewed the inscriptions, and in a less degree from the incorrectness of the transcripts with which we have been furnished. This unfortunate state of things has prevented Dr. Kern from attempting in the mean time to supply a restored text of the whole of the Inscriptions. Those which are for the most part, or in regard to the main points, intelligible, and with which in consequence he has been able to deal, amount to more than the half.

I am glad to learn that there is a prospect of our being by-and-bye put in possession of more accurate transcripts of these Inscriptions.

Prof. Kern concludes his Dissertation with the following paragraphs:– "The Edicts included in this Dissertation give an idea of what the king did for his subjects in his wide dominions, which extended from Behar to Gāndhāra, from the Himālaya to the coast of Coromandel and Pāṇḍya. They are not unimportant for the criticism of the Buddhistic traditions; but the number of the data which they present regarding the condition of the Buddhist doctrine, and its adherents, is extremely small. The king in his eleventh year went over to Buddhism. He was a zealous Buddhist; he busied himself with the spiritual interests and even with the catechism of his co-religionists; at the proper time and place he makes mention in a delicate and becoming manner of the doctrine which he had embraced. But in his measures as a ruler nothing of a Buddhistic spirit is to be traced: from the commencement of his reign he was a good prince. His ordinances regarding the sparing of animal life are more in unison with those of the heretical Jains than with those of the Buddhists. Thus although the Edicts of Aśoka the Humane are only in part of direct importance for the history of Buddhism, the labour spent on persuing them is not lost, because the traits of the Aśoka, with whom we become acquainted from his own words, effectually counterbalance the caricature which, in the works of the Buddhists and others, is presented to us as the figure of the noble king." The points which are here summarized are more fully treated in the preceding pages.

The entire dissertation affords fresh proofs of the learning, ingenuity, and ability of Prof. Kern.

References

1. Over de Taartelling der Zuidelijke, Buddhisten en de Gedenkstukken van Açoka den Buddhist, door H. Kern. Uitgegeven door de Koninklijke Academie van Wetenschappen te Amsterdam. C.G. Van der Post, Amsterdam, 1873, pp. 120, 4to.
2. If Aśoka began to reign in 270 B.C. and the Nirvāṇa took place only 100 years before that, we only obtain 370 as the date of the latter. This miscalculation, as I learn from a communication of Prof. Kern himself, must have arisen from his having had in his thoughts the number 110, which according to the Northern Buddhists represented the period between the Nirvāṇa and the second council in the reign of Aśoka. The error, however, he remarks, does not affect his conclusion, as he has not assumed, nor does he suppose the Southern Buddhists meant, that the rough number 100 denoted the exact number of years between the Nirvāṇa and Aśoka. –J.M.

24

Three New Edicts of Aśoka

G. Bühler

The subjoined three edicts from part of the splendid discoveries which General Cunningham has been making in Northern and Central India during the last years, and will shortly be published in facsimiles in the first volume of his *Corpus Inscriptionum Indicarum.* General Cunningham sent me last autumn plate XIV. of his work which contains them. With the help of a photograph also furnished by him I soon succeeded in deciphering the very simple Sahasrām edict. But the more important Rūpnāth inscription. I was unable to make out completely, until, I received two rubbings, which General Cunningham was good enough to take at my request. On my communicating my final results he very generously gave me permission to publish the text with my translations, and thus enabled me to make these most important inscriptions at once generally accessible.

The great historical value of the new edicts lies herein: –

1*stly* – That they absolutely fix the length of time which elapsed between Buddha's *nirvāṇa* and Aśoka;

2*ndly* – That they prove the accuracy of the chronology of the southern Buddhists, *as far as India is concerned;*

3*rdly* – That their data, together with the information of the Greek historians, prove Buddha's *nirvāṇa* to have taken place between the years 483-82 and 472-71 B.C.; and

4*thly* – That they indicate the direction in which future efforts to find the exact date of Buddha's *nirvāṇa* ought to be made.

These assertions may appear bold and over-confident, as the inscriptions neither give the name of the king who caused them to be incised, nor show any of the common epithets of Buddha. But nevertheless I feel confident that a careful consideration of the contents of the edicts will cause their correctness to be admitted.

In the Sahasrām inscription a person who calls himself 'the Beloved of the gods' states that he was for a long time an *upāsaka,* or worshipper, without exerting himself much for his faith; that afterwards, in consequence of strenuous exertion *during a year and more,* he made the inhabitants of Jambudvīpa, *i.e.* India, abjure the gods in whom they believed formerly. He then quotes a passage in favour of 'exertion' from a 'sermon,' and adds that this sermon was delivered by the *Vivutha,* 'the Departed,' two hundred and fifty-six (years) before, and that its substance has been incised on rocks and stone pillars. In the Rūpnāth edict 'the Beloved of the gods' enlarges the first two statements by adding that the time of his being an *upāsaka* included *more than thirty-two years and a half;* and that during the period of exertion, lasting *upwards of a year,* he was a member of the *saṁgha,* or of the community of asçetics. This last point is also preserved in the fragment of the Bairāṭ inscription. In the date the Rūpnāth edict shows, besides, an important addition. It says, '256 (years) from the departure of the *Sata*, the Teacher.'

Now it is quite clear that the individual who calls himself 'the Beloved of the gods' must be a *king*. For, the fact that this epithet occurs before the names of the three kings Piyadasi-Aśoka, Daśaratha, and Tishya, and that in the Jaugada separate edicts it is used by itself to denote the first ruler, proves that it was an ancient royal title corresponding nearly to the modern 'by the grace of God,' and the Roman Augustus, and was used in the third century before Christ. Secondly, the boast that the writer caused a change of religion throughout India, – the result not of his *greatness,* but of his *zeal*, – and that he caused the matter of the sermon to be incised on rocks and pillars, can only proceed from a great ruler, who held the whole or a great part of India in subjection. Both the title of the writer, and the alphabet which the edicts show, make it very probable that this king belongs to the third century before Christ, and to the

Maurya dynasty. For it has hitherto not been proved that the title was used by later kings, or that the so-called Aśoka or Lāṭ characters were adopted by any one but the Mauryas, their subjects and contemporaries.

The next point to be determined is the faith to which the writer belonged. The statements that he destroyed the belief in the gods until then considered to be true, and that he was first an *upāsaka* or *sāvaka,* and later a member of the *saṁgha*, show that he must have been either a Bauddha or a Jaina. Both these sects apply the former two terms to their lay brethren, and the latter to the brotherhood of their ascetics. If thus the choice lies between the Jainas and Bauddhas, it cannot be doubtful that the latter are meant. For though the Jainas existed in the third century before Christ, and even occur in Piyadasi-Aśoka's inscriptions under their ancient name Nigaṇṭha, *i.e.* Nirgrantha,[1] no proof has hitherto been found for their own assertion that they were patronized by one of the Maurya kings;[2] on the contrary, there is every reason for adhering to the generally received opinion that both Aśoka and his grandson Daśaratha, and the other later Maurya princes, were Buddhists or patrons of Buddhism.

If the 'Beloved of the gods' war a Buddhist, it follows that the *sermon* which he quotes must be a Buddhist sermon, and the Vivutha of the Sahasrām edict, or Vyuṭha of the Rūpnāth edict, must be the Buddha himself. The word is not one of the common names of Śākyamuni-Gotama, but its etymological import is such as to make it a fitting epithet for him. I take *vivutha* for a representative of Sanskṛit *vivṛitta,* and of Pali *vivutta* or *vivaṭṭo.* As not one of these or of the formerly published inscriptions of Piyadasi shows double letters, but always substitutes single ones,[3] *vivutha* is in reality equivalent to *vivuttha,* and this form differs from the Pali *vivutta* only by the aspiration of the second *t.* This difference, however, does not matter much. For, firstly, there are other instances of irregular aspirates in the language of the edicts. Thus we have *kichhi,* 'something,' for Sanskrit *kiṁchit* and Pali *kiṁchi.*[4] Secondly, the letter *r* causes in Pali sometimes the aspiration of a preceding *ta, e.g.* in *tattha*=*tatra,*[5] and it is therefore not astonishing that the vowel *ṛi* should have exercised the same influence in a cognate dialect.

But irrespective of these phonetic considerations the identity of *vivutha* with Sanskrit *vivṛitta* becomes almost certain from the immediately following sentence of the Sahasrām edict, *duve sapaṁnālātisatā vivuthā,* –literally 'two hundred *(years)* exceeded by fifty-six have *elapsed.'* The sense of this passage, which is further confirmed by the phrase of the Khandagiri inscription (line 5)[6] *tatho vivuthe vase,* 'then after a year had elapsed,' makes it impossible to take *vivuthā* for anything else than *vivṛittāni* or rather *vivṛitte* (nom. dual neuter). As these two examples, as well as the etymology, show, *vivutha,* if applied to a person, means originally 'the *Departed,'* or' *he who has passed away.'* [7] Such a name fits Śākyamuni very well, as he is considered to be the first who passed away *beyond the circle of births.* The Rūpnāth form *vyuṭha* arose, in my opinion, from the substitution of *u* for *vu,* and the consequent change of the *i* of the prefix *vi* to *y* in accordance with the laws of Sanskrit phonetics. Its lingual *ṭh* has been caused by the lost *ṛi,* which in Pali too, as the form v*aṭṭo* shows, has the same effect.[8]

From the identification of the *Vivutha,* the preacher of the sermon, with Śākyamuni, it follows further that the era in which the inscriptions are dated is that of the *Nirvāṇa.* For, the *ti, i.e. iti,* which stands at the end of the sentence *duve sapaṁnālātisatā vivuthā ti,* shows that it is governed by the preceding sentence. *iyaṁ sāvane vivuthena.* Anybody who is acquainted with the use of the Sanskrit *iti* will see the truth of this remark, and will translate *idaṁśrāvanaṁ vivṛittena (kṛitam) dve shaṭ panchāśadadhikaśāte vivṛitte iti,* by "this sermon was preached by the *Departed* two hundred and fifty-six years ago." The date of the Rūpnāth inscription confirms the above explanation. It says, 256 *satavivāsā ta (i.e. ti),* lit. "256 from the departure of the *Sata, thus."* Here the word *sata* requires special notice. It may stand for Sanskrit *Śata,* 100, or, as the inscription does not note double consonants for *saptan,* 'seven,' *śakta,* 'able,' *śapta,* 'cursed;' or, as the inscription frequently leaves out the *anusvāra*[9], for *santa, i.e. sat,* pres. part. of *as,* 'good,' *śānta,* 'quiescent,' *śrānta,* 'tired;' or, finally, because the inscriptions do not always aspirate *t̃* followed by *r* or preceded by *s,*[10] for *śasta,* 'praised,' *śastra,* 'a weapon,' *śāstra,* 'institutes of science,' and *śāstṛi, 'a teacher.'* I select from these numerous possibilities the last explanation, because in Pali *satthu*[11] = Sanskrit *śāstṛi* is a common designation of Śākyamuni. The translation of the date is therefore, "256 *(years)* since the departure of the *Teacher* (have elapsed)." The final *ta,* which I believe to represent *ti,* indicates here probably that the inscription is finished.

The result which has now been gained is that the inscriptions proceeded from a Maurya king, or from a contemporary of the Mauryas, who was a Buddhist lay-brother during thirty-two years and a half, and a member of the *saṁgha* for upwards of a year, *i.e.* who was a Buddhist for more than thirty-three and a half, and *that in the thirty-fourth year of his adherence to the Buddhist faith* 256 *years after the Nirvāṇa* had elapsed, or in other words *the* 257th *year after the Nirvāṇa corresponded to the second half of the* 34th *year after his conversion.* Now we know of no Indian princes who made any great efforts for Buddhism in the third century after the *Nirvāṇa* besides Aśoka and Daśaratha, his grandson. But the latter cannot be the author of the inscriptions, as he reigned only seven years. There remains, therefore, nobody but Aśoka, whose reign lasted more than thirty-seven years. This inference is fully confirmed by the *Mahāvaṁśa,* which, provided a certain line of interpretation is adopted, gives the years of Aśoka's reign after his conversion as upwards of 34, and places his death in 257 Buddhæ.

The chronological dates regarding Aśoka which occur in the Ceylonese chronicle are as follows:—

1. Interval between Bindusāra's death and Aśoka's *abhisheka*... ... ... *(upwards of)* 4 years.[12]
2. Interval between Aśoka's *abhisheka* and his *conversion* to Buddhism ... ... *(upwards of)* 3 years[13]
3. Conversion of Tishya, the *Uparāja* ... ... in the 4th year of Aśoka's reign.[14]
4. Ordination of Mahendra and Sanghamitrā ... ... in the 6th year.[15]

5. Death of the Sthaviras Tishya and Sumanas ... ...in the 8th year.
6. The third Buddhist convocation ... ... in the 17th year.[16]
7. Planting of the Bodhi-tree in Ceylon ... ... in the 18th year.
8. Death of queen Asandhimitrā ... ... 12th year after the last event.
9. Aśoka's marriage with her attendant ... ... 4th year after the last event.
10. Destruction of the Bodhi-tree ... ... 3rd year after the last event.
11. Death of Aśoka ... ... 4th year after the last event.
12. Total of Aśoka's reign. . . . 37 years.[17]

There are two points connected with these dates which require consideration, viz, if the years of Aśoka mentioned under Nos. 3-7 are to be counted from the death of Bindusāra or from Aśoka's *abhisheka,* and, secondly, how the dates under 8-11 can be reconciled with the statement No. 12, that Aśoka ruled 37 years.

As regards the first question, the common custom of the Hindus to reckon the years of their kings from the date of their *abhisheka,* and not from their actual accession to the throne, is a strong argument for taking all the years mentioned under Nos. 3-7, as well as the total under No. 12, to refer to the period after Aśoka's *abhisheka*. This argument is further strength ened by the consideration that if the 4th year, in which Aśoka's brother Tishya entered the *saṁgha*, and the 6th year, in which his (Aśoka's) son Mahendra and his daughter Sanghamitrā were ordained, had to be counted from Bindusāra's death, both these events would fall *before Aśoka's conversion to Buddhism.* For his conversion cannot have taken place earlier than the 8th year after Bindusāra's death. Now Indian princes were, and are, no doubt, great latitudinarians in religious matters, and it would not be extraordinary to find that the brother of a Brahmanical king had turned Buddhist with his sanction. But it seems extremely improbable that a Brahman should persuade, or even give permission to, a son and a daughter to become ascetics of another sect than his own. For this reason also I can come to no other conclusion but that the dates of Tishya's and of Mahendra's and Sanghamitrā's ordinations fall in the 4th and 6th years after Aśoka's *abhisheka, i.e.* in the 1st and 3rd years after his conversion. If that is conceded in the case of these two events, it follows that all the other dates have to be taken in the same manner. The second question—as to how the dates given under 8-11 are to be reconciled with the statement under 12, that Aśoka reigned 37 years—has attracted the attention of Professor Lassen, who is of opinion that the *Mahāvaṁśa* contradicts itself. He maintains that as the death of Asandhimitrā fell in the 12th year after the 18th year of Aśoka's accession, the marriage of Aśoka in the 4th year after that event, the destruction of the Bodhi-tree in the 3rd year after the marriage, and the death of Aśoka in the 3rd year after the destruction of the Bodhi-tree, the total of Aśoka's years ought to be 41, instead of 37.[18] The *Mahāvaṁśa* certainly does express itself very loosely, but still its statements may be reconciled with each other. For it does not assert that the last four events took place at intervals of 12, 4, 3, and 4 years, but at intervals of—

11 years + *x* months or days.
3 years + *x* ,, ,, ,,
2 years + *x* ,, ,, ,,
3 years + *x* ,, ,, ,,

Nor does it say that the Bodhi-tree was sent to Ceylon 18 years after Aśoka's *abhisheka,* but in the 18th year, *i.e.* after 17 years and *x* months or days had elapsed. If we now assume that the number of the months or days in excess of the full years elapsed on the occurrence of each of the last five events does amount to more than one entire year and to less than two entire years, and if we concede that, as Turnour and others have already conjectured, the total of Aśoka's reign, 37 years, refers only to the number of *completed* years, and leaves out odd months and days, then the two statements will agree perfectly. In order to make my meaning plainer, I will, merely for argument's sake, put down definite figures for the unknown number of months or days, and the agreement of the two statements will appear at once:–

		Yrs.	m.
(7)	The Bodhi-tree planted in Ceylon in the 18th year after *abhisheka*...	17	7
(8)	Asandhimitrā died in the 12th year after that	11	7
(9)	Aśoka married her attendant in the 4th year after that	3	3
(10)	The Bodhi-tree was destroyed in the 3rd year after that	2	4
(11)	Aśoka died in the 4th year after that	3	1
		----	----
	The total of Aśoka's reign was then...	37	10
		----	----

and that is just what the *Mahāvaṁśa* says, provided its total 37 is taken to refer to completed years only.

The figures assigned for the months are, as I have stated, entirely fictitious, and, as far as the statements of the *Mahāvaṁśa* are concerned, the surplus over 37 years may be just as well ten days as ten months. But it seems obvious to me that the above interpretation of the passage is more accurate, and more in accordance with the literal meaning of the text than that proposed by the *Ṭīkā,* which declares it necessary to avoid counting the last year of each period twice.[19]

If we now turn to consider the adjustment of Buddha's years and of Aśoka's, we shall again find an element of uncertainty in the statement of the *Mahāvaṁśa*. But it will also appear that, under certain suppositions which the text by no means disallows, the statements of the *Mahāvaṁśa* and of those of the new inscriptions completely agree. The *Mahāvaṁśa* says, V. 21, that 218 years after the *Nirvāṇa had passed* when Aśoka's *abhisheka* took place. This obviously means, according to our manner of expressing ourselves, that the *abhisheka* was performed in 219 A.B. The text leaves it doubtful if the 218th year had only just closed, or if a number of months had elapsed since its completion. On this point, regarding which, I repeat it, no certainty can he gained from the *Mahāvaṁśa,* as well as on the other point, which according to the preceding discussion is equally uncertain, the amount of the excess over the total of 37 years, depends the determination of the year of the *Nirvāṇā* in which Aśoka died. If at the time of the *abhisheka* 218 years of the *Nirvāṇa* plus a few months, say two or three only, had elapsed, and if the excess of months over the total of 37 years of Aśoka's reign amounts likewise to a few months, say two or three only, then the death of Aśoka will fall in the year 256 of the N*irvāṇa*. For 218 years and 2 months + 37 years and 2 months makes 255 years and 4 months. Under this supposition Aśoka died in the first half of the year 256 of the *Nirvāṇa*.

But if many months, say 10 or 11, of the 219th year of the *Nirvāṇa* had passed at the time of the *abhisheka,* and, if many months, say ten or eleven, have to be added to the total of the years of Aśoka's reign, then his death falls in the year 257 after the *Nirvāṇa* For 218 years and 11 months + 37 *years and* 11 *months* makes 256 years and 10 months. It is also apparent that in order to bring about an agreement between the inscriptions and the *Mahāvaṁśa* this second interpretation has to be adopted. For only in case Aśoka died towards the end of 257 A.B. will it be possible to allow that he may have caused an inscription to he incised *when* 256 years *after the departure of the Teacher had passed.*

Now only one more point, the probable date of Aśoka's conversion, remains to be considered in order to complete the agreement between the inscriptions and the *Mahāvaṁśa*. The cquation of the former is 33 years 6 months and x days=256A.B. + x months or days. The *Mahāvaṁśa*, says, V. 34, "The father (of Aśoka), being of the Brahmanical faith, used to feed (daily) sixty thousand Brahmans. He himself did so *for three years.*" Now this may mean either that the interval between Aśoka's *abhisheka* and his conversion was filled by three years exactly, or that some months and days have to be added. The equation in the new inscriptions makes it necessary to add at least eight months, because the middle of the thirty-fourth after the conversion could not fall under any other supposition in the 257th year after the *Nirvāṇa*. But if this addition is made the dates of the inscription and of the *Mahāvaṁśa* agree perfectly. For then we obtain—

Aśoka's *abhisheka* 218 years after the *Nirvāṇa* and say 11 months, *i.e.* at the cud of 219 A.B.

Aśoka's conversion 3 years after the *abhisheka* and say 8 months, *i.e.* in the middle of 223 A.B.

Date of the inscriptions 33 years and 6 months and odd days after conversion, *i.e.* in the beginning of 237 A.B.

Death of Aśoka 37 years and say 10 months after *abhisheka, i.e.*, in the end of 257 A.B.

The agreement which has thus been shown to exist between the inscriptions and the *Mahāvaṁśa* is, in spite of the uncertainty introduced by the neglect of the odd months in the latter work, sufficiently close to prove that the *Mahāvaṁśa*'s statements regarding the history of India and of the beginnings of Buddhism are more than fanciful inventions of the monastic mind. They must be regarded as genuine historical dates, derived from contemporary evidence.

The necessary consequence of this discovery is that all attempts to adjust the Ceylonese chronology to that of the Greeks by means of a reduction or of a lengthening of the distance between the *Nirvāṇa* and Aśoka have to be given up. Henceforth it must be accepted as a fact that the *abhisheka* of Aśoka took place in 219 A.B., and that he was alive in the beginning of 257 A.B. If the identification of Aśoka's grandfather Chandragupta with the Sandrokyptos of the Greeks, and Aśoka's own relations to Antiochus, the Antiyoka or Antiyoga of the rock inscriptions, prove that the Ceylonese date of the *Nirvāṇa* 543 B.C. has been placed 60 to 70 years too early, the fault must lie either in the period after Aśoka, or in the adjustment of the dates of the Indian history and of the Ceylonese kings. It is possible that either some kings have been erroneously inserted After *Devānāṁpriya Tishya*, the contemporary of Aśoka, or that the reigns of Tishya, as well as of his predecessor and successors, have been intentionally expanded. The latter alternative seems to me most likely, because, as Mr. Turnour[20] and other Orientalists have shown, the dates of Pāṇḍukābhaya, of Mutaśiva and of his four sons, are extremely suspicious. It seems impossible that these kings, who represent three generations, should have reigned 200 years. This suspicion becomes stronger through other circumstances, especially through the fact that Vijaya's landing is made to fall on the day of the *Nirvāṇa*. I am not prepared to risk any definite statement as to the manner in which the reigns of the Ceylonese kings ought to be reduced, or on the exact amount of the reduction, as I think it very likely that Dr. P. Goldschmidt's collection of Ceylonese inscriptions will completely clear up the question. For all practical purposes the date for the *Nirvāṇa,* 477-78 A.D., fixed by Professor M. Müller, by General Cunningham, and others, is perfectly sufficient. The new inscriptions show that it cannot be very far wrong. The two outside termini for the beginning of Chandragupta's reign are 321 B.C. on the one side, and 310 B.C. on the other. For this reason, and because the Ceylonese date for the beginning of the Mauryas, 163 A.B., must now be considered to he genuine, the *Nirvāṇa* must fall between 483-82 B.C. and 472-71 B.C. If, therefore, the date 477-78 for the *Nirvāṇa* should eventually be proved to be wrong, the fault cannot be more than five or six years one way or the other.

Certainty regarding the date of the *Nirvāṇa,* as already stated, will probably he obtained from the Ceylonese inscriptions. But there is a chance that the same goal may be reached by a different road. If a perfectly trustworthy account of the interval between Aśoka's death and the beginning of the Vikrama or of the Śaka eras could be obtained either from Indian inscriptions or from books, then the question would also be solved. I must add that an account of this kind exists, though I should be sorry to call it trustworthy on the evidence hitherto adduced. The Śvetāmbara Jainas place Mahāvīra s *nirvāṇa* in 470[21] before the era of Vikramāditya 56-7 B.C., and the beginning of the Mauryas in 216 after Mahāvīra, or in 311 B.C. This date agrees well enough with the statements of the Greeks, and I should be prepared to adopt it if the manner in which the Śvetāmbaras arrived at it agreed with the Buddhist chronology, and the age of the *gāthā* in which it occurs were better authenticated. But the Jaina account of the dynasties in the 6th and 5th centuries B.C. differs from those of the

Bauddhas and of the Brahmāns. The *gāthā says* that Mahāvīra died on the night in which king Pālaka of Ujjain was installed on the throne; that Pālaka ruled 60 years; that, next, the Nandas held India for 155 years, and that the latter were succeeded by the Mauryas. Thus the Śiśunāgas are left out altogether—a point which makes the dates suspicious. Under these circumstances I give the Jaina account merely as a curiosity, and in order to warn against its being used, without further inquiry, as a means to find the exact date of Chandragupta's accession and of the *Nirvāṇa*.

The additions to the history of the last years of Aśoka which the new inscriptions furnish are of great interest. We now hear for the first time that Aśoka's zeal for the Buddhist faith produced towards the end of his reign something very like bigotry. His boast that he caused the people of Jambudvīpa to abjure their ancient gods, which probably must be taken to mean only that he did his best to bring about such a result, stands in strange contrast to his earlier toleration.[22] The change finds its explanation partly in the increasing age of the monarch, and the domestic difficulties which, both according to Buddhistic and Jaina accounts, he had with the queen whom he married after Asandhimitrā's death, and partly by his turning ascetic. This fact is likewise new and of great interest, as Aśoka, in spite of his asceticism, apparently continued to govern the country. It indicates that the Buddhists allowed, just like the Jainas in exceptional cases, an intermediate stage between the *Śrāvakas* or lay brethren and the *Bhikshus* or monks. The Gujarāt chroniclers assert that the Chaulukya king Kumārapāla, to whom they even give the title *saṁghādhipāti,* 'lord of the Saṁgha,' took at various periods of his reign vows of continence, of temperance, of abstention from animal food, and of *apratigraha, i.e.* to renounce the confiscation of the heirless property of Vāṇiās. I am not aware that other instances of royal Bauddha ascetics, occur who continued to administer the affairs of their kingdoms.

There is yet another question for which the new inscriptions are of the utmost importance;— the history of the ancient Nāgarī numerals. Hitherto the oldest inscriptions showing them were the Mathurā inscriptions of Kanishka, the Śātavāhana inscriptions on the Nānāghāṭ, and the inscriptions of the Andhrabhṛityas. It is satisfactory to find now that these numeral signs are contemporaneous with the oldest known form of the Indian alphabet. But the form of the sign for 200 is still more important, as it furnishes the clearest proof for the correctness of Pandit Bhagvānlāl Indrajī's discovery of the syllabic origin of the Nāgari numerals. The sign for 200 employed in The Sahasrām edict is 𑀲𑀼 and, if the right-hand side-stroke denoting the second hundred is left out of consideration, closely resembles the sign for 100 in the Nānāghāṭ inscriptions and the fifth Gupta sign.[23] But in the Rūpnāth edict the common sign for the syllable *su* 𑀲𑀼 appears in its stead, slowing, however, an unusual elongation of the left-hand vertical stroke. It is obvious that the elongation of the vertical stroke serves[24] here the same purpose as the side-stroke in the Sahasrām figure, *i.e.* to denote that 200, not 100, must be read. But the fact that the common sign for the syllable *su* is employed, instead of the differentiated form used in the Sahasrām edict, proves that the engraver knew it to be a syllable, and pronounced it as such.

I take this opportunity to give an attempt at an explanation of the very curious fact that in the syllabic notation of numerals 200 is expressed by the syllable *su or śu* plus one stroke, and 300 by *su or śu* plus two strokes, which latter are attached, according to the fancy of the writer, either at the right-band side both high up and low down, or even placed at the top. This manner of notation is not easily explicable on the supposition that the side-strokes represent *ankas* of figures. For in that case we ought to find two side-strokes for 200, and, three for 300. I propose, therefore, to take them as marks intended to show that in the case of 200 the syllable *su* had to be pronounced long, *sū*, and in the case of 300 *pluta, i.e., sū-u*. This explanation holds good for the Andhrabhṛitya and Vākaṭaka signs for 1,000, 2,000, and 3,000 also, which may be read *dhu, dhū,* and *dhū-u,* respectively. It is confirmed by the fact that in the case of 400 the sign for the syllable expressing 4, *khka* or k*i* according to Bhagvānlāl, is attached to *su.* The

Hindu grammarians allow syllables of three *mātrās* only, and it was therefore impossible to employ an additional stroke in order to denote 400.

The sign in the two edicts for 50 also deserves attention. Rūpnāth shows the form used in the Kshatrapa and Valabhī inscriptions, while Sahasrām gives that of the Eastern plates and of the MSS.

Inscription* on a *Rock at Sahasrām.

From General Cunningham's facsimile, revised according to photograph

Transcript and Restoration of the Sahasrām Edict.[25]

Devānāṁ piye hevaṁ ā[hā sātilekāni aḍhit]i yāni savachhalāni, | aṁ upāsake sumi, | na cha bāḍhaṁ palakaṁte. – 1 –

Saviṁchhale sādhike |, aṁ [sumihakā bādhaṁ palakaṁ]t[e].

Etena cha aṁtalena | jaṁbudīpasi aṁmisaṁ, devā[hu]saṁ, ta – 2 –

munisā | misaṁ deva kaṭā | Pala [kamasi hi] iyaṁ phale [n]o [cha i]yaṁ mahatatā-vachakiye pāvatave. | Khudakena hi pala – 3 –

kamamīnenā vipule suag[e] [sa]kiye ālā[dha yita]v[e]. | Se etāye aṭhāye iyaṁ sāvāne | : khudakā cha uḍālā cha pa – 4 –

lakamaṁtu, aṁtā pi chaṁ jānaṁtu |; chila-ṭhitīke cha palakame hotu|. Iyaṁ cha aṭhe vaḍhisati|, vipulaṁ pi cha vaḍhisati, – 5 –

diyāḍhiyaṁ avaladhiyenā diyaḍhiyaṁ vaḍhisati | Iyaṁ cha savane vivuthena; duve sapaṁnālāti- – 6 –

satā vivuthā ti (sū ṅ phra) 256. Ima cha aṭhaṁ pavatesu likhāpayā thāya; [yata] vā a- –7–

thi hete silāthaṁbhā tata pi likhāpaya tha-yi. –8–

Translation

The Beloved of the gods speaketh thus: (*It is*) [*more than thirty-two*] years [*and a half*] that I am a worshipper (*of Buddha*), and have not exerted myself strenuously. (*It is*) a year and more [*that I have exerted myself strenuously*]. During this interval those gods that were (*held to be*) true gods in Jambudvīpa have been made (*to be regardedas*) men[26] and false. For through strenuous exertion comes this reward, and it ought not to be said to be an effect of (*my*) greatness. For even a small man who exerts himself can gain for himself great rewards in heaven. Just for this purpose a sermon has been preached: "Both small ones and great ones should exert themselves, and in the end they should also obtain (*true*), knowledge. And this spiritual good will increase; it will even increase exceedingly; it will increase one (*size*) and a half, at least one (*size*) and a half." And this sermon (*is*) by the *Departed*. Two hundred (*years*) exceeded by fifty-six, 256, have passed since; and I have caused this matter to be incised on the hills; or where those stone pillars are, there too I have caused it to be incised.

Transcript of the Rūpnāth Edict.[27]

Devānāṁ piye hevaṁ āhā: sātirakekāni aḍhitisāni va[sā], ya sumi pākā sa[va]ki, no cha bāḍhi pakatc. Sātilckc chu chhavachhare, ya sumi haka saṁgha-papite –1–

bāḍhi cha pakate. Yi imāya kālāya jambudipasi amisā devāhusu te dāni masā kaṭā. Pakamasi hi esa phale, no cha esā mahatatāpā-potave. Khudakenā hi ka –2–

pi parumaminenā sakiye pipule pi svage ārodhave. Etiya aṭhāya cha sāvane kaṭe: khudakā cha uḍālā cha pakama ṁtu ti, atā pi cha jānaṁtu. Iyaṁ pakāre cha –3–

kiti? chiraṭhitike siyā. Iya hi aṭhe vaḍhi vaḍhisiti, vipula cha vaḍhisiti, apaladhiyenā diyaḍhiyaṁ vaḍhisati. Iya cha aṭhe pavatisu lekhāpeta vālata hadha cha; aṭhi –4–

silāṭhubhe śilāhaṁbhasi lākhāpeta vayata. Etinā cha vayajanenā yāvatakatu paka ahāle, savara-vivase tavāyati. Vyuṭhenā sāvane kaṭe. (sū ṅ phra) 256 sa – 5 –

ta-vivā sā ta – 6 –

Translation

The Beloved of the gods speaketh thus: (*It is*) more than thirty-two years and a half that I am a hearer (*of the law*), and I did not exert myself strenuously. But it is a year and more that I have entered the community (*of ascetics*) and that I have exerted myself strenuously. Those gods who during this time were considered to be true (*gods*) in Jambudvīpa, have now been abjured. For through exertion (*comes*) this reward, and it cannot be obtained by greatness. For a small (*man*) who exerts himself somewhat can gain for himself great heavenly bliss. And for this purpose this sermon has been preached: "Both great ones and small ones should exert themselves, and should in the end gain (*true*) knowledge, and this manner (*of acting*) should be, what? Of long duration. For this spiritual good will grow the growth, and will grow exceedingly, at the least it will grow one (*size*) and a half." And this matter has been caused to be written on the hills; (*where*) a stone pillar is, (*there*) it has been written on a stone pillar. And as often as (*man brings*) to this writing ripe thought, (*so often*) will he rejoice, (*learning to*) subdue his senses.[28] *This* sermon has been preached by the *Departed.* 256 (*years have elapsed*) since the departure of the *Teacher.*

Transcript of the Bairāt Edict.[29]

Devānaṁ piye āhā sāti[lekāni]................*i.e.* sa......... – 1 –

vasā-naṁ ya haka upāsake n[o] cha bāḍhaṁ.............. – 2 –

aṁ mamayā saṁghe papayite [bā]ḍha[ṁ] cha............. – 3 –

jaṁbudipasi amisā-naṁ deva-hi.......vi........[pala]kamasi esa[pha]le – 4 –

(n)o hi ese mahatane vachakaye...............[pala]rumamimenā ya............pa – 5 –

vipule pi śvaṁge [sa]kye ālādheta(v)e.............[khuda]kā cha uḍālā cha palakamatu ti – 6 –

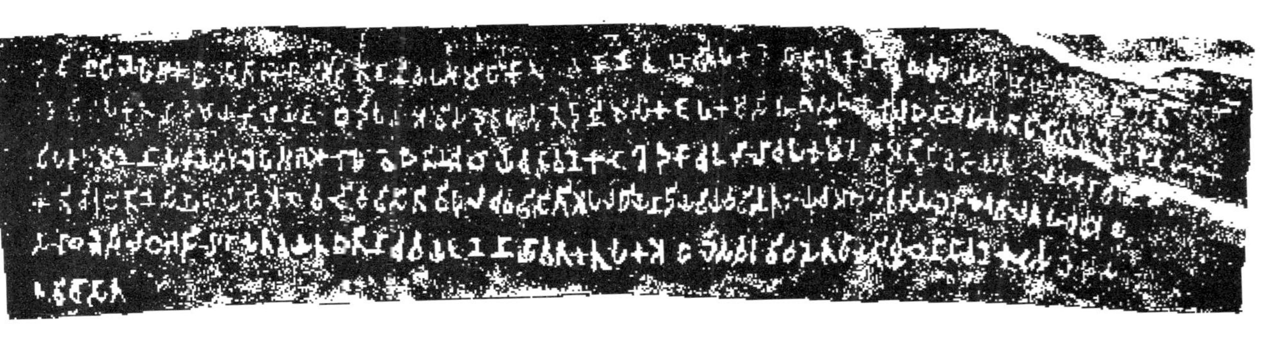

Plate I : Photo-Zincograph of General Cunningham's impression of the Rūpnāth Edict. (Facing Page 170)

aṁte pi janaṁtu ti chilathiti[ke]...........[vi]pulaṁ pi vaḍhisati –7–

diyaḍhiyaṁ vaḍhisati (ṅ phra) 56................–8–

Index of Words occurring in the three Edicts[30]

Aṁ, S. 1, 2; B. 3=Sansk. *yat:* compare Dhauli VI. 3, 5; sep. ed. I. 2, &c.

Aṭhaṁ, S. 7, *aṭhāya*, S. 5, R. 4, *aṭhe;* S. 5, R=Sansk. *artha*, Pali *aṭṭho*: compare Dhauli IV, 7, V. 7, &c. and pillar edicts.

Aṭhi, R. 4=Sansk. *asti*: compare Dhauli IX. 1, &c.

[*Aḍhit*]iyāni, S.1, a vicarious form for the following=**aḍhitihāni;* compare Panjābī *tīh*, thirty, and *ikattī*, thirty-one, *bīh*, twenty, and *panjī*, twenty-five, &c.

Aḍhitisāni, S.1=Sansk. *ardhadvi-triṁsāni*, Gujarāti *aḍhitīs:* compare also *aḍha-(kosikyāni)*, Delhi sep. ed. 2. Regarding Sansk. *ardha=sārdha* see *Pct. Dict.* s.v. *ardha. Aḍhi* or closely allied forms occur in all the modern Prakrits.

Atā, R.3=*aṁtā*=Sansk. *amtāt.*

Athi, S.7=Sansk. *asti* with meaning of the plural *santi:* compare Childer's *Pali Dict.* .s.v. *atthi*, and Delhi sep. ed. 11, *ata athi silāthaṁbhāni.*

Aṁtalena. S.2=Sansk. *antareṇa*: compare Dhauli, *e.g.* IV. 1, and pillar edicts.

Aṁtā, S.5=Sansk. *antāt.*

Aṁte, B.7=Sansk. *ante.*

Apaladhiyenā, R.4=Sansk. *aparārdhyena.*

Amisā, R.2=Sansk. *amishāt.*

Amisā-naṁ, B.4= amishāt+*nanu*, *Aṁmisaṁ*, S.3, mistake or vicarious form for *amisaṁ*=Sansk. *amisham*: compare, regarding nasalization, Kuhn, *Beitrage Pali Gram*, p. 33, and Dhauli II. 3. *Aṁni=āni=yāni*, &c.

Avaladhiyenā, S.6=Sansk. *avarārdhyena.*

Ahāle, R.5=Pali *āhāro*: see Childer's *Dict.* s. v. For the change in the quantity of the initial *ā* compare Kuhn, *loc. cit.* pp. 20-30, Dhauli IX. 1, *abādhesu=ābādhesu*, &c.

Ahusaṁ, ahusu: see *husaṁ, husu.*

Ārodhave, R.3, mistake for *ārādhave*=Sansk. *ārāddhavyaḥ:* compare Girnār VI. 12.-*Tave, i.e. tavve*=Sansk. *tavyaḥ,* occurs in the pillar edicts.

Ālā(dhayita)v(e), ālādhetave, S.4, B.6: see the preceding, and compare Dhauli IX, 7, &c.

Āhā, S.1. K.1, B.1=Sansk. *āha.*

Ima, S.7=*imaṁ*=Sansk. *imam.*

Imāya, R.2=Sansk. *asmai*: compare Girnār III. 3.

Iya, R. 4=*iyaṁ.*

Iyaṁ, S.3, 5, 6; R.3=Sansk. *ayam* and *idam*: compare Khālsī XII. 13, *iyam mule;* Delhi III. 17, *iyaṁ kayāne,* &c.

Uḍālā, S.3, R.3, B.6=Sansk. *udārāḥ,* Pali *uḷārā.*

Upāsake, S.1, B.2=Sansk. *upāsakaḥ,* Pali *upāsako.*

Etāye, S.4=Sansk. *etasmai;* compare Girnār III. 3, &c.

Etinā, R.5=Sansk. *etena.*

Etiya, R.3=*etāye.*

Etena, S.2=Sansk. *etena.*

Esa, R.2, B.4=Sansk. *esha,* Pali *esa*: compare Dhauli sep. ed. I.2, &c.

Esā, R.2, probably a mistake for *esa* or *ese.*

Ese, B.5=Sanks. *esha,* Pali *eso,* Māgadhī *eśe.*

Kaṭā, Ś.3, R.2=Sansk. *kṛitāḥ,* Pali *kaṭā*: compare Dhauli V. 3, &c.

Kaṭe, R. 3, 5=Sansk. *kṛitam* (neuter): compare Dhauli V. 1, &c.

-Katu, in *yāvata-katu,* R.5=Sansk. *kṛitvaḥ* and Pali *khattuṁ.*

Kapi, R.2,3=Sansk. Pali, *kiṁapi,*—possibly a mistake for *kipi.*

Kālāya, R. 2=*kālāya* with sense of *kāle.*

Kiti, R.4=Śansk. *kimiti,* Pali *kiṁti;* rock edicts usually *kiṁti,* but Khālsī N. face XIII. 12 *kiti.*

Khudakā, S.4, R.3, B.6=Sansk. *kshudrakāḥ,* Pali *khuddakā.*

Khudakena, S.3, *-kenā,* R.2=Sansk. *kshudrakeṇa.*

Cha, S.1, 2, 4, 5, 6, 7; R. 1, 2, 3, 4, 5; B.3, 6=Sansk. and Pali *cha.*

Chaṁ, S.5, mistake for *cha.*

Chā, B. 6, mistake for *cha.*

Chiraṭhitike, R.4=Sansk. *chirasthitikaḥ,* Pali *chiraṭṭhitiko.*

Chilaṭhitīke, S.5; see the preceding: compare Dhauli V.8, VI. 6.

Chilathiti (*ke*), B.7; see the preceding.

Chu, R.1=Sansk. *tu:* compare Dhauli VI.7, sep. ed. I.10.

Chhavachhare, R.1=Sansk. *saṁvatsaraḥ,* possibly a mistake for *sava*⁰; but compare *kāchhati*=**kassati*=Sansk. *karishyati,* in the pillar edicts.

Janaṁtu, B.7; probably a mistake for *jānaṁtu.*

Jambudipasi, R.2, B.4,=Sansk. *jambudvīpe,* Pali *jambudīpe.*

Jaṁbudīpasi, S.2; see the preceding.

Jānaṁtu, S.5, R.4=Sansk., Pali, *jānantu.*

-Thiti, S.5, R.4 (in *chila-ṭhitike*)=Sansk. *sthiti,* Pali *ṭhiti.*

Ta, S.2, mistake or vicarious form for *te,* which see.

Ta, R.6, for *ti*=Sansk. *iti.*

Tata, S.8=Sansk. *tatra,* Pali *tattha*: compare Delhi sep. ed. 3, &c.

Tavāyati, R.5; probably a mistake for *tapayati*=Sansk. *tarpayati,* Pali *tappeti.*

Ti, S.7, R.3, B.6, 7=Sansk. *iti,* Pali *ti.*

Te, R.2=Sansk., Pali, *te* (nom. pl. m. of *tad*).

Thayi, S.8, probably for *athāyiṁ*=Sansk. *asthām* (1st per. sing. aor. act. of *sthā*).

Thāya, S.8, a variant of the preceding.

Dāni, R.2=Sansk, *idānīm,* Pali *dāni.*

Diyaḍhiyaṁ, S.6, R.4, B.8=Sansk. *dvyardham,* Pali *diyaḍḍhaṁ*: compare *diyāḍha,* Khālsī XIII. 35.

Diyāḍhiyaṁ, S. 6; a vicarious form for the preceding.

Duve=Sansk, *dve,* Pali *duve.*

Deva, S.3, B.4, probably mistake for *devā.*

Devā, S.3, R.2=Sansk. *devdḥ.*

Devānaṁ, B.1=Sansk. *devānām,* Pali *devānaṁ.*

Devānāṁ, S.1, R.1, a mistake or variant for the preceding.

Na, S.1=Sansk., Pali, *na.*

Naṁ, B.2 (in *vasā-naṁ*), B.4 (in *amisā-naṁ*)=Sansk. *nanu,* Śaur., Māg., *ṇaṁ,* Hemach. IV. 283, 302, ed. Pischel.

No, S.1, 3, R.1, 2, B.2, 5=Sansk., Pali, *no*: compare Dhauli V. 3, &c.

Paka, R.5=Sansk. *pakvaḥ,* Pali *pakko.*

Pakate, R.1,2=Sansk. *prakrāntaḥ.* Pali *pakkanto,* but with the meaning of *parākrānta.*

Pakamaṁtu, R.3=Sansk. *prakrāmantu,* Pali *pakkamantu.*

Pakamasi, R.2=Sansk. *prakrame.*

Pakāre, R. 3=Sansk. *prakāraḥ,* Pali *pakāro,* but possibly a mistake for *pakame.*

Papaye or *papayite,* B.3=Sansk. *prāpitaḥ.*

-Papite, R.1 (in *saṁgha-pa*)=Sansk. *prāpitaḥ.*

Parumaminenā, R.3, mistake for *pakamaminenā*=Sansk. *prakramamāṇena.*

Palakaṁte, S.1, 2=Sansk. *parākrāntaḥ,* Pali *parakkanto.*

Palakamatu, B.6, a variant of the following.

Palakamaṁtu, S.5=Sansk. *parākrāmantu,* Pali *parakkāmantu*: compare also Dhauli VI. 6, &c.

Palakamamīnenā, S.3,4=Sansk. *parākramamāṇena*: for the termination-*mīna* compare *sampaṭapādayamīne,* Dhauli sep. ed. I. 15.

Palakamasi, S.3, B.4=Sansk. *parākrame.*

Palakame, S.5=Sansk. *parākramaḥ*: compare Dhauli VI. 7.

Palarumaminenā, B. 4,5, a mistake for *palakamaminenā.*

Pavatisu, R.4, a *varia lectio* for the following.

Pavatesu, S.7=Sansk. *parvateshu,* Pali *pabbatesu.*

Pākā, R.1, a mistake for *hakā.*

Pāpotave, R.2 (in *mahatatāpā*[0])=Sansk. *prāptavyam,* but formed from a new root, *pāpo*: compare Pali *pappoti,* and *pāpovā,* Delhi VI. 3.

Pāvatave, S.3=Sansk. *pravaktavyam:* for the lengthening of the first syllable compare Pali *pāvachanam.*

Pi, S.5, 8, R.3, B.6=Sansk. *api,* Pali *pi.*

Pipule, R.3, a mistake for *vipule.*

Piye, S.1, R.1, B.1=Sansk. *priyaḥ,* Pali *piyo.*

Phale, S.3, R.2, B.4=Sansk. *phalam,* or possibly=*phalaḥ,* a rare form for *phalaṁ: vide* the *Pet. Dict.* s.v. *Phalāni* occurs Khālsī II. 6.

Bāḍhaṁ, S.1, B.2, 3=Sansk. *bāḍham*: compare rock edicts VII, end.

Bāḍhi, R.1, 2, B.2, 3 (?), a vicarious form for the preceding. For *am=e=i,* compare also Delhi V.8, *sūkali.*

Mamayā, B.3=Sansk. *mayā*: compare Dhauli VI. 1, Delhi sep. ed. 3.

Masā, R.2=*misā*=Sansk. *mishāt.*

Mahatatā, S.3, R.2=Sansk. *mahattā,* Pali *mahantatā.*

Mahatane, B.5=Sansk. *mahattvam,* Prāk. *mahattaṇaṁ:* compare Var. IV. 22.

Misam, S.3=Sansk. *misham.* For the meaning of *mishaṁ kṛi* see *Pet. Dict.* s.v. *misha.*

Munisā, S.3=Sansk. *manushyāḥ*: compare Dhauli II. 3, &c.

Ya, R.1, B.2=Sansk.*yat,* Pali *yaṁ.*

Yāvatakatu, R.5=Sansk. *yāvatkṛitvaḥ.*

Yi, R.2=Sansk., Pali, *ye* (nom. pl. m. of *yad*).

Lākhāpeta, R.5, a mistake for *lekhāpeta.*

Likhāpaya, -yā, S. 7,8=Sansk. *lekhitvā; -aya=ya*; compare Pali *likhāpeti,* and for the construction of *ṭhā* with the absolutive, Childers' *Dict.* s.v. *tiṭṭhati, ṭhāti.*

Lekhāpeta, R.4=Sansk. *lekhitaḥ*: compare Dhauli II. 3, *lopabeta* and *lopapita*=Sansk. *ropitāni.*

Vaḍhi, R.4=*vṛiddhim* (acc. sing.), Pali *vaḍḍhiṁ.*

Vachakaye, B.5, *-kiye,* S.3 (in *mahatatāva*^{0})=Sansk. *vāchaka* enlarged by the affix *īya* (?).

Vaḍhisati, S.5, 6, R. 4, B.7, 8=Pali *vaḍḍhissati*: compare pillar edicts, *e.g.* Delhi I.6, &c.

Vaḍhisiti, R.4, a vicarious form for the preceding.

Vayajanenā, R.5=Sansk., Pali, *vyanjanena*: see Childers' *Dict.* s.v. See also rock edicts III., end. As to *i* represented by *a,* see Kuhn, *loc. cit.* p. 24, and compare Khālsī XIII. 38, *vayāsanaṁ=vyasanaṁ.*

Vayata, R.5—probably a mistake for *thāyi ta=asthāyi* (*sthitaḥ*) *iti.*

Va (*sā*), R.1=Sansk. *varṣhāṇi.*

Vasā-naṁ, B.2=Sansk. *varshāṇi nanu*: compare above, *naṁ.*

Vā, S.7=Sansk., Pali, *vā.*

Vālata, R.4, possibly a mistake for *pālata,* but=Sansk. *paratra*: compare pillar edict *pālataṁ=pāratrikam.*

Vipula, R.4=Sansk., Pali, *vipulam.*

Vipulaṁ, S.5, B.8=Sansk. *vipulam.*

Vipule, S.4, B.6=Sansk. *vivulaḥ*: compare also *pipule,* and rock edicts VII.

Vivase, R.5 (in *savaravi*⁰)=Pali *vivaso,* Sansk. *vivaśah.*

Vivāsā, R.6 (in *satavi*⁰)=Sansk. *vivāsāt.*

Vivuthā, S.7=Sansk. *vivṛittāni,* Pali part, of *vaṭṭati,* is sometimes *vutto:* compare also Khandagiri inscr. 1.5, *Jour. Beng. Br. R. As. Soc.* vol. VI, p. 1050, *tatho vase vivuthe.*

Vivuthena, S.7=Sansk. *vivṛittena.*

Vyuṭhenā, R.5, a vicarious form for the preceding, caused by the substitution of *u* for *vu.*

Śvaṁge, śvage, B.6=Sansk. *svaragaḥ.* Similar substitutions of *ś* for *s* occur particularly often in the latter half of the Khālsī edicts, *e.g.* XI. 129 *śo* for *so,* XI. 30 *mitaśaṁthutāna=mitrasaṁstutānāṁ,* XII. 34, *śiyā=siyā=syāt,* &c.

Savachhalāni, S.1=Sansk. *saṁvatsarāḥ:* compare also *chhavachhare* and *saviṁchhale.*

Sakiye, -kye, S.4, R.3, B.6=Sansk. *svakīyaḥ,* Pali *sakiyo.*

Saṁgha, R.1, *-ghe,* B.3=Sansk. *saṁghaḥ,* Pali, *saṁgho.*

Satavivāsā, R.5, 6=Sansk. *śāstṛivivāsāt,* Pali *satthuvivāsā.*

-Satā, S.7=Sansk. *śatāni.*

Sapaṁnālātisatā, S.7=Sansk. *shaṭpan chāśadatiśatāni.* For *sa=shaṭ*: compare *saḍu-(vīsati)* in the pillar edicts. For the use of *ati=adhi* compare *atiratha, rājātirāja,* &c.

The *la* of *paṁnāla* is inexplicable, ad one feels tempted to read *paṁnāha* instead, 𑀳 for 𑀮.

Sa(va)ki, R.1=Sansk. *śrāvakaḥ,* Pali *sāvako.*

Savara-, R.5=Sansk., Pali, *saṁvara.*

Savane, S.6, a mistake for *sāvane.*

Saviṁchhale, a mistake for *saṁvachhale.*

Sātirakekāni, R.1, a mistake for *sātilekāni.*

Satileke, R.1=Sansk. *sātirekaḥ,* Pali *sātireko.*

Sādhike, S.2=Sansk. *sādhikaḥ.*

Sāvane, R.3, 5=Sansk. *śrāvaṇam,* Pali *sāvanaṁ*: compare Delhi VII. 20.

Sāvāne, S.4, a mistake for the preceding.

Siyā, R.4=Sansk. *syāt*: compare Gir.III.3, &c.

Silāṭhaṁbhasi, R.5=Sansk. *śilāstambhe.*

Silāthubhe, R.5=Sansk. *śilāsthambhaḥ.*

Silāthaṁbhā, S.8=Sansk. *śilāstambhaḥ*: compare *silāthaṁbhāni,* Delhi sep. ed. 11.

Suag(e), S.4=Sansk. *svargah.*

Sumi, S.1, R.1.=Sansk. *asmi* (1st per. sing. pres. of *as*): for the insertion of *u* compare Kuhn, *Beit, Pali Gram.* p. 45.

Se, S.4=Pali *se*: compare Dhauli IV. 1, VI. 1, Delhi II.16, R.2, &c.

Svage, R.3=Sansk. *svargaḥ.*

Haka, R.1, B.2=Sansk. *aham.* Māgadhī, *hage*: compare also *pākā,* and Dhauli VI. 5 and *passim.*

Hadha, R. 4=Sansk. *iha,* Pali *hidha*: compare pillar edicts, *e.g.* Delhi I. 3, *hida-ta.*

Hi, S.3, R.2, B.5=Sansk., *Pali, hi.*

-*Husu*, (*hu*)*saṁ*, R.2, S.2=*abhūvan*: compare *a-huṁsu*, and *husa*, Delhi VII. *12*.

Hete, S.8=Sansk., *Pali*, *ete* (nom. m. of *etad*).

Hevaṁ, S.1, R.1, B.1=Sansk., Pali, *evam:* compare Dhauli VI. 4 and *passim*.

Hotu, S.5=Sansk. *bhavatu*: compare Dhauli V.8, &c.

References

1. See Lassen, *Ind. Alt.* vol. II. p. 468, 2nd ed., and Delhi separate edict, 1.5.
2. According to their accounts, Samprati or Sampadi, the son of Kuṇāla and grandson of Aśoka, covered the earth with Jaina *chaityas*. See, *e.g.*, Hemachandra, *Pariśishtaparva*, Sargas X, XI.
3. Compare, *e.g.*, '*diyaḍhiyam*' with Pali *diyaḍḍho, tata* with Pali *tattha, aṭhe* with Pali *aṭṭho*, etc.
4. Compare also the irregular aspirates in Pali words, like *kuntha, phalita*, &c. enumerated by E. Kuhn, *Beitrāge zur Pali Grammatik*, p. 40.
5. Compare Kuhn, *loc. cit.* p. 50.
6. *Jour. As. Soc. Beng.* vol. VI. p. 1090.
7. Another *possibility* to explain *vivutha* as a corruption of *vivṛita*, and to take this as a synonym of *nirvṛita*, Pali *nibbuto*, I reject on account of the two cases where it is construed with the word *vaso*, 'a year'.
8. Compare also E. Kuhn, *loc. cit.* p. 49, and the form *kaṭe* for *kṛitaḥ*.
9. Compare, *e.g.*, *pakate=prakrāntaḥ, atā=āntāt*, &c.
10. Compare *tata*, Sah. 1.8=*tatra* and Pali, '*ta=asta*: Kuhn, *loc. cit.* p. 53.
11. *Vide* Childers' *Pali Dict.* s.v.
12. *Mahāvaṁśa*, V. 17-20, –Turnour, pp. 21-22.
13. *Mahāv.* V. 35, –Turnour, p. 23. In this passage and the preceding one the author says that *three* and *four* years respectively had elapsed when the second event took place; the latter fell, therefore, in the 4th and 5th years Mr. Turnour translates *chatuhi vassehi* (V. 20) wrongly by 'in the fourth year'.
14. *Mahāv.* V. 168-172, –Turnour, p. 34.

15. *Mahāv.* V. 215, – Turnour, p. 37.

16. *Mahāv.* V. 286, – Turnour, p. 42.

17. For the last dates see *Mahāv.* XX. 1.6, – Turnour, p. 122.

18. Lassen, *Ind. Alt.* vol. I, p. 283. 2nd ed. He has over-looked the fact that the *Tikā* of the *Mahāvaṁsa* – Turnour, Introd. p. xlvii, – warns against this 'laughable mistake.'

19. Turnour, *Mahāv,* Introd. p. xlvii.

20. *Mahāv.* Introd. p. xli.

21. See *Ind. Ant.* vol. II. p. 362, and *Jour. Bo. Br. R. As. Soc.* vol. IX. p. 147. Kern in his *Jaartelling,* p. 28, gives 466 before Vikrama as the date of Mahāvīra's *nirvāṇa,* on the authority of Professor Weber's extracts from the *Śatrunjayamāhātmya.* That work is a wretched forgery by some *yati* of the 13th or 14th century, as the chapter on Kumārapāla of Aṇahilapāṭaka, 1144-74 A.D., and the numerous *Gujaraticisms,* show. The Śvetāmbaras *mean* the era of Vikramāditya of 56-7 B.C. when they say 470 before Vikrama. The Digambaras place Mahāvīra's *nirvāṇa* in 605 before Vikrama, and refer to the so-called Śaka era.

22. See Lassen, *Ind. Alt.* vol. II. p. 275, 2nd ed.

23. *Ind. Ant.* vol. VI, p. 45, col. 1 and col. 5.

24. In the case of 300 the Jainas also place the second stroke above the syllable, and write [illegible].

25. Materials used: Plate XIV. of General Cunningham's *Corp. Inscr. Ind.* vol. I. and a photograph supplied by General Cunningham.

L. 1. The facsimile and photograph show that seven or eight syllables have been lost. The restoration of the first six is absolutely certain on account of the identical readings of *R.* and *B.* [*aḍhit*]*iyāni* is less certain. I take it for a representative of *aḍhitisāni,* caused by the change of *s* to *h* and its subsequent loss, just as in Panjābī *tīh,* thirty and *ikattī,* thirty-one.

L. 2. Read *saṁvachhale,* R. Six or seven letters have been lost. *R.* and *B.* have two sentences, corresponding to this lacuna, containing sixteen letters. *S.* can have had one sentence only. The sense requires the sentence given above. Read *amisaṁ,* according to *R.* Read *devā-husaṁ* as *R.* has *devā-husu* and a verb is required. The vertical stroke in the facsimile is the left-hand part of the [illegible]. This emendation I owe to Paṇḍit Bhagvānlāl Indraji. Read *te* for *ta,* according to *R.*

L. 3. Read *devā.* The *pala* before the lacuna is probable from the photograph. The restoration is certain on account of the corresponding passage in *R.*, which here, as everywhere, substitutes the root *pakam* for *palakam.* The second and third lacunas have been filled in according to *R.*

L. 4. Restoration according to *R.* and *B.* –Read *sāvañe.*

L. 5. Read *cha jānaṁta.*

L. 6. Read *sāvane;* the facsimile has *dute,* but according to the photograph *duve,* which the sense requires, is at least probable, if not certain.

L. 7. Restoration suggested by the fact that two syllables have been lost, and a relative pronoun is desirable, though not absolutely necessary. The date had been read by General Cunningham before I received the inscription.

26. This phrase probably alludes to the Buddhist belief that the *devas* also have shorter or longer terms of existence, after which they die and are born again in other stages of existence according to their *karma.*

27. Materials used: two rubbings forwards by General Cunningham.

L. 1. Read *sātilekāni,* the letter looks blurred and is a mistake for . For *pākā* read *hakā.* There is a faint mark between *sa* and *ki* which may be *va,* –*sāvaki* is required as synonym for *upāsake; saṁgha ushite* is a possible reading, as the letters appear to be half effaced. The reading given above is supported by *B.*

L. 2. Under the *vā* of *devā-husa* there is a vertical stroke, resembling an *u* . Probably it is intended to indicate the absorption of the initial *a* of *chusu,* and is the oldest form of the *Avagraha* . Read *esa* for *esā.* A letter may have stood between *khudakeṅā hi* and *ka.* But I rather think the marks in the impression are accidental scratches.

L. 3. Read *pakamaminenā; vipule; ārādhave;* the long *ā* in *pakāre* is not quite certain.

L. 5. Read *lekhāpeta ṭhāyi ti; tapayati* for ; but possibly the reading on the stone may be *tapāyati,* as the lower part of *vā* does not quite form a circle. Possibly *vyaṭhenā.* The two last figures of the date had been read by General Cunningham before I received the inscription.

L. 6. Probably *ti* for *ta* to be read.

28. The original has a double meaning. The other meaning is, "And as often as (*a man seasons his*) boiled rice with this condiment he will be satisfied, falling into a state of *saṁvara, i.e.* that state of

intense satisfaction and repletion in which he closes his eyes from pleasure, and suspends the activity of the senses generally.

29. Materials used: Cunningham, *Corp. Inscr.* vol. I. plate XIV., and a cloth copy made by Paṇḍit Bhagvānlāl Indrajī.

L. 1. Cloth copy; *devānāṁ*. The remnants of three letters towards the end of the line are also from the latter.

L. 2. *Corp. Inscr.: paka*. Cloth copy shows lower part of *n*(*o*). *Corp. Inscr.: bāḍhi*. Cloth copy has remnants of these letters towards the end of the line.

L. 3. *Corp. Inscr.: payaye ate* and *bādhi*. In the cloth copy the top of *dha* is wanting.

L. 4. Cloth copy: *amisā-na deve pi* and omits *vi*. I conjecture *amisā-naṁ deva-ki*[*su te dā*]*ni*. Portions of the letters *laka* appear on the cloth copy; *Corp. Inscr.: masi*.

L. 5. *Corp. Inscr.* begins the line *ha hi,* the cloth copy shows *o* clearly. *Corp. Inscr.: mapātane*. I think *mahatana* should be read, as the word forms a compound with *vachakaye*. Read [*pala*]*kamaminenā*. The cloth copy omits *ya..........pa,* which are not easily explained.

L. 6. Cloth copy: *vipule hiṁ śvage takye; Corp. Inscr.: vipule pi śvaṁge kiye*. The above reading is conjectural, but supported by the analogy of *S.* and *R.* Possibly *sakiye* may be the right form. Towards the end *Corp. Inscr.* reads [*khuda*]*kā che,* which is incorrect.

L. 7. Cloth copy omits *aṁ*(*te*), shows half a *ta* instead of *ti* in *chilathiti*(*ke*), and omits *pu* in (*vi*)*pulaṁ*.

L. 8. Cloth copy: *diyaḍhiya. vadhasati,* and omits the numeral signs. I must confess that I doubt the correctness of the latter, on account of their position.

30. The references to be published edicts refer to Mr. Burgess's Girnār facsimiles, and to the plates of General Cunningham's *Corp. Inscript. Ind.* vol. I, which he has kindly forwarded to me.

25

The Three New Edicts of Aśoka

G. Bühler

My translation and analysis of General A. Cunningham's new Aśoka edicts, published in vol. VI pp. 149ff of the *Indian Antiquary,* have called forth two reviews in the London *Academy,* one by Mr. Rhys Davids,[1] and one by Professor R. Pischel,[2] in which my explanation of several important words have been found fault with, and the correctness of the historical inferences drawn from the inscriptions has been disputed. Mr. Rhys Davids has also devoted a couple of pages to the new edicts in an appendix to his work "On the coins and measures of Ceylon" (*Numismata Orientalia,* Part VI. pp. 57-60). As the latter work contains an analysis of the statements regarding Buddhistic chronology, given in the *Dīpavaṁsa* and *Mahāvaṁsa,* as well as a very ingenious attempt to fix the date of the Nirvāṇa somewhere about 410 B.C., the author very naturally felt it necessary to deal with the somewhat inconvenient three edicts, which, if the interpretation given by me were right, would make his deductions valueless. The importancc of thc questions connected with the new inscriptions, and the consciousness that in my first notice some important points have been either entirely omitted, or rather touched than fully discussed, induce me to reply to the strictures passed on my article.

For the sake of ready reference I reprint the texts of the Sahasrām and Rūpnāth edicts.[3]

Sahasrām

Devānāṁ piye hevaṁ ā[*hā: sātilekāni aḍhit*]i-yāni savachhalāni, aṁ upāsake sumi, na cha bāḍhaṁ palakaṁte.

Saviṁchhale sādhike, aṁ [*sumi bāḍhaṁ palakaṁ*]t[*e*].

Etena cha aṁtalena jambudīpasi aṁmisaṁ devā[*hu*]saṁ, ta munisā misaṁ deva kaṭā.

Pala [*kamasi hi*] iyaṁ phale, [*n*]o [*cha i*]yaṁ mahatatā-vachakiye pāvatave.

Khudakena hi palakamamīnenā vipule suag-[*e*] [*sa*]kiye ālā[*dhayita*]v[*e*].

Se etāye aṭhāye iyaṁ sāvane:

Khudakā cha uḍālā cha palakamaṁtu, aṁtā pi chaṁ

janaṁtu; chilaṭhitīke cha palakame hotu.

Iyaṁ cha aṭhe vaḍhisati, vipulaṁ pi cha vaḍhisati, diyāḍhiyaṁ avaladhiyenā diyaḍhiyaṁ vaḍhisati.

Iyaṁ cha savane vivuthena; duve sapaṁnālātisatā vivuthā ti (*su ṅ phra*) 256.

Ima cha aṭhaṁ pavatesu likhāpayā thāya; [*yata*] vā athi hete silāthaṁbhā tata pi likhāpayā thayi.

Rūpnāth

Devānāṁ piye hevaṁ āhā: sātirakekāni aḍhitisāni va[*sā*], ya sumi pākā sa[*va*] ki, no cha bāḍhi pakate.

Sātileke chu chhavachhare, ya sumi haka saṁgha-papite, bāḍhi cha pakate.

Yi imāya kālāya jambudipasi amisā devāhusu, te dāni masā kaṭā.

Pakamasi hi esa phale, no cha esā mahatatāpāpotave.

Khudakenā hi kapi parumaminenā sakiye pipule pi svage ārodhave.

Etiya aṭhāya cha sāvane kaṭe:

Khudakā cha uḍālā cha pakamaṁtu ti, atā pi cha

jānaṁtu; iyaṁ pakāre cha kiti? chiraṭhitike siyā. Iya hi aṭhe vaḍhi vaḍhisiti, vipula cha vaḍhisiti, apaladhiyenā diyaḍhiyaṁ vaḍhisati.

Iya cha aṭhe pavatisu lekhāpeta vālata hadha cha; aṭhi silāṭhubhe silāthaṁbhasi lākhāpeta vayata.

Etinā cha vayajanenā yāvatakatu paka ahāle, savara-vivase tavayati. Vyuṭhenā sāvane kaṭe; (*s ū ṅ phra*) 256 satavivāsā ta.

In my analysis of these edicts I stated–

Firstly, that the author must be a king, because he uses the ancient royal title, *Devānāṁpiye,* speaks of his greatness, and asserts that he caused a change of religion throughout India, and incised his edicts on rocks and pillars.

Secondly, that this king probably belonged to the third century B.C., and to the Maurya dynasty, on account of the title, which we know to have been a Maurya title, and on account of the alphabet employed in writing the inscription.

Thirdly, that he must have been a Buddhist, because the Mauryas were patrons of that sect, and because we have no evidence that the Jainas, the only other known sect which the terms employed in the inscriptions would fit, were patronized by a Maurya.

Fourthly, that as the author of the inscription was a Buddhist, the author of the sermon which the inscription quotes, the Vivutha or Vyuṭha, must be Śākyamuni Buddha, and that *vivutha* must mean 'the Departed,' or 'he who has passed away,' on account of the phrase *duve sapaṁnālātisatā vivuthā* (Sah. 6, 7), and that the word *probably* corresponded to Sanskrit *vivṛitta.*

Fifthly, that if the Vivuṭha was Buddha, the era used must be that of the Nirvāṇa, and that the explanation of *satavivāsā* by *śāstṛi-vivāsāt,* 'from the departure, *i.e.* the death, of the teacher,' which I regarded as *probable,* confirmed this view.

Sixthly, that as the inscription belonged to a Buddhist and Maurya king, no one but Aśoka could be the author, as no other Maurya had ruled as long as thirty-four years, or been for so long a time a Buddhist; and

Seventhly, that the statements of the *Māhāvaṁśa,* if correctly interpreted, showed that Aśoka had been a Buddhist for about thirty-four years, and might have been alive during the greater part of the year 257 after the Nirvāṇa.

In his first review (*Academy,* July 14th; 1877) of my article, Mr. Rhys Davids demurred to one point only, viz. to the explanation of the word *vivāsa* by 'death', preferring to render it, *'in accordance with classical usage,'* by *'abandoning his home'* or 'becoming an ascetic,' and assumed that the era used was not that of Buddha's Nirvāṇa, but that of the Great Renunciation. He further stated that even if my interpretation were correct, and the era used were that of the Nirvāṇa, the inscription would only prove that the Buddhists *believed* the Nirvāṇa to have taken place 257 years before the 34th of Aśoka's conversion, and *not* that it *actually did* take place at that time. He finally suggested that the opening sentence of the edicts might mean that the gods of Jambudvīpa, who had hitherto held aloof from men (*i.e.* the Buddhistic deities), had been caused to mingle with them.[4]

Next, Professor Pischel, in a note on the inscription (*Academy,* Aug. 11, 1877) objected to my view that the edicts belonged to Aśoka. He declared my explanations of *vivutha, vyuṭha,* and *sata* to be inadmissible. The former two words he identified with the Sanskrit *vyushita,* the past part. pass. of *vivas,* 'to depart,' and translated them by 'he who has departed from life.' *Sata* he declared to be the Sanskrit *sattva,* 'life,' and explained the phrase *satavivāsā* by *sattvavivāsāt,* 'since his departure from life.' He further contended that, as neither of these terms nor any other word was clearly of Buddhistic origin, nothing remained to connect the inscriptions with Aśoka. He therefore took them to the Jaina, and expressed his conviction that the *Vivutha* must be Mahāvīra, for which view he adduced a phrase, '*from the departure,*' occurring in Stevenson's *Kalpasūtra*, p. 95. He finally ascribed the inscriptions to Aśoka's grandson Sampadi, whom, as I had stated, the Jainas represent to have been a patron of theirs.

Finally, Mr. Rhys Davids, in the appendix to the *Numismata Orientalia*, Pt. VI. pp. 57-60, once more reviews the whole question. Influenced by Professor Pischel's criticism, he no longer confidently attributes the edicts to Aśoka, but thinks that my arguments for that view are not sufficient. He repeats Professor Pischel's assertion that the terms employed in the edict may be Jaina as well as Buddhistic; he also points out that *Devāṇuppiya*, the Jaina form of *Devānāṁpiye*, is used by the latter as a polite form of address to inferiors and women. Hence he thinks that my strongest argument for the identity of the author of the edicts with Aśoka, drawn from the fact that he was the only Devānāṁpiye who in the third century of the Buddhist era was a zealous Buddhist, and reigned more than thirty-four years, falls to the ground. He, however, does not go so far as to absolutely reject the authorship of Aśoka; but he would, in case that were proved, adhere to his former explanations of *vivāsa* by *abhinikkhamaṇa,* or 'turning ascetic,' and take *vivutha-vyuṭha* for an equivalent of *vyushita-vyushṭa,* and in the sense of *pravrajita.* He combats Prof. Pischel's explanation of *satavivāsā,* and he also gives Professor Jacobi's authentic text of the passage from the Jaina *Kalpasūtra* to which Professor Pischel had referred, and shows that it affords no countenance to the identification of the *Vivutha* with Mahāvīra or, to call him by his correct name, Nirgrantha Jñātiputra.[5] The result at which Mr. Rhys Davids arrives is that the inscriptions afford no assistance for determining the date of the Nirvāṇa, that they may be either Jaina or Buddhistic, and that everything connected with them is exceedingly uncertain and doubtful.[6]

These reviews contain the following points which require consideration:—(1) whether the inscriptions really contain nothing that connects them with Aśoka, and shows them to be Buddhistic; (2) the etymology of the terms *Vivutha-Vyuṭha* and *Sāta*; (3) the explanation of the word *vivāsa* by *abhinikkhamaṇa,* 'the Great Renunciation.' To the discussion of these points I shall have to add an inquiry regarding Mr. Rhys Davids's adjustment of the date of the Nirvāṇa. For it is evident that if his deductions from the texts of the *Dīpavaṁśa* and of the *Mahāvaṁśa* are correct, and the Nirvāṇa has to be placed about 410 B.C., the Ceylonese date for Aśoka's coronation, 219 A.B., with which, according to my interpretation, the date of the inscriptions agrees, must necessarily be wrong. I shall also have to consider his remark that in the most favourable case the new edicts prove only the belief prevailing in Aśoka's time regarding the date of the Nirvāṇa, not the actual date itself; and to add a few further facts bearing on the interpretation of the edicts, which I omitted in my first notice.

As regards the first point, I regret that I cannot agree either with the method employed by my critics in their discussion of the authorship of the edicts, nor with their results. In my opinion, the question if the terms *saṁgha, upāsaka, sāvaka, vivutha-vyuṭha, sata, Devānāṁpiye* are exclusively Buddhistic, or if they have been used by Jainas, Brahmans or other sects also, as well as the etymology of *vivutha-vyuṭha* and *sata,* affect the chief problem very little. I have myself stated that some of these words were used by two sects, and I have no doubt that all of them were current in the fourth and third centuries B.C. among the adherents of various sects. In some cases actual proof for this belief can be furnished. I have given two *possible* etymologies for *vivutha*, and nine for *sata,* and I now regret that I did not add two more for the former word, as my doing so might have made it clearer how little I relied on them. The chief problem—the question *who* was the author of the new edicts—has to be solved in an entirely different manner, viz, by a careful comparison of the old Aśoka edicts, and of the other known Prakrit inscriptions with the new edicts. If that comparison is duly made, I think it will be found that there is a good deal to connect the new inscriptions with Aśoka, and that their authorship is not even doubtful. If my critics, in answer to this defence, charged me with having neglected to state my case clearly, and to put forward in a prominent manner all the points which prove Aśoka to be the author of the three edicts, I should feel obliged to plead guilty. But I should urge in extenuation that I trusted to their knowledge of the old Aśoka edicts, which would enable them to recognize at once the family likeness existing between the old and new sets, and to supply my omissions. I must also confess that the decided opinion of General Cunningham, who, long before the inscriptions came into my hands, recognized their origin,[7] as well as the agreement of other eminent epigraphists with his and my conclusions, influenced the manner in which I put the case. I can now only express my regret that I have not been explicit enough, and arrange the decisive arguments in the proper manner. The case may be stated as follows:—

We possess a large number of inscriptions which, according to the *consensus communis* of all competent scholars, belong to the Maurya Aśoka. These inscriptions are written in the peculiar characters which are usually called Pali or Lāṭ, and which I prefer to style Maurya. These inscriptions, further, are written in a number of Prakrit dialects, which differ from all those known from other sources, and which vary according to the provinces where they are found. They are distinguished by a very peculiar style, and by their moralizing, sermonizing contents. In the latter respect they are unique, utterly different from the inscriptions of all other Indian princes. They are further incised both on rocks and pillars, in slightly varying recensions. Their author calls himself usually Devānāṁ Piye Piyadasi, and in some cases simply Devānāṁ Piye.

If we now turn to the new edicts, we find that they closely resemble the old ones in every one of the details mentioned. The new edicts, too, are written in the Maurya characters; they, too, show different dialects, according to the districts where they were incised. Their vocabulary is, with the exception of two or three words, identical with that of the old edicts. The grammar of the Sahasrām edict perfectly agrees with that of Aśoka's Māgadha edicts. The Rūpnāth edict, which comes from the Central Provinces, agrees in some particulars more with the Saurāshṭra inscriptions of Girnār, and is in other respects independent, though it comes nearer to the Aśoka forms than to any other. As regards the style, we find the well-known formulas and turns: "The beloved of the gods speaketh thus", "This manner of acting should be what? of long duration", and so forth. The contents, too, agree so far with those of the old pillar or rock inscriptions that they are a sermon,—not historical matter, such as we are accustomed to find in other inscriptions. The new edicts, just like the old ones, further give variations of one and the same text, and contain the explicit statement that they too were incised on rocks and pillars. Finally, their author, too, calls himself Devānāṁ Piye.

Where we have so many points of agreement between two sets of inscriptions, the obvious inference is that both proceed from the same author. The only way to bar this conclusion would be to show that the facts on which it is based are susceptible of some other explanation. My critics have not done much in this respect. Professor Pischel is entirely silent regarding the close resemblance of the new edicts to the old ones. Mr. Rhys Davids occupies himself only with the title *Devāṇāṁ Piye,* which he thinks may have been used by Jaina kings and others also. In support of the latter assertion he adduces the Jaina-Prakrit term *Devāṇuppiya,* which in the *Āgamas* of the Jaina sect is frequently used as a polite form of address. I, too, believe that *Devānāṁ piye* was not a title peculiar to Buddhist kings, but one common to the Mauryas and their contemporaries, whether they were Buddhists or not. Originally, it seems to me, it must have been invented by Brahmans, because Buddhists or Jainas would hardly care much whether they were the beloved of the gods, *i.e.* of beings to whom they paid but little reverence, and whom they considered perishable like themselves.[8]

That, however, is not very important. Taken by itself the title does not prove much. It merely shows that the author was a king of the fourth or third century B.C. But it is of great value if taken as a link in the long chain of circumstantial evidence which connects the inscriptions with Aśoka. The same remarks apply to the alphabet used. Other kings besides Aśoka did use it, and its occurrence in the new edicts shows only, like the title *Devānāṁpiye,* the period to which the inscriptions belong. It may also be contended that other kings besides Aśoka used some of the words and the grammatical forms occurring in the two edicts. We have some evidence to this effect in the Khandgiri and the Daśaratha inscriptions, and the supposition is not more than reasonable. But with respect to the peculiar turns of expression and the style of the inscriptions, the same reasoning does not hold good. The style of a man reveals, as is generally allowed, his individuality as much as his handwriting or his general deportment. If, therefore, particular resemblances in this respect are observable between two sets of compositions, something more definite than a vague assertion that others too *may* have employed phrases like *Devānāṁ piye hevaṁ āhā, vipule svage sakiye ārādhave* or *iya pakāre kiti chiraṭhitike siyā,* is required in order to preclude the obvious inference to be drawn from their occurrence in both. In like manner, there is only one way to account for the fact that both sets of edicts contain sermons preached by a ruler of "all the Indias" to his subjects, and that both give original texts, different redactions of which were placarded, so to say, in different places and dialects on "rocks and pillars" for the enlightenment of the multitude. We have many hundreds of Indian inscriptions, issued by hundreds of different kings, but there is not one document which resembles Aśoka's edicts in this respect, and there is not one king who tried to convert his subjects to a particular creed, and to keep them in the paths of virtue and morality by means of *affiches officielles.* Here, too, the individuality of the author reveals itself, and, as long as it is not shown that others besides Aśoka actually adopted the same plan, the resemblance of the two sets of edicts in this respect admits only of one explanation, viz. that they belong to the same author. If, now, the other points mentioned above, the identity of the alphabet, of the vocabulary and grammar, and of the author's title, are taken into account, it is, I think, not too much to say that the edicts not only contain *something* connecting them with Aśoka, but that they furnish as strong proof as circumstantial evidence can afford that they actually proceeded from the great Maurya Buddhist.

As regards the question whether the edicts contain any Buddhist terms, I will point out one word, which my critics have overlooked, viz. *ahāle* (R. 5). I have translated this by 'thought,' relying on the explanation of *āhāra* given in Childers' *Pali Dictionary.*[9] I do not think that the passage can be taken otherwise than I have done, and the silence of my critics seems to indicate that they agree with me. But if that is so, then *ahāle* is a specially Buddhistic word, which in this sense has been traced neither in Brahmanical nor in Jaina books. The matter is, however, of small importance. For, as the inscriptions belong to Aśoka, all the doubtful terms most be Buddhistic. *Upāsaka* and *sāvaka* must mean 'a lay Buddhist,' *saṁgha* must denote the community of Buddhist ascetics, and the *Vivutha* or *Vyuṭ ha,* whatever the etymology of the words may be, must be Śākyamuni-Gautama.

In turning to the consideration of Professor Pischel's criticisms on my explanation of these two terms, I must premise that I fully agree with his assertion that Sanskrit *vyushita* and *vyushṭa* phonetically correspond to *vivutha* and *vyuṭha.* I may add that this phonetic correspondence was known to me from Childers' *Pali Dictionary* when I wrote my first article, as well as the phonetic identity of Sanskrit *vyuttha (vi+ut+sthā+a)* with the same two terms of the edicts, and that several scholars had pointed it out to me before Professor Pischel's letter appeared. But I must demur to Prof. Pischel's statement that, on account of this phonetic identity, my explanation is "quite untenable." For, considering the fact that Prakrit words are corruptions, which may have originated in many ways, and that all Prakrits, but especially those used in the inscriptions, frequently show a want of fixedness both as to orthography and grammar, phonetic identity is neither the only nor even the chief point to look to in the interpretation of doubtful words. In attempting to explain *Vivuthenā* and *Vyuṭhenā,* the correct method is to begin, not with the etymology, but with the sentence *duve sapaṁnālātisatā vivuthā,* in which, as well as in the parallel passage of the Khandgiri inscription, *tatho vivuthe vase, vivutha* is used, not as an appellative noun, but as a verbal form, and cannot mean anything but 'passed, gone.' This is a translation, with which neither Professor Pischel nor Mr. Rhys Davids finds fault. The next question is whether the same meaning answers in the case of *Vivuthenā.* There can be no doubt that it does. For Buddha may fitly be called 'the Departed,' or 'he who has passed away,' since at his death he obtained freedom from future births by entering *Nirvāṇa,* whatever notion the early Buddhists may have connected with this term. This is the way in which I arrive at the meaning 'by the Departed' for *Vivuthenā,* which of course must also be that of *Vyuṭhenā.* I do not rely on any etymology, as Professor Pischel thinks. As the meaning of the term is thus fixed by the aid of parallel passages, the etymology has only a secondary importance, though, of course, it must be looked to. Now the Sanskrit *vyushita* or *vyushṭa,* no doubt, phonetically corresponds to *vivutha-vyuṭha.* This etymology might also suit the noun *vivutha,* but it does not fit the participle *vivuthā,* in the Sahasrām date. For *dve shaṭpanchāśadatike śate vyushite* or *vyushṭe* is a phrase inadmissible in Sanskrit, where *vivas* is not used for 'to elapse,' and *vyushṭa*—a derivative of *vas* 'to shine,'—means 'having broken or begun.' Nor has it been shown that the verb acquired this meaning in any of the Prakrits. It is therefore necessary to look for some other etymology, and the verb the past participle of which comes nearest to the two forms, is the Sanskrit *vivṛit.* In the Prakrits of the dramas *vṛit* usually makes *vutta,* and in Pali *vutta, vatta,* or *vaṭṭa.* The compound verb *vivṛit* means in Sanskrit 'to turn round, to roll away, to pass,' and the meaning of its past participle exactly corresponds to the sense which *vivutha* has in the Sahasrām date, and in the passage of the Khandgiri inscription. This etymology also fits the noun *Vivutha-Vyuṭha* perfectly. For, though Śākyamuni is now here called *vivutta* or *vivaṭṭa,* still the neuter *vivaṭṭam,* according to Childers' *Dictionary,* means 'absence of *vaṭṭa* or transmigration, Nirvāṇa.' Hence the masculine *vivaṭṭo* or *vivutto,* whether taken as past part. of *vivaṭṭ*, or as a compound formed of the particle *vi* and the noun *vaṭṭa*, is a suitable name for Śākyamuni, and it may be reasonably expected that a more complete investigation of the Bauddha *Āgamas* will show its actual occurrence. But, whether this expectation is fulfilled or not, the existence of the neuter affords a powerful support to the proposed etymology.[10] The phonetic difficulty which the latter presents, viz, the irregular appearance of an aspirated *tha* i.e. *ttha,* instead of unaspirated *ta (tta),* appears less important in consequence of the following considerations. Firstly, in the various Prakrit dialects aspirated letters *do* frequently appear for the corresponding unaspirated ones. Secondly, there are several cases where this change is observable in past part. pass. Thus we find in Jaina-Prakrit *pasaḍha* for *prasṛita, ūsaḍha* for *utsṛita,* and *samosaḍha* for *samavasṛita* (Müller, *Jaina Prakrit,* p. 26). Further, in modern Gujarātī there is a whole series of verbs which form their past participles in *dho, dhī, dhuṁ:* e.g. *khā-vuṁ, khādho, pī-vuṁ, pīdho, de-vuṁ, dīdho.* The last example is most to the point, as *dīdho* stands for an ancient Prakrit form *ditta,* which, though hitherto not traced, can be inferred from Kaśmīrī *dyutu,* genitive *dit-is,* and also, from the corresponding Sindhī form. Thirdly, it must not be forgotten that in all Prakrits the letters *r* and *ṛi* cause aspiration, though the dialects of Aśoka's edicts do not usually show this influence, like the Pali and the dialects employed in the dramas and poetry. The *ṛi* or *r* which stood in the original of *vivutha* may therefore also have contributed to the development of the aspirate. Finally, the derivation of the two forms from *vivṛitta* has this advantage, that it will fit *vyaṭ ha,* which *may* be read, and has been read by General Cunningham, instead of *vyuṭha.* For we have in Jaina-Prakrit *viyaṭṭa* for *vivṛitta.* I have adopted the reading *vyuṭha* in the transcript of the text, because a little stroke seems to protrude under the *vy,* but the reading is not beyond doubt. I do not think that it can be settled definitively without a fresh and very careful examination of the stone. It may remain doubtful even after that has been done, as the group of letters seems to be damaged. In concluding this discussion I will repeat that I do not consider the etymology proposed very important for my chief point, and will add that I consider it is a *pis aller.* I should prefer one where the phonetic correspondence with the Sanskrit would be exact, if it were suitable in other respects. If it could be shown, for instance, that *vivas* had the meaning of 'to elapse,' I should be ready to accept the derivation from that verb. Without that proof I feel unable to rely entirely on the phonetic laws, because, as stated above, the Prakrit dialects, and especially those of Aśoka's inscriptions, are deficient in that fixedness of orthography and grammar which is required in order to give to phonetic correspondence a paramount importance.

Professor Pischel's rendering of the last word of the Rūpnāth edict, *satavivāsā,* I am likewise unable to agree to, though I admit that *sata* does phonetically correspond to *sattva,* and ought to be added to my list of possible Sanskrit equivalents. The sense requires that the first part of the compound should contain the designation of the person whose *vivāsa* or departure is referred to. *Sattvavivāsāt* would mean 'since the departure of life,' *prāṇasya apagamāt,* not 'since his departure from life,' as Professor Pischel renders it. The numerals together with this compound form one sentence, and are not connected with the preceding *vyuṭhenā sāvane kaṭe.* Hence the *his* does not readily suggest itself. If, however, it is considered too unsafe to interpret *sata* by *śāstṛi*, it may be taken as an equivalent of *śānta* or *sat,* which both suit Buddha very well, and which, according to the analogy of *pakate* for *pakrāntaḥ,* and *yāvata (katu)* for *yāvanta,* would exactly correspond to *sata.* I, for my part, however, adhere to the explanation by *śāstṛi*, which, as Pali *atta* for *asta* shows, *might* become *satta* or *sata.*

I, now, come to the meaning of the word *vivāsa,* which Mr. Rhys Davids, appealing to classical usage, takes as an equivalent of *abhinikkhamaṇa,* 'the departure from home,' 'the renunciation of domestic life.' I am unable to understand on what classical usage he bases his interpretation. I have never found the verb *vivas* or any of its derivatives used as a synonym for *pravraj,* nor has Mr. Rhys Davids brought forward any passages supporting his notion of the classical usage of *vivas.* As far as I know, *vivas* has only one technical meaning, viz. 'to go into exile,' and its causative *vivāsay* accordingly means 'to banish.' If Mr. Rhys Davids is unable to bring forward passages which show that our dictionaries are defective, and that *vivas* means also 'to renounce domestic life, to turn ascetic,' his appeal to classical *usage* is useless. Classical usage supports neither his nor my rendering. But analogous transitions of meaning in the case of other verbs may be brought forward in support of both translations. Some Sanskrit verbs which mean 'to depart, to go forth,' acquire the secondary signification 'to renounce domestic life,' and some develop the meaning 'to die.' To the first class belong *pravraj* and *nishkram,* 'to go forth,' as well as *abhinishkram,* literally 'to go forth towards.' The second change is much more common. We have firstly *pra-i,* 'to go forth,' which is one of the commonest terms for 'to die.' There is secondly *gam*, which, like the compound *vigam,* means 'to die,' while *anugam* means 'to die after a person,' and *sahagam* 'to die with somebody.' *Prasthā,* too, and its derivative *prasthāna* are used for 'to die' and for 'death.' *Pravas* also appears to have developed the same secondary meaning (though I find no passages quoted for it), as *pravāsanā,* a derivative on its causal, is stated to mean 'killing.' This list might be enlarged, but the examples quoted are sufficient to show that Sanskrit, like all other languages, uses words meaning 'to depart' for 'to die.' I may add, however, that even in the present day it is usual among Pandits, when peaking of the decease of Gurus or parents, to use the tenderer and more reverential expressions, *svargavāsī abhūt, kailāsaṁ gataḥ,* or *prasthitaḥ para lokaṁ gataḥ* instead of the more matter-of-fact *mṛitaḥ.* If we now return to the phrase *sata-vivāsā,* both Mr. Rhys Davids and myself agree that the first part of the compound denotes a person—either Śākyamuni or somebody else. The second part cannot, therefore, have its etymological and primary meaning 'departure, or starting.' It must have been used in a secondary sense. Now, as has just been shown, on purely philological grounds two explanations are possible. *Vivāsa* may either mean 'the renunciation of domestic life' or 'death.' Which, then, is the one to be adopted? I answer the latter, because we know that both Bauddhas and Jainas began their eras with the death of their founders. If Mr. Rhys Davids wishes to make his explanation probable, he will have to show that the Bauddhas, or at least some other Indian sect, reckoned also from the Great Renunciation of their founders. The same objection must be made to his explanation of *Vivutha-Vyuṭha.* Supposing it were proved that these two terms corresponded to *vyushita-vyushṭa,* they could only be rendered by 'the Departed,' or 'he who is dead.' These remarks will suffice to show that neither Professor Pischel's objections, which are quite worthy of his reputation as a grammarian, nor Mr. Rhys Davids' new rendering of *vivāsa,* can exactly be called unanswerable, or be said to render my explanation of the edicts untenable.

I now turn to the consideration of Mr. Rhys Davids' date of the Nirvāṇa, which, if correct, would entirely destroy the remarkable agreement between the edicts as interpreted by myself and the statements of the Ceylonese chronicles. This agreement is visible especially in two points:—

1stly, in the length of membership of the Buddhist sect assigned to Aśoka both by the edicts and by the chronicles; and

2ndly, in the fact that the year 257 AB., which I have taken to be the date of the edicts,[11] apparently was, according to the statements of the *Mahāvaṁsa,* the last year of Aśoka's life.

The force of the former point has been acknowledged by Mr. Rhys Davids, who declares (*Num. Or.* VI. p. 59) the fact that while the Devānāṁ Piye of the new inscriptions speaks of his having been an *upāsaka* for thirty-three years and a half, and that we know of no king of the *third century* A.B. but Aśoka who reigned more than 34 years, – to be my strongest argument for the identification of the two. I have already stated that the strongest argument for the identification of our Devānāṁ Piye with Aśoka lies in the family likeness of the old and the new edicts. But, as we have a case of circumstantial evidence only, it is no doubt indispensable that the results gained by interpretation should agree with the facts known from other sources. I do not consider this agreement, therefore, as a matter of small importance. It is, on the contrary, as essential as the arguments given above. In order to show the full importance of the fact mentioned in the edicts, that *Devānāṁpiye,* a ruler of the whole of Jambudvīpa, was a member of an heretical sect for more than thirty-three years, I will point out that according to the Buddhistic chronicles the only kings in the *first three centuries* A.B. who reigned longer than thirty-three years were Bimbisāra and Aśoka, and that according to the Purāṇas *no Maurya king except* Aśoka occupied the throne for so long a period.

The second point, the very remarkable fact that, while the inscriptions are dated in the year 257 A.B., the statements of the Ceylonese chronicles permit us to infer that Aśoka was alive during a portion of the year 257, has not been noticed at all by Mr. Rhys Davids. The reason for this omission probably is his distrust of the date, 219 A.B., which the *Dīpavaṁsa* and the *Mahāvaṁsa* give for Aśoka's coronation. According to Mr. Rhys Davids, this is an invention of the southern Buddhists, or rather a mistake caused by an erroneous addition of certain figures in their list of Theras. The real distance between the Nirvāṇa and Aśoka's accession to the throne is, according to his calculation, not upwards of 218 years, but 150 years only. If Mr. Rhys Davids were right, and the genuine tradition of the southern church showed the shorter period only, the agreement between the edicts and the chronicles would certainly be of no importance for my view. It would, on the contrary, tend to prove that my explanation must be wrong. For the latter can only hold good if the date 219 A.B. for Aśoka's coronation either is really genuine, or at least is derived from a calculation made during the reign of Aśoka and before the incision of the three edicts. It must be wrong if the coronation date had been settled later in Ceylon and were based on a mistake. Under these circumstances I am compelled to examine closely Mr. Rhys Davids' chapter on the Ceylonese date of Buddha *(Num. Or.* VI. paras. 82-124), and to institute an inquiry as to whether his objections to the date 219 A.B. for Aśoka are really valid.

Mr. Rhys Davids begins his essay by giving a few facts which make the early use of the now prevalent Ceylonese era of the Nirvāṇa, and the general acceptance of its initial date 543 B.C., somewhat doubtful. He shows that even modern inscriptions in Ceylon are not always dated in the era of Buddha, while the oldest known in which that era occurs, belongs to the twelfth century, and that the Chinese pilgrim Fa Hian, who visited Ceylon in 412 A.D., speaks of a Ceylonese proclamation or sermon in which the Nirvāṇa was mentioned as falling 1497 years earlier. Adverting, then, to the fact that the elements of the calculation for the date of the Nirvāṇa are contained in the *Dīpavaṁsa* and in the *Mahāvaṁsa,* he further points out that its beginning in 543 B.C. depends on three periods, viz, the period from Duṭṭhagāmini, 161 B.C., down to the present time; the period from the coronation of Devānāṁpiya Tissa, 236 B.C., to Duṭṭhagāmini, 161 B.C.; and the period from the Nirvāṇa to Devānāṁpiya Tissa, —the total of the three (236+146+161) being 543. Accepting the period which begins with Duṭṭ hagāmini as correct, he proceeds to an examination of the other two. Travelling over oft-trodden ground, he shows, with the help of the Greek notices of Chandragupta and of Aśoka's inscriptions, that an error of more than sixty years exists in the Ceylonese chronology of the oldest period of 236 years, as the latter places Chandragupta's accession in 381 B. C., and Aśoka's in 325 B.C. Next, turning to the second period of 146 years, he finds that the great number of years assigned to Mutasīva and his nine sons likewise indicates the existence of a serious error, —a point which other scholars, too, have noticed, —and that the statements of the chronicles regarding Mahinda and Sanghamittā show Devānāṁ-Piya Tissa's reign to have been doubled. Mahinda and Sanghamittā were ordained in the sixth year of Aśoka, when they were respectively twenty and eighteen years old, they came to Ceylon 12½ years afterwards, and died there, at the ages of sixty and fifty-nine, in the eighth and ninth years after Tissa. Hence it may be concluded that Mahinda lived in Ceylon 27½ years, eight of which were subsequent to Tissa. The reign of the latter must therefore have lasted twenty, not forty years as stated in the chronicles. Mr. Rhys Davids remarks that Turnour and his Pandits, who are apparently supported by a passage of the *Dīpavaṁsa,* have got over the difficulty with Mahinda by explaining the figures 60 and 59 to refer to Mahinda's and his sister's spiritual ages, but that under this supposition, too, there is a discrepancy of two years, as the correct number for Sanghamittā would be 61 (12+40+9). Mr. Rhys Davids next expresses a doubt regarding the correctness of the period of 218 years stated to have elapsed between the Nirvāṇa and Aśoka's coronation, because the number of kings and of patriarchs or chiefs of the Buddhist church placed between the two events is too small for the length of the period. Taking first into consideration the list of the Māgadha kings, who fill the space between Buddha and Aśoka, he admits that it involves no absurdities. But it appears suspicious to him, because a number of kings are said to have murdered their fathers, and because the years assigned to some are multiples of 4 and 8, and finally because the Purāṇas have a shorter list. The list of the kings of Ceylon between 1 and 236 A.B., which he takes up next, clearly shows traces of an undue lengthening of the reigns, as only five kings are named, the lust of whom, Mutasīva, must have reached the respectable age of 147 years. After this, Mr. Rhys Davids passes to the list of the *Theras* or Buddhist patriarchs from 1 to 285 A.B. He extracts the data regarding them from the *Dīpavaṁsa,* and, reducing all the years given there, according to the reigns of the Ceylonese and Māgadha kings to years of the Buddha era, he arranges them in tabular form as below:—

Name	**Dt. of Birth**	**Dt. of Upasam -padā,**	**Age at Upasam -pada of successor**	**Len. of Member ship**	**Age at Death**	**Dt. of Death, A.B.**
Upāli	44 Bef. B.	...	60	...	74	30
Dāsaka	14 A.B.	16	40	50	64	80
Sonaka	60 A.B.	59	40	44	66	124
Siggava	100 A.B.	100	64	55	76	176
Tissa	158 A.B.	164	66	68	86	234
Mahinda	204 A.B.	224	...	60	89	285

This table, as Mr. Rhys Davids points out, abounds in absurdities, as it places the birth and the ordination of most Theras too close together, and in the case of Sonaka the latter event before the former. He, however, thinks that the absurdities may be removed by taking the statements, which are merely based on the *Therāvali* by themselves, and by separating them entirely from those of the first two and the last columns, which depend on the *Rājāvalis* of Ceylon and Māgadha. After doing this he finds that the figures no longer involve any absurdity, and that by deducting the difference between the ages of the four Theras beginning with Dāsaka at the ordination of their pupils (col. 3) and their ages at their death (col. 5) from the number of years during which they were members of the church (col. 4) the length of time may be found during which each was head of the church. If to the total of these figures the sixteen years are added which elapsed between Buddha's death and the ordination of the second Thera, Dāsaka (col. 2), as well as the eighteen years which lie between the sixth, Mahinda, and Aśoka's council, the interval between the Nirvāṇa and Aśoka's council is not 236, but 168 years. As the council took place after Aśoka had ruled eighteen years, the coronation falls in 150 A.B. These calculations are embodied in a second table, which, for clearness', sake, I reprint:—

Name	Age when he performed the Upasaṁpadā	Age when he died	No. of yrs. he was a full member	Years during which he and his successor were full members	Years of his full membership before his successor's admission
Upāli	60	74	...	...	...
Dāsaka	45	64	50	19	31
Sonaka	40	66	44	26	18
Siggava	64	76	55	12	43
Tissa	66	86	68	20	48
			—		—
			217		140
Dāsaka admitted to full membership					16 A.B.
The second council was in the twelfth year of Mahinda's full membership					12
					—
					168
Date A.B. of Aśoka's council					18
					—
Date A.B. of Aśoka's coronation					150

It thus appears that in reality the *Dīpavaṁsa,* in its *Therāvali* portion, allows for 168 years only as having elapsed between the Nirvāṇa and Aśoka's council. At the same time the same work places the council explicitly in 236 A.B., and Aśoka's 'coronation in 218 (?) A.B. The question now arises whether the shorter or the longer period is the more credible one. Mr. Rhys Davids declares himself in favour of the former, because the number of the Theras (five) is not sufficient to fill a period of 236 years; because, further, the number of the Ceylonese kings is also too small for more than two hundred years; and because, finally, the Brahmanical lists of the kings of Māgadha which place the Siśunāgas before Bhātiya and his descendants, likewise speak in favour of the shorter interval. Mr. Rhys Davids further shows that the Buddhists possessed a number of ancient works which probably contained the *Therāvalis,* and that the latter have therefore a claim to be considered historical. He, also, points out that according to the Ceylonese chronicles the Siśunāgas reigned just 68 years, and that if they are placed before Bhātiya and Bimbisāra and their descendants the number of years of the Māgadha kings down to Aśoka will be exactly 150, and thus fully agree with the sum of years gained by the adjustment of the *Therāvali*. An explanation may be offered for the insertion of the longer period also. For as the sum of the figures in column 3 of the second table makes 217, it becomes not improbable that Buddhist chronologists, in calculating the distance of Aśoka from the Nirvāṇa, by mistake added up the periods during which each Thera was *upasampanna,* instead of those during which he was sole teacher of the *Vinaya,* or head of the church.

On first reading Mr. Rhys Davids' deductions, it is impossible to avoid being fascinated by his eloquent and ingenious pleading, to which my abstract does but scant justice. Still one cannot help feeling a certain distrust against so very startling results, and the discovery that the ancient Buddhists must have been such utter fools. A number of objections against, and difficulties with, certain details also present themselves at once. Thus, with respect to the alleged inconsistency of the chronicles regarding the ages of Mahinda and Sanghamittā and the reign of Devānāṁ-piya Tissa, one cannot help seeing that it has only been caused by Mr. Rhys Davids' method of interpretation. Both the *Dīpavaṁsa* and the *Mahāvaṁsa* state that Mahinda and Sanghamittā received the first or *pabbajjā* ordination at the end of or in the sixth year of Aśoka, and that Mahinda alone received the second or *upasampadā* ordination at the same time. Afterwards it is alleged that Mahinda died in Ceylon, 'having completed sixty years,' in the eighth year of king Uttiya;[12] and Sanghamittā, 'after having completed fifty-nine years', in the ninth year of the same king. Now as Aśoka was crowned *after* the completion of the 218th year of the Nirvāṇa era, his sixth year corresponds to 224-225 A.B., and the eighth year of Uttiya to 284-285 A.B. The interval between Mahinda's *upasampadā* and his death is thus exactly sixty years, as stated by the chronicles. It is clear that the sixty years can only be referred, as Mr. Turnour has done, to the spiritual age, or the period after the *upasampadā,* —not to the natural age, as Mr. Rhys Davids wishes to do. This explanation is confirmed, as Mr. Rhys Davids himself has shown, by a verse of the *Dīpavaṁsa* where it is stated that Mahinda had completed twelve years when he came to Ceylon.[13] The case of Sanghamittā is no less clear, if the statement that she died 'after completing fifty-nine years' is referred to the period after her second or *upasampadā* ordination. The interval between the sixth year of Aśoka, 224-225 A.B., Uttiya's ninth year, and 285-286 A.B, is, as Mr. Rhys Davids has stated, 61 years. But as Sanghamittā was in 224-225 only eighteen years old, she had to wait two years before she could receive the second ordination, which gave her full membership. If we deduct these, the figures agree, and she really had completed fifty-nine years after the *upasampadā* at the time of her death. There can be no doubt that this is the correct interpretation of the seemingly inconsistent statements of the chronicles. We shall see, further on, that the latter, when speaking of the ages of *Theras* or *Upasampanna Sādhus always* refer to the period after the *upasampadā,* or, to adopt Mr. Rhys Davids' appropriate term, to the spiritual ages just as references to the *ages* of anointed kings refer to the time after their *abhisheka.*

If we now turn to the chief portions of Mr. Rhys Davids' calculations, it becomes impossible to accept without a re-examination the statements contained in his first table, though they agree with Mr. Turnour's analysis of the *Dīpavaṁsa.*[14] As it has been found that the seeming contradictions in the case of Sanghamittā disappeared, as soon as the chronicles were correctly interpreted, the question arises whether a reconsideration of the text of the *Dīpavaṁsa* would not clear away the stupendous absurdities contained in the table which gives the data regarding the Theras. But even supposing the first table to be correct, a consideration of Mr. Rhys David's second table raises numerous difficulties. One cannot help asking how he gets the sixteen years between Buddha and Dāsaka without the help of the *Rājāvali,* which he considers to be unworthy of reliance; or how, if he gets them from that source, he can reconcile that with his promise to rely on the *Therāvali* alone. One must further ask why he adds the sixteen years in col. 5 of table II., and not in col. 3, where they are evidently also required. If he had added the sixteen years in col. 3, the total would become 233, and it would have appeared at once that the chroniclers could not have made the mistake imputed to them. (paras. 115, 116). Finally, on comparing the two tables a serious discrepancy is observable between the figures given for Dāsaka's age at Sonaka's *upasampadā* in col. 3 of the first, and col. 1 of the second table. In the former place it is stated to be 40, and in the second 45, and no explanation is offered. Similar vacillations occur, too, in the date of Aśoka's coronation, which sometimes is stated to have occurred *after the completion* of the 218 years of the Nirvāṇa era *(i.e.* in 219 A.B.), and sometimes in 218 A.B.,[15] and that the latter incorrect statement is used in order to convict the chroniclers of an inaccuracy (para. 114).

These and other doubts which it would be too long to enumerate induced me to ask Dr. Oldenberg, who is preparing an edition of the *Dīpavaṁsa*, for the loan of his text, and to examine the work once more. A cursory inspection showed to me that Mr. Rhys Davids' first table does not accurately represent the statements of the *Dīpavaṁsa*, but, besides a number of minor inaccuracies, contains three important mistakes. The heading of col. 4 ought to be "*Chiefship of the Vinaya* (*vinayaṭṭhāna* or *pāmokhatta*);" the heading of col. 5 should be "*Spiritual Age at Death, i.e.,* Age reckoning from the *upasampadā* ordination," and hence the figures put against the names of the first five Theras in col. 1 ought to be removed. I found that the *Dīpavaṁsa* left not the slightest doubt on the necessity of these alterations, and that, if it is interpreted rightly, its history of the Theras contains to absurdities. The text, though less corrupt in the *Therāvali* than in other portions, nevertheless shows a few mistakes in the figures which can be easily corrected. In order to enable the reader to judge if my interpretation is correct, I give the text of the chief passage, *Bhāṇavāra* V. 76-106, in full, together with a translation. The text is Dr. Oldenberg's,[16] with whose permission it is published. The translation is my own:—

nibbute lokanāthassa vassāni soḷasam ahū | samasaṭṭhi tadā hotī vassaṁ Upāli paṇḍitaṁ |76|[17]

Ajātasattuchatuvīsaṁ Vijayassa soḷasaṁ ahū | Dāsako upasampanno Upālitherasantike |77|

chattālīs'eva vassāṇi Dāsako nāma paṇḍito | Nāgadāse dasavasse Pakuṇḍakassa vīsati |78|[18]

upasampanno Sonako thero Dāsakatherasantike | chattālīsavasso dhīro thero Sonakasavhayo |79|[19]

Kālāsokassa dasavasse Tambapaṇṇi-antarāvāse vassaṁ ekādasaṁ bhave | Siggavo upasampanno Soṇakatherasantike |80|

Chandaguttassa dve vasse cḥatusaṭṭhi Siggavo tadā | aṭṭ hapaññāsa vassāni Pakuṇḍakassa rājino | upasampanno Moggaliputto Siggavatherasantike |81|

Asokadhammassa chhavasse chhasaṭṭhi Moggaliputto ahū | aṭ ṭhachattārīsa [vassāni] Mutasīvassa rājino | Mahindo upasampanno Moggaliputtassa santike |82|[20]

uggahesi vinayaṁ cha Upāli Buddhasantike | Dāsako vinayaṁ sabbaṁ Upālitherasantike |uggahetvāna vāchesi upajjhāyo va sāsane |83|

vāchesi Dāsako thero vinayaṁ Sonakassa pi | pariyāpuṇitvā vāchesi upajjhāyassa santike |84|

Sonako buddhisampanno dhammavinayakovido | vāchesi vinayaṁ sabbam Siggavassa anuppadaṁ |85|

Siggavo Chandavajjo cha Sonakasaddhivihārikā| vāchesi vinayaṁ thero ubho saddhivihārike |86|

Tisso Moggaliputto cha Chandavajjassa santike | vinayaṁ uggahetvāna vimutto upadhisaṁkhaye |87|

Moggaliputto upajjhāyo Mahindaṁ saddhiviharikaṁ | vāchesi vinayaṁ sabbaṁ theravādaṁ anūnakaṁ |88|

parinibbute sambuddhe Upālithero mahājuti | vinayaṁ tāva vāchesi tinsa vassaṁ anūnakaṁ |89|

saddhivihārikaṁ theraṁ Dāsakaṁ nāma paṇditaṁ | vinayaṭṭ hāne ṭhapetvāna nibbuto so mahāmati |90|

Dāsako Sonakaṁ theram saddhivihāriṁ anuppadaṁ |katvā vinayapāmokkhaṁ chatusaṭṭhiṁhi nibbuto |91|

Sonako chhaḷabhiññāno Siggavaṁ ariyatrajaṁ | vinayaṭṭhāne ṭhapetvāna chhasaṭṭhimhi cha nibbuto |92|

Siggavo ñāṇasampanno Moggaliputtañ cha dārakaṁ | katvā vinayapāmokkhaṁ nibbuto so chhasattati |93|

Tisso Moggaliputto cha Mahindaṁ saddhivihārikaṁ | katvā vinayapāmokkhaṁ chhāsītivassamhi nibbuto |94|[21]

chatusattati Upāli cha chatusaṭṭhi cha Dāsako | chhasaṭṭhi Sonako thero Siggavo tu chhasattati | asīti Moggaliputto sabbesaṁ upasampadā |95|

sabbakālamhi pāmokkho vinaye Upālipaṇḍito | paññāsaṁ Dāsako thero chatuchattārīsaṁ cha Sonako | panchapaññāsavassaṁ Siggavassa aṭṭhasaṭṭhi Moggaliputtasavhayo |96|[22]

Udayo soḷasa vassāni rajjaṁ kāresi khattiyo | ehhavasse Udayabhaddamhi Upālithero nibbuto |97|

Susunāgo dasavassaṁ rajjaṁ kāresi issaro | aṭṭhavasse Susunāgamhi Dāsako parinibbuto |98|[23]

Susunāgass' achchayena honti te dasa bhātaro | sabbe bāvisativassaṁ rajjam kāresu vaṅsato | imesaṁ chhaṭṭhe vassānam Sonako parinibbuto |99|

Chandagutto rajjaṁ kāresi vassāni chatuvīsati | tasmiñ chuddasavassamhi Siggavo parinibbuto |100|

Bindusārassa yo putto Asokadhammo mahāyaso | vassāni sattatiṇsaṁ pi rajjaṁ kāresi khattiyo |101|[24]

Asokassa chhavīsativasse Moggaliputtasavhayo sāsanaṁ jotayitvāna nibbuto āyusaṁkhye |102|[25]

chatusattativassaṁhi thero Upālipaṇḍito | saddhivihārikaṁ theraṁ Dāsakaṁ nāma paṇḍitaṁ | vinayaṭṭhāne ṭhapetvāna nibbuto so mahāgaṇī |103|

Dāsako Sonakaṁ theraṁ saddhivihārikaṁ anuppadaṁ katvā vinayapāmokkhaṁ chatusaṭṭhimhī nobbuto |104|

Sonako chaḷabhiññāno Siggavaṁ ariyatrajaṁ | vinayaṭṭhāne ṭhapetvāna chhasaṭṭhimhi pari nibbuto |105|[26]

Siggavo ñāṇasampanno Moggaliputtañ cha dārakaṁ | katvā vinayapāmokkhaṁ nibbuto so chhasattati |106|

Tisso Moggaliputto so Mahindaṁ saddhivihārikaṁ | katvā vinayapāmokkhaṁ chhāsītivassamhi nibbuto |107|[27]

Translation

76. Sixteen year had elapsed after the protector of the world (*Buddha*) had entered Nirvāṇa, then the learned Upāli had just completed sixty years;[28]

77. Then twenty-four years of Ajātaśatru's (*reign*) and sixteen of Vijaya's had elapsed, (*and then*) Dāsaka received the *upasampadā* ordination from Thera Upāli.

78. The learned Dāsaka (*had completed*), just forty years, when Nāgadāsa (*had reigned*) ten years, and twenty (*years of*) Pāṇḍurāja's (*reign had passed*);

79. (*Then*) Thera Sonaka received the *upasampadā* ordination[29] from Thera Dāsaka.

The wise Thera called Sonaka had completed forty years.

80. When Kālāśoka had completed ten years, and the eleventh year of the interregnum in Ceylon was (*the current one*), (*then*) Siggava received the *upasampadā* ordination from Thera Sonaka.[30]

81. Two years of Chandragupta's (*reign had passed*), then Siggava (has completed) sixty-four years, (*and*) fifty-eight years of Pakuṇḍaka's (*reign had elapsed*). Then Tissa-Moggaliputta received the *upasampadā* ordination from Thera Siggava.[31]

82. When Dharmāśoka had (*reigned*) six years, (*then*) Moggaliputta had completed sixty-six years, (*and*) forty-eight years of king Mutasīva had passed. (*Then*) Mahinda received the *upasampadā* ordination from Moggaliputta.

83. And Upāli learned the *Vinaya* from Buddha; Dāsaka, having learnt the whole *Vinaya* from Thera Upāli, recited (*it*) like (*his*) teacher in the Faith.

84. Dāsaka, the Thera, instructed Sonaka also in the *Vinaya*, (*and he*), having mastered it, repeated it before his teacher.

85. Sonaka, endowed with intelligence and acquainted with the law and the *Vinaya*, taught Siggava the whole *Vinaya*, sentence by sentence.

86. Siggava and Chandavajja (*were*) the pupils of Sonaka. The Thera taught both his pupils the *Vinaya*.

87. And Tissa-Moggaliputta, having learnt the *Vinaya* from Chandavajja, was emancipated by the destruction of the *substrata* (*i.e., became an Arhat*).

88. Moggaliputta, the teacher, taught Mahinda, his pupil, the whole *Vinaya,* the whole, entire doctrine of the Theras.

89. After the Sambuddha had entered Nirvāṇa, Thera Upāli, endowed with great lustre, taught the whole *Vinaya* during thirty years.

90. Having appointed his pupil, thera Dāsaka, to the office of (*Chief of the*) *Vinaya,* that high-souled man entered Nirvāṇa.

91. Dāsaka made his pupil, Thera Sonaka, in his turn, Chief of the *Vinaya,* and died in (*his*) sixty-fourth year.[32]

92. Sonaka, possessed of the six supernatural faculties, appointed Siggava, of honourable descent, to the office of (*Chief of*) the *Vinaya,* and died in (*his*) sixty-sixth year.

93. Siggava, possessed of (*true*) knowledge, made Moggaliputta, the youth, Chief of the *Vinaya,* and died after (*completing*) seventy-six years.

94. And Tissa-Moggaliputta made his pupil Mahinda Chief of the *Vinaya,* and died in (*his*) sixty-eighth year.[33]

95. And Upāli, seventy-four, and Dāsaka sixty-four, Thera Sonaka sixty-six, but Siggava seventy-six, Moggaliputta eighty (that is, *the number of years elapsed between*) *the* upasampadā *ordination of each* (*Thera and his death*).

96. The learned Upāli is chief of the *Vinaya* for all time. Thera Dasaka (*held that office*) fifty (*years*), and Sonaka forty-four, Siggava fifty-five years, and he who is called Moggaliputta sixty-eight.

97. The Kshatriya Udaya reigned sixteen years; when Udayabhadra had (*completed*) six years, Thera Upāli died.

98. Śiśunāga, the lord, reigned ten (?) years; when Śiśunāga had (*completed*) eight years, Dāsaka died.[34]

99. After Śiśunāga's death came those ten brothers; according to hereditary custom, they reigned all (*together*) for twenty-two years. In the sixth year of their (*reign*) Sonaka died.

100. Chandragupta reigned twenty-four years; when he had (*completed*) fourteen years Siggava died.

101. Famous Dharmāśoka, the son of Bindusāra, of royal race, reigned thirty-seven years.

102. When Aśoka had (*completed*) twenty-six years, he who is called Moggaliputta died of old age, after having exalted the Faith.

103. The learned Thera Upāli, the great chief of the school, died in his seventy-fourth year, after appointing the learned Thera Dāsaka, his pupil, to the office of (*Chief of the*) *Vinaya*.

104. Dāsaka, in his turn, made his pupil, Thera Sonaka, Chief of the *Vinaya,* and died in (*his*) sixty-fourth year.

105. Sonaka, endowed with the six super-natural qualities, appointed Siggava, of honourable descent, to the office of (*Chief of the*) *Vinaya,* and died in (*his*) sixty-sixth year.

106. Siggava, possessed of (*true*) knowledge made young Moggaliputta Chief of the *Vinaya,* and died, having (*completed*) seventy-six years.

107. Tissa-Moggaliputta made his pupil, Mahinda, Chief of the *Vinaya,* and died in (*his*) eighty-sixth year.[35]

This passage contains:–

1. The dates of the *upasampadā* of each of the five Theras, from Dāsaka to Aśoka's son Mahinda, according to the chronology of Māgadha and of Ceylon, together with the spiritual age of the teacher who performed the ordination–*vv.* 76-82.
2. A statement of the teachers under whom each of the six Theras studied the *Vinaya*–*vv.* 83-88.
3. A statement regarding the persons who appointed each to the office of Chief of the *Vinaya,* or head of the church–*vv.* 89-94.
4. A statement of the number of years which elapsed between the *upasampadā* ordination and the death of each, *i.e.* the length of the life of each while full member of the Saṁgha–*v.* 95.

5. A statement of the number of years during which Dāsaka, Sonaka, Siggava, and Tissa were Chiefs of the *Vinaya* or heads of the church, – which must be completed as far as Upāli is concerned from *v.* 89-96.
6. The dates of the Māgadha kings in whose reigns the five Theras died, together with the year of the death – *vv.* 97-102.
7. A repetition of the information given above under 3 and 4.

Two other passages of the *Dīpavaṁsa* (IV. 27-46 and V. 69-73) give the same details, – the first regarding Upāli, Dāsaka, Sonaka, Siggava, and Chandavajja; and the second regarding the last two teachers and tissa-Moggaliputta. These two passages mostly agree word for word with that given above. But they add a few particulars and show some variations, which it will be necessary to quote. Firstly (IV. 31), it is said that Buddha himself appointed Upāli to be Chief of the *Vinaya*: –

saṁghamajjhe visākāsi Buddho Upālipaṇḍitaṁ |
aggo vinayapāmokkho Upāli mayha sāsane |31|

Secondly, it is stated (IV. 41) that Dāsaka's spiritual age was *forty-five* years, instead of *forty,* when he ordained Sonaka. Thirdly, the date of the ordination of Siggava is specified more exactly as having taken place ten years and half a month (according to the *varia lectio* of bad MS., 'and eight months') after Kālāśoka's coronation: –

chattārīśeva vasso so thero Sonakasavhayo |
Kālāsokassa dasavasse aḍḍhamāsañ cha sesake[36] |41|

A corrupt verse adds the statement that at that time eleven years and six months of Pakuṇḍaka – Pandukābhayāa's interregnum had elapsed, –

sattarasannaṁ vassānāṁ thero āsi paguṇako |[37]
atikkantekādasavassaṁ chhamāsaṁ chāvasesake |42|

The information regarding the career of Aśoka's son, Mahinda, finally, is completed in the following passages: –

(1) VI. 20, where his birth is stated to have taken place after 204 years of the Nirvāṇa, –

dve vassasatāni honti chatuvassaṁ pan' uttari |
samantaramhi so jāto Mahindo Asokatrajo |20|

(2) VII. 21-24, where it is said that Mahinda became an ascetic when he was full twenty years old, and when Aśoka had reigned six years (after his coronation); that Mahinda received the *upasampadā* ordination at the same time; and that Moggaliputta was fifty-four years old when Aśoka's coronation took place, and six years. The last verse is, however, corrupt, and must be corrected as proposed below:—

paripunnavīsativasso Mahindo Asokatrajo |
Saṁghamittā cha jātīya vassaṁ aṭṭhārasaṁ bhave |21|
chhavassamhi Asokassa[38] *ubho pabhajitā paja* |
tatheva upasampanno Mahindo dīpajotako |22|
Saṁghamittā tadā yeva sikkhāyo vaśam ādiyi |
ahu Moggaliputto va theravādo[39] *mahāgani* |23|
chatupaññāsavassamhi Asokadhammo abhisitto |
Asokass' ābhisittato chhasaṭṭhi[40] *Moggalisavhayo* |
tato Mahindo pabbajito Moggaliputtassa santike |24|

(3) XVII. 91-93, where the date of his death is given as occurring after the completion of the eighth year of Uttiya, and of the sixtieth year after his ordination,—

Uttiyo dasavsassamhi rajjaṁ kāresi khattiyo |91|
aṭṭhavassābhisittassa nibbuto dīpajotako |
akāsi sarīranikkhepaṁ Tissārāme puratthime |92|
paripuṇṇadvādasavasso Mahiṇḍo cha idh' āgato |
saṭṭhivasse paripuṇṇe nibbuṭo Chetiyapabbate |93|

The contents of these passages are most easily intelligible if they are given in tabular form, and it is therefore advisable to imitate Mr. Rhys Davids in this respect. It will also be advisable to exhibit the information of the *Dīpavaṁsa* exactly in that form in which it is given, without correcting any of the inconsistencies of the text. If that is done we obtain the following results:—

Name	Date of Upasampada	Spiritual Age at Pupil's Upasampadā	Spiritual Age at Death	Date of Death	Length of Chiefship of Vinaya
1. Upāli	41	60 years [*D*. IV. 27, V. 76].	74th year [*D*.V. 103]. [74 year [*D*.V. 95].	Udayabhadra 6=30 A.B. [*D*. IV. 38, V. 97].	30 years [*D*. IV. 34, V. 89].
2. Dāsaka	Ajātaśatru 24=Vijaya, 16 A.B. [*D*. IV. 26, 27; V. 76, 77.]	40 years [*D*. V. 76]. 45 years [*D*. IV. 41].	64th years [*D*.V. 91, 104; IV. 43]. 64 years [*D*. V. 95].	Siśunāga, 8=80 A. B. [*D*. V. 98.]	50 yrs. [*D*. V. 96].
3*a*. Sonaka	Nāgadāsa 10=Paṇḍurāja 20=58 A.B. *D*. V. 78, 79].	40 years [*D*. IV. 44; V. 70].	66th year [*D*. V. 92, 66 years [*D*. V. 95].	Nandas 6=124 A. B. [*D*. V. 99]	44 yrs. [*D*. V. 96].
3*b*. Chandavajja	The Same	Not Stated	Not Stated	Not Stated	Not Stated
4. Siggava	Kālaśoka 10, or 10+½ month = Interregnum, 11 or 11+ 6 mos.=100 A.B. [*D*. IV. 44, 45; V. 80]	64 years [*D*. V. 69, 81].	75 years [*D*. V. 93, 106].	Chandragupta 14=176 A.B. [*D*. V. 73, 100].	55 yrs. [*D*. V. 96]
5. Tissa-Mog -galiputta	Chandragupta 2=Pakuṇḍa 58=164 A.B. [*D*. V. 69, 81].	66 years [*D*. V. 82, VII. 24].	86th [*D*. V. 94, 107]. 80th [*D*. V. 95, 107]. 38th [*D*. V. 94].	Aśoka 26=244 A.B. [*D*. V. 102].	68 yrs. [*D*. V. 96]
6. Mahinda, 204 A.B. [*D*. VI. 20.]	Aśoka 6=224 A.B. [*D*. V. 82, VII. 22-24].	Not Stated	60 years [*D*. XVII. 93].	Uttiya 8=284 A.B. [*D*. XVII. 93].	Not stated but may be calculated at 40 yrs.

The first glance at this table shows that the figures given there are intended to form a chain, each link of which is closely connected with some of the others. The connexion is established in this wise, that the difference between the dates of each teacher's and his pupil's *upasampadā* gives the age of the former at the latter ceremony; that, further, the difference between the date of the *upasaṁpadā* and of the death gives the length of the spiritual life; and that finally the difference between the dates of the teacher's and the pupil's death gives the length of the latter's chiefship of the *Vinaya.* But the most cursory inspection also shows that some of the figures given are corrupt and do not answer.

In the case of Upāli the date of the *upasampadā* os not given, but may be calculated by deducting the length of time during which he was Chief of the *Vinaya* after Buddha's death from his spiritual age: 74-30=44. His spiritual age at the *upasampadā* of Dāsaka, sixty years (col. 4), is given, and the correctness of the statement can be controlled by the dates for his own and his pupil's *upasampadā,* the difference between which—44 B.B. and 16 A.B.—must, and does give exactly 60. The length of his spiritual life, which is once given as full seventy-four years and as the seventy-fourth year, *i.e.* seventy-three years *plus* an indefinite number of months, can be tested by the figure given for his spiritual age at Sonaka's *upasampadā* and the difference between the date of the latter and the date of Upāli's death, which together amount to 60+14=74. The discrepancy between the two statements which mention both the seventy-fourth year and seventy-four years, may be got over by assuming that he died in his seventy-fourth year, but that his death took place towards the *end of the year.* As the author of the *Dīpavaṁsa* nearly throughout uses round figures, he found it more practical to substitute in his calculation seventy-four full instead of seventy-three full years. This explanation applies also to the spiritual ages of Dāsaka, Sonaka, and Tissa. In the case of Siggava seventy-six complete years (*chhasattati*) are given everywhere. Hence it may be concluded that his death occurred either exactly at the end of the seventy-sixth year or in the beginning of the seventy-seventh. The same remark holds good for Mahinda, whose age is always given as sixty years.

In the case of Dāsaka, the date for his spiritual age at Sonaka's *upasampadā* has not been given correctly in the text, which in one passage reads forty years, and in the other forty-five years. The correction can be made only with the help of the dates of Dāsaka's own and Sonaka's *upasampadā*. The former is placed in Agātaśatru 24=Vijaya 16=16 A.B., and the three periods agree exactly. The date of Sonaka's *upasampadā* is given as having taken place Nāgadāsa 10 and Paṇḍurāja 20. The former date corresponds with 58 A.B. and tha latter, if it is taken to refer to *completed* years, with 59 A.B. For Vijaya ruled full thirty-eight years; after his death came an interregnum of one year, and then only followed Paṇḍuvāsa's *abhisheka.*[42] The *Dīpavaṁsa* (XI. 10) says also expressly that Nāgadāsa had completed twenty-one years when Panduvāsa died; *ekavīsaṁ Nāgadāso Paṇḍuvāso tadā gato.* The text of the *Dīpavaṁsa* does not seem to be corrupt in the two passages which contain the equation Nāgadāsa 10=Paṇḍuvāsa 20 (IV. 41 and V. 78, 79). Still the date 58 A.B. is required for Sonaka's ordination, as he is said to have died at the end of Nanda 6=124 A.B., and the difference between 58 and 124 A.B. exactly agrees with the length of his spiritual life, or nearly sixty-six years. The discrepancy therefore, must be, either real and owing to a slip of the author, or it may have been caused by his using round numbers instead of exact dates in his calculations. An author who talks as loosely as the Ceylonese chroniclers do might perhaps say that at the close of Buddha 58 Nāgadāsa had ruled ten years, and Paṇḍuvāsa twenty, though in reality the former counted three or four months in excess of ten years, and the latter seven or eight months less than twenty. He further might assert that eleven years later, at the close of 69 A.B., ten year of Nāgadāsa's reign had elapsed, and that Paṇḍuvāsa died after ruling thirty years. This explanation appears to me the most likely. For it may be considered certain that in very few cases only the initial dates of the reigns of the Māgadha kings and of the Ceylon kings fell on the initial dates of the corresponding years of Buddha. It seems also, from the case of the date of Siggava's ordination, which will be discussed below, that the chroniclers possessed more exact figures, but mostly thought it unnecessary to use them. If now the ordination of Sonaka must be placed at the end of 58 A.B., and that of Dāsaka fell at the close of 16 A.B., the age of the latter at Sonaka's *upasampadā* must have been forty-two years, not forty of forty-five. The number 42 has therefore to be entered in col. 4, and in the text of the *Dīpavaṁsa dvechattālisa* has to be written for *panchattālisa* (IV. 41) and for *chattālīśeva* (V. 76). The emendation suits the metre in both passages.

The length of Dāsaka's spiritual life, (*nearly*) sixty-six years, corresponds with the difference between the dates of his *upasampadā* 16 A.B. (col. 3) and of his death 80 A.B. (col. 6). The length of his chiefship of the *Vinaya,* too, agrees with the difference between his own and Upāli's death: 80 A.B. − 30 A.B. = 50 years (col. 7).

In the case of Sonaka all the figures agree, with the exception of that for his spiritual age at the *upasampadā* of Siggava, which, though twice give as forty, must be forty-two. For the difference between the dates Nāgadāsa 10 = Paṇḍurāja 20 = 58 A.B., and Kālāśoka 10 = *interregnum* 11 = 100 A.B., is 42 years. The text of the *Dīpavaṁsa* again may be altered accordingly, viz. —

IV. 44. *dvechattālīsavasso so* thero sonasaka-savhayo, instead of the nonsensical *chattārīśeva vasso so,* &c.

V. 76. *dvechattālīsavasso so* thero sonakasa-vhayo| instead of *chattālīsavasso dhīro thero,* &c. The latter alteration recommends itself, because corresponding passages are mostly given in exactly the same words.

As regards Siggava the date of his *upasampadā* requires a remark. In one passage (V. 80) we have the equation Kālāśoka 10 = *Interregnum* (Ceylon) 11: in the other passage (IV. 44-46) Kālāśoka 10 + ½ month = *Interregnum* 11 + 6 months. Immediately after the last verse it is further stated that "But at that time, forsooth, one hundred years after Buddha's death," the Vesāliya schism occurred.[43] It seems, therefore, that the author meant to place Siggava's ordination just at the end of the first century after Buddha. The discrepancy in the dates of the kings may be adjusted by assuming that the beginning of Kālāśoka's reign, as well as that of the *Interregnum,* did not fall exactly in the beginning of the ninety-first and of the ninetieth year of Buddha, but that the former began fifteen days, and the latter six months, after the beginning of the corresponding year of Buddha. If that was the case, it would seem that the author gave in the first passage the exact figures, and in the second, according to his usual manner, round figures only. The difference between Siggava's *upasampadā* (100 A.B.) and Tissa's *upasampadā* Chandragupta 2=Pakuṇḍaka 20=164 A.B., is exactly 64, and agrees with the number of years allotted to him in col. 4. The length of his spiritual life (seventy-six years) likewise corresponds with the difference between the dates for his *upasampadā* and for his death. But he cannot have been Chief of the *Vinaya* for fifty-five years, as the difference between his death and that of his predecessor amounts to fifty-two years only. It seems certain that in this case also we have to deal with a corruption of the text only. Besides the total of the figures entered in col. 7 for the first five Theras must agree with the date of the last in col. 6,—244 A.B. The agreement can only be obtained if we substitute 52 for 55. If the latter number is retained, we get 247=244, which is obviously nonsense. Finally the half-verse (V. 96*b*) in which the date occurs is obviously corrupt. I propose to read for

panchapaññāsavassam Siggavassa aṭṭhasaṭṭhi Moggaliputtasavhayo |

paññāsavassaṁ Siggavo aṭṭhasaṭṭhiṁ Moggalisavhayo |

In order to make out the metre, it is necessary to elide the first syllable of *aṭṭhasaṭṭhiṁ,* and to make a disyllable of *Moggali,* as has to be done in other cases.

In the case of Tissa the figure given for his spiritual age at the *upasampadā* of Mahinda is wrong. For the difference between Chandragupta 2=Pakuṇḍaka 58=164 A.B. and Aśoka 6-224 A.B. is sixtyyears, not sixty-six as given in the text and in the table. Though the faulty figure occurs in two passages (V. 82 and VII. 24*c*), still the latter verse 24*a* contains a certain proof that the mistake belongs to the copyists, not to the author, of the *Dīpavaṁsa.* For in that line it is explicitly stated that Moggaliputto was *fifty-four* years old at Aśoka's coronation. It is obvious that six years later he could not be sixty-six years old, but must be sixty. The length of his spiritual life (co. 5) is given variously as 86, 80, and 38 years. The second date is the correct one, because this figure agrees with the difference between the dates for his *upasampadā* and for his death. The dates given for Mahinda all agree, and require no remark or rectification. The subjoined second table gives a summary of this discussion, and shows the corrected figures, as well as the faulty ones in brackets.

Name	**Birth**	**Dt. of Upas-ampadā**	**Spiritual Age at Upas-ampadā of Pupil**	**Spiritual Age at Death**	**Dt. of Death**	**Len. of Chief-ship of Vinaya**
Upāli	Not stated	44 bef. B	60	cir. 74 yrs.	30A.B.	30 yrs.
Dāsaka	Do	16A.B.	42 yrs. (40, 45)	cir. 64 yrs.	80A.B.	50 yrs.
Sonaka	Do	58A.B.	42 yrs. (40)	cir. 66 yrs.	124A.B.	44 yrs.
Siggava	Do	100A.B.	64 yrs.	76 yrs.	176A.B.	52 yrs(55)
Tissa	Do	164A.B.	60 yrs. (66)	80 yrs. (86, 38)	244A.B.	68 yrs.
Mahinda	204A.B.	224A.B.	Not stated	60 yrs.	284A.B.	40 yrs.

If we compare the above passages of the *Dīpavaṁsa* with Mr. Rhys Davids' first table and his remarks thereon, the mistakes which I imputed to him, and to Mr. Turnour before him, are perfectly clear. The terms *Vinayapāmoskkha,* 'Chief of the *Vinaya,*' and *Vinayaṭṭhāna,* the office (of Chief) of the *Vinaya,* occur frequently, and in V. 96 the former is expressly connected with the periods of 50, 44, 52 (55), and 68 years which occur in col. 4 of his first table, and in col. 3 of his second table. Further *Dīp*. V. 95 precludes the possibility even of the doubt whether the natural or the spiritual age of the Theras is indicated by the figures in col. 5 of Mr. Rhys Davids' first table. The period after the *upasampadā* ordination alone can be referred to. Hence the whole basis for Mr. Rhys Davids' deductions, by which the chronicles are shown to give really 150 years, not 218 years, as the interval between the Nirvāṇa and Aśoka, disappears. The *Dīpavaṁsa* gives, on the contrary, a very simple history of six Theras, the fifth of whom was a contemporary of Aśoka, and died about the middle of his reign. If the four corrections proposed by me are accepted, the story shows not only no absurdities, but not even the slightest inconsistency. As regards the date of Aśoka's coronation, 219

A.B., it is clear that it cannot be the result of an absurd mistake in addition, made, as Mr. Rhys Davids supposes, by the Ceylonese Buddhists.

It is no less evident that this date is the only one for the coronation of Aśoka which the Ceylonese tradition supports, and that the *Dīpavaṁsa* does not contain any evidence in favour of a shorter interval between the Nirvāṇa and Aśoka's accession. Nor do I think that the other points which Mr. Rhys Davids brings forward in order to show its incredibility carry much weight. When he points out that the number of Theras enumerated in the *Dīpavaṁsa* is too small to fill a space of more than two hundred years, the obvious answer is that the correctness of this list is by no means proved, and that, as Mr. Turnour[44] has pointed out and he himself admits, another and longer list is in existence. But even if the shorter list were proved to be correct, it could not be said that the account of the *Dīpavaṁsa* involves impossibilities. If we assume that each of the five Theras received the *upasampadā* ordination at the legal age of twenty, the longest-lived among them would have reached the age of one hundred years, and the shortest-lived the age of eighty-four. The succession of five very long-lived Chiefs of the *Vinaya* would certainly be something remarkable, but it is not absolutely impossible. Again, Mr. Rhys Davids' objection drawn from the small number of Ceylonese kings (para. 107) who are stated to have reigned between the *Nirvāṇa* and Aśoka has very little weight. He himself, like all other scholars who have written on the subject, has seen that the Ceylonese history from Vijaya to Duṭṭhagāmini is untrustworthy. It is impossible that Mutasīva lived to the age of 147 years, and that his sons reigned after him, with interruptions, 102 years. Hence no portion of a story which contains such statements can be used in order to discredit another independent tradition, or to support an adjustment. It is quite true that the number of kings is too small for the interval of 236 years stated to lie between Vijaya and Devānāmpiya Tissa. But instead of reducing that interval, we may just as well assume that Vijaya's invasion falls later than the Nirvāṇa, or that the chroniclers did not possess the names of all the princes who ruled between Vijaya and Duṭ ṭhagāmini, and were tempted by the legend of the synchronism of Vijaya's conquest and Buddha's death to spread the scanty materials over too large an area. Finally, it seems inadvisable to bring forward (para. 110) the Brahmanical tradition in order to prove that Siśunāga, Kālaśoka and his ten sons reigned before Bhātiya, and to allow the number of years given by the Buddhists to stand. An indiscriminating combination of portions of two contradictory traditions, however much its results may agree with preconceived notions, has not hitherto been recognized as being in accordance with the principles of historical criticism.

These remarks may suffice to show that hitherto no evidence, be it external or internal, has been brought forward which proves the date 219 A.B. for Aśoka's coronation to be spurious. It *may,* therefore, be either really historical, or at least go back to Aśoka's own time, *i.e.* have been calculated by the Indian Buddhists from the Māgadha *Rājāvalis* and their *Therāvalis,* when Aśoka became a patron and adherent of their faith, and have been carried by the missionaries to Ceylon. Several points can be adduced in favour of the latter hypothesis. Firstly, it seems only reasonable to suppose that the Buddhists, who, through Aśoka's protection, obtained a fresh start in the race for spiritual influence, should have tried to ascertain the distance of the royal *dāyāda* or 'relative' of their faith from their first teacher. If their account of this period is at all to be trusted, their sect was, just about the time of Aśoka's conversion, in a somewhat fallen condition. Quarrels had taken place among the Bhikkhus, and not less than eighteen mutually hostile sects had arise. Aśokas conversion at first made matters only worse, as it induced numerous followers of other faiths to pass themselves off for disciples of Buddha in order to participate in Aśoka's bounty, and to create confusion in the Buddhist doctrines. The resistance of the orthodox ascetics against this state of things led to the council in Aśoka's seventeenth year. Its immediate consequence was a purification of the Buddhist Church from the foreign intruders, and a new redaction of the sacred texts. Another result was the appointment of missionaries for the conversion of foreign, and even Mlechchha, countries,—an undertaking which in later times gave to

Buddhism a place among the great religions of the world. It seems only natural that the Buddhist Theras, at such a period, the importance of which for their faith they must have fully felt, should have revised, together with their sacred books, the lists of their teachers, and of the data referring to the chief events of their spiritual career, and that they should have connected the history of their patron and of his predecessors in Māgadha with the history of their sect. These considerations make it, in my opinion, more probable that a *Therāvali* and a Māgadha *Rājāvali* similar to, if not identical with, that which the Ceylonese chronicles give, were arranged in India and carried to Ceylon by the first missionaries, than that fragmentary materials only, out of which the Ceylonese later manufactured their account, came over from the continent. This hypothesis, though it would not prove that every one of the figures and events contained in the Ceylonese chronicles has remained unchanged, would make it probable that some considerable portion of the southern tradition might be ancient and of Indian origin. The date of Aśoka's coronation, against which no particular objection can be urged, would probably have to be included in the latter category.

Secondly, a much stronger argument for the Indian origin of the same date is furnished by a fact which first has been brought forward by M. Burnouf (*Introd. ā l'Hist. du Bouddh.* pp. 432-36), but has received little attention. This is the statement of a fragment of an *Avadāna,* entitled *the Council,* —that Aśoka lived not, as the northern Buddhists usually assert, one hundred, but *two hundred* years after the Nirvāṇa. The story begins: "Deux cent ans après que le bienheureux Buddha fut entré dans le Nirvāṇa complet régnait dans la ville de Pātaliputra un roi nommé Aśoka." It contains in the sequel an account of the birth of Kuṇāla and the story of Sundara, which agree with the common northern traditions. M. Burnouf has pointed out that this fragment shows that the northern Buddhists, too, originally recognized two Aśokas, of whom most of their books have made one person, and that it confirms the authenticity of the southern tradition. I do not see how this conclusion can be avoided, and how it can be denied that the date for Aśoka's coronation, according to the era of the Nirvāṇa, must have been settled in India before Buddhism was introduced into Ceylon. As the assertion of the southern Buddhists that the conversion of the Ceylonese took place during Aśoka's reign has not been doubted, and as there is no reason to doubt it, the date, if calculated in India, must have been calculated just during Aśoka's own reign, and must be, as far as the belief of those times is concerned, perfectly genuine. The effect of this conclusion on the question of the authorship of the new edicts is obvious. As the date of the edicts agrees with the date for the coronation of Aśoka in 219 A.B., and as the latter is shown to have been settled during Aśoka's reign, the agreement of the dates itself becomes a strong additional proof for the correctness of the proposed interpretation of the edicts.

I do not see that there is at present any possibility of saying, whether the belief, prevailing in Aśoka's time, that between the Nirvāṇa and the king's coronation upwards of 218 years had elapsed, deserves implicit credence or not. That would depend on a knowledge of the nature of the materials which were at the disposal of the Buddhist chronologists, and this knowledge we do not possess. Mr. Rhys. Davids is therefore right in pointing out that the new edicts do not absolutely prove the length of the interval between the Nirvāṇa and Aśoka, but merely the belief on this point entertained by Aśoka and his contemporaries. But the smallness of the period, sixty years of which are besides covered by the reigns of Chandragupta and Bindusāra, where Brahmans and Buddhists agree in the figures, makes a considerable deviation from the truth improbable, and for practical purposes the number of years given by the Buddhists may be accepted as a fact.

References

1. *The Academy,* July 14, 1877, p. 37.
2. *Ib.* Aug. 11, 1877, p. 145.

3. Corrections and vv. II.: –

Sahasrām

Savachhale – amisaṁ, – devā, – cha jānaṁtu, – sāvane. Mr. Rhys Davids in addition reads *sapaṁnātātisatā,* a correction regarding which I am still as doubtful as when I wrote my first article. – *Num. Or.* VI. p. 57, note. I.

Rūpnāth

sātilekāni, – hakā – pakamaminenā, – vipule – ārādhave – pakare? – lekhāpeta ṭhāyi ti – tapayati? tapāyati? – vyaṭhenā? –

Mr. Rhys Davids suggests for *sa*(*va*)ki, *su-ko,* I think unnecessarily. His correction *vyuṭhena*, is also unnecessary as the inscriptions show three instr. in *en ā.* The real reading of the inscription is *kaṭ e,* not *kaṭa* as he supposes. – *Num. Or.* VI. p. 57, note 2.

4. As I shall not recur to this remark, I may as well state that the explanation of *misam,* by *miśra,* seems to me very improbable.
5. The discovery of the real name of the founder of the Jainas belongs to Professor Jacobi and myself. The form Jñātiputra occurs in the Jaina and Northern Buddhist books; in Pali it is Nātaputta, and in Jaina-Prakrit Nāyaputta. Jñāta or Jñāti appears to have been the name of the Rajput clan from which the Nirgrantha was descended.
6. Mr. Rhys Davids does not discuss Professor Pischel's conjecture which makes Sampadi the author of the edicts. I shall follow him in this respect, and merely remark that Sampadi is, according to the Buddhists and the Jainas, the grandson of Aśoka, and that the first author of certain date who gives the history of his conversion to Jainism by Suhasti and of his benefactions is Hemachandra, the contemporary of Kumārapāla (1173 A.D.). Hemachandra's account is purely legendary and unhistorical. The tradition that Sampadi was a protector of the Jainas is, however, old. Sampadi may be merely another name of Daśaratha, who appears in his stead in the Brahmanical *rājāvalis,* or he may be a distinct person. But the information regarding him is too vague to afford a basis for *any* historical speculations.
7. See now *Corp. Inscr. Ind.* vol. I, pp. 20 *et. seq.*, which were printed before my article was written.
8. Though I thus agree with Mr. Rhys Davids in his chief statement, I regret that I cannot see the force of the argument employed by him. I am unable to understand what the Jaina address *Devāṇuppiya,* which, as far as my observation goes, is invariably used by superiors speaking to inferiors, – *e.g.* by Yatis speaking to their pupils or to

Śrāvakas, by husbands to their wives, &c., – is to prove with respect to the self-given title of great kings. It seems to me that the royal title, the Jaina mode of address, and the Brahmanical use of *Devānāṁ priya* to dentoe 'an idiot,' are caused by three entirely different currents of thought, and that a derivation of the one from the other is very improbable. *Devānāṁ priya* means, etymologically,' dear to the gods.' The early Indian kings, who elsewhere are declared to be incarnations of deities, called themselves 'dear to the gods' in order to indicate their divine right. The early Jainas employed it as a form of polite, or rather humane address, recommending thereby the person spoken to the protection of the gods, – 'you who *may* be dear to the gods.' Compare the use of *āyushman,* 'you who may this name, because such persons were considered to stand in the particular keeping of the gods.

9. See also Sp. Hardy, *Manual,* pp. 499, 500.

10. This will become clearer by a comparison of *santa=śānta,* the neuter of which *santaṁ* means *Nirvāṇa,* while the masculine *santo* is used as an epithet of Buddha, and occasionally as a proper name, Now *santaṁ*: *santo=vivaṭṭam*: *vivaṭṭo*.

11. I must add that the date of the inscriptions *may* be 256 A.B., if we assume that the figure refers to the current year. In my first article I referred it to the number of completed years in accordance with Prinsep's *dictum,* Essays, II. 165, note 1. I did this, not because I was fully convinced of the correctness of Prinsep's rule, but because I wished to take the most unfavourable alternative.

12. According to the *Dīpavaṁsa,* 'when Uttiya had completed eight years: see below.

13. Compare also *Dīp*. VII. 27, where it is stated that Mahinda was *four* years of age (*i.e.* spiritual age) when Aśoka had ruled ten years: –

    Asokassa dassavasamhi Mahindo chatuvassiko | sabbaṁ sutaparīyattiṁ gaṇipāchariyo ahu |27|

14. *Jour. As. Soc. Beng.* vol. VII, pp. 919 seqq.

15. The first date occurs, *e.g.* paras. 84, 86, and the second 114 (twice).

16. Dr. Oldenberg, very judiciously, has not attempted a restoration of the original work, but merely of the *codex archetypus,* from which the existing modern MSS. have been prepared. He has collected a good many various readings, from which I have selected a few particularly important ones.

17. Second half probably corrupt, – perhaps *samasaṭṭhī tadā hoti thero Upāli paṇḍito,* or *saṭṭhivasso t. h. samam Up.*

18. The first line is corrupt, see below. For *Pakuṇḍakassa, Paṇḍurājassa* must be read, as *Pakuṇḍaka* is a name of Paṇḍukābhaya.

19. The second line is corrupt, see below.

20. Corrupt, see below.

21. 94*b*. Corrupt, see below. – v. 1, *aṭṭhatiṁsamhi.*

22. 96*b*. Corrupt, see below.

23. The first line seems to be corrupt, as the figure is wrong. Perhaps *aṭṭha cha* has to be read for *issaro.*

24. Probably *'Dhammasoko'* should be read.

25. Perhaps *Moggali-savhayo* is to be read.

26. Probably *nibbuto* to be read.

27. Corrupt, see below. v. l. *asītivassamhi.*

28. This construction is apparently a mixture of the loc. and gen. absol., and occurs frequently.

29. *Upasampadā, i.e.,* second or full ordination.

30. Regarding these dates more will be said below.

31. Pakuṇḍaka is another name of Paṇḍukābhaya.

32. The years are to be counted from the *upasampadā*: see below, *v.* 95.

33. v. l. in his 38th year.

34. See note to text.

35. v.l., in his eightieth year.

36. v.l. *aṭṭhamāsañ cha sesake.*

37. Dr. Oldenberg's very probable emendation is, *choro āsi Pakuṇḍako.*

38. The genitive stands for the locative, as above.

39. v.l., and the correct one, *theravāde.*

40. Dr. Oldenberg proposes *Asokābhisitte chhavasse,* and I read in addition *saṭṭhi* for *chhasaṭṭhi,* as required by the metre and the sense.

41. Not stated, but 44 before B. may be obtained by deducting length of chiefship from spiritual age.

42. *Dīpavaṁsa* IX. 42, XI. 2, X. 6, and XI. 3-10.

43. tena kho samayena vassasataṁ hi nibbute bhagavate vesālikā Vajjiputtakā, &c.

44. *Jour. As. Soc. Beng.* vol. VII. p. 791; compare also Lassen, *Ind. Alt.* vol. II, p. 92, 2nd ed.

26

The Buddhist Inscription at Keu-Yung-Kwan

S. Beal, B.A.

Attention has elsewhere been drawn to the ancient Buddhist inscription at[1] Keu-yung-kwan, a small village about five miles to the north of the Nankow Pass. This inscription is engraved in the characters of six different nations, viz., Mongol or Bāshpah, Uīghūr, Nyuchih, Chinese, Devanāgari, and Tibetan. On examination it is found to contain certain Buddhist *dhārani* or incantations, which in the paper alluded to (*Jour. R. A. Soc.*, vol. V. pp. 14ff.)[2] have been translated by Mr. Wylie and Dr. Haas for the benefit of the English reader. These *dhāranis* are found in various Buddhist works, and are supposed to represent the highest and most potent charms which words proceeding from the top of the illustrious diadem (*chūḍa*) of Buddha's head are able to convey. This "honoured diadem of Buddha's head" refers to the well known conceit of the Buddhists that form the top of the cranium of their master proceeded an elongated excrescence (*ushṇīsh*),[3] the top of which reached to the highest heaven. In all probability this imaginary formation is pictured in the Amarāvati sculptures as the "pillar of glory surmounted by Om" proceeding from the throne supposed to be occupied by Bhagavat (see particularly pl. lxxi, figs. 1 and 2, *Tree and Serpent Worship*). These pillars of light are also referred to by Spence Hardy (*Manual of Buddhism,* 1st ed. pp. 180, 207), and perhaps originated in the idea of the Liṅga and its worship. Be this as it may, it is curious to trace as far back as we can the origin of such a peculiar idea; and for this purpose we have appended the translation of a *Sūtra* attributed to the Shaman Buddhavara (*Fo-to-po-li*) of the Yang dynasty.

The Sūtra of the Dhārani of the Illustrious Diadem of Buddha's Surmounting Head

"Thus have I heard. At one time Bhagavat was residing at Śrāvastī, in the garden of Jeta, the friend of the orphans, together with 1250 great Bhikshus, his disciples, and with upwards of 12,000 great Bōdhisattwas and priests. At this time there was amongst the Dêvas of the Trayastrinśas Heavens, one in the Assembly of the Saddharma Hall, called Shen-chu. This Dêva, whilst wandering to and fro in the celestial gardens, with the company of Dêvīs who attended him, had heard a voice proceeding from space, and warning him that in a few days hence he should be called to give up his heavenly estate and be born in hell, after which he should receive a succession of births all more or less miserable and painful. On this, the Dêva hastened to Śākrarāja, and with doleful voice and many tears laid the case before him, asking and beseeching for advice and escape. Then Śākrarāja, having heard the words of Shen-chu, at once entered into a state of profound abstraction, and, perceiving that the case was to be with Shen-chu even as the voice had declared, he resolved at once to repair to the place where Buddha was residing, even to the garden of Jeta, and there having presented him with suitable gifts, to seek his counsel and advice on the point. Accordingly having done so, and having saluted the foot of Bhagavat and seven times circumambulated him, he stated the circumstances of Shen-chu's destiny, and humbly asked the advice of the World-honoured one."

Then Buddha caused to proceed from the top of his head every kind of glorious light, which spread itself from world to world through all space. Then this light again returned to the presence of Buddha, and having revolved around him three times entered through his mouth. Then the World-honoured gave a gentle smile, and addressed Śākrarāja as follows :–"Heavenly king, there are certain *dhārani* called the 'honoured diadem of Buddha's head,' which are able to deliver from every kind of evil birth, and to destroy every possible sorrow. If a man once hears these, and if they once pass through his ears, then all the evil deeds he has ever done shall be cancelled and their punishment remitted; if he writes them on a wall, or reads them, so written, to others, then shall the same consequences follow and full deliverance be obtained."

On this Śākrarāja entreats Buddha to repeat these charmed words, on which he did so.

The *dhārani* are much shorter than those on the Keu-yung gate, but contain the same leading words; we do not repeat them, our object being merely to show the purpose of their being placed on this barrier gate, through which Mongols and Thibetans must enter the empire, and doubtless were glad to be so easily assured of deliverance by the repetition of the words.

"Śākrarāja, having heard these words, thankfully received them; and having saluted the World-honoured one, forthwith departed."[4]

References

1. It belongs to the Mongol age, cir. 1345 A.D.
2. See also Yule's *Marco Polo*. vol. I, pp. 29, 444. –ED.
3. The word *ushṇīsha* usually means a 'turban,' but is used by the Buddhists as a technical term for the top-knot on Buddha's head, by which all figures of him are distinguised; he is never represented in Indian sculpture with any sort of covering on his head – ED.
4. *The Oriental,* Oct. 9, 1875.

27

Sanskṛit and Old-Canarese Inscriptions

J. F. Fleet, Bo. C. S., M.R.A.S.

No. CXVI.

The present inscription is from a stone-tablet lying near a small ruined Jain temple in the fort at Ḍambaḷ, in the Gadag Tālukā of the Dhārwāḍ District. A transcription is given in the Elliot *MS. Collection,* Vol. I, p. 356; but my text is edited from an ink-impression made by Mr. H. Cousens, of the Government Archæological Survey.

The emblems at the top of the stone are, – in the centre, a female figure, evidently the Tārā or Tārādêvi of the inscription, seated in a shrine, and facing full front, and holding in her left hand a water-lily just expanding, and in her right hand something which I cannot identify from the drawing; on her right hand, a cow and calf, with the sun above them; and on her left hand, a standing figure with his hands joined and held to his face in the act of salutation, the flower of an eight-leaved water-lily in front of his hands, two lamp-stands, with burning flames, behind him, and the moon above him. The body of the inscription, which is in the Old-Canarese language and in finely engraved an excellently preserved characters of the period to which it refers itself, covers a space of about 3' 1'' high by 2' 1'' broad. But there are also two long lines of writing, in the same characters and containing three verses in the Sanskṛit language, round the top of the tablet.

The body of the inscription is of the time of the Western Chālukya king Tribhuvanamalla or Vikramāditya VI; and it is dated in the Yuva *saṁvatsara,* the nineteenth year of the Chālukya-Vikramavarsha established by him and dating from the commencement of his reign,[1] *i.e.* in Śaka 1017 (A.D. 1095-6). It gives us the name of one of his queens, Lakshmādêvī, who at this time was governing the district called the Eighteen *Agrahāras* and the city of Dharmāpura. She is called here the *piriy-arasi,* or 'senior queen'; but this title corresponding to the Sanskṛit *agra-mahishī,* was borne also by one or two others of his consorts. The Eighteen *Agrahāras* appear to have been a group of towns somewhere in the north of Maisūr or in the south of the Dhārwāḍ District; but I think that they have not yet been actually identified. Dharmāpura, or, as it is also called in this inscription, Dharmavoḷal, meaning, in either form, 'the city of religion', is evidently Ḍambaḷ itself. In connection with the Jain religion, this inscription is of interest as recording the existence at Ḍambaḷ of a *vihāra* or temple of Buddha, which had been built by the sixteen *Seṭṭis*[2] of that place, and of another *vihāra* of Tārādêvī, which had been built by the *Seṭṭi* Saṁgavayya of Lokkiguṇḍi or the modern Lakkuṇḍi. The object of the inscription is to record certain grants to these two *vihāras.* It is worthy of note that these *Seṭṭis,* who built and endowed a Bauddha *vihāra,* and who were therefore Jains, belonged to the *Vīra-Baḷañja*[3] sect, or the class of merchants and traders, by which principally the Liṅgāyat religion of Basava was subsequently adopted.

Transcription

[1] Namô Buddhāya ||* Hari-kari-śikhi-phaṇi-taskara-nigaḷa-jaḷ-ārṇṇava-shi(pi)śāchabhaya-sa(śa)mani(nī) sa(śa)si(śi)-kiraṇa-kānti-

[2] dhāriṇi bhagavati Tārê namas=tubhyaṁ ||* Yā jñān-ārṇṇava-maṁthanāt=samuditā Prajñ=êti yā kathyatê yā Buddhasya

[3] vibhūti-dā tri-bhuvanê bôdhi-svarūpā parā yā hri(hṛi)d-byô(vyô)mni Tathāgatasya vasati ḥpthītīva[4] chāndrī kaḷā sā

[4] Tārā bhava-tāpa-duḥkha-sa(śa)manī prāsi(śā)shṭu(stu) vas=sarvvadā ||* Svasti Samastabhuvanāśraya śrī-pri(pṛi)thvīvallabha mahā-

[5] rāj-ādhirāja paramêśvaraṁ paramabhaṭṭārakaṁ Satyāśraya-kuḷa-tiḷakaṁ Chāḷuky-ābharaṇaṁ śrīmat-Tribhuva-

[6] namalladêvara vijaya-rājyam=uttarôttar-ābhivri(vṛi)ddhi-pravarddhamānam=ā-chandrārkka-tāraṁ baraṁ salluttam-ire ||*

[7] Svasty=Anavarata-parama-kallyā(lyā)ṇ-ābhyudaya-sahaśra(sra)-phaḷa-bhôga-bhāgini dvitiya-Lakshmī-samāne parivāra-ni-

[8] dhāne dāna-chintāmaṇi samast-āntaḥpura-mukhamaṇḍani śrīmat[T*]ribhuvanamalladêva-viśāḷa-vaksha[ḥ*]sthaḷa-nivā-

[9] siniyar=appa śrīmat piriy-arasi Lakshmādêviyaru Padinemṭ-agrahāramuṁ(mumaṁ) Dharmmāpuramuman=āḷdu sukha-saṁ-

[10] kathā-vinôdadiṁ rājyaṁ-geyyuttam-ire ||* Svasty=Anêka-guṇa-gaṇ-āḷaṁkri(kṛi)ta-satya-śauchā[chāra*]-chārucharitra-naya-vine(na)-

[11] ya-śīḷa-saṁpannaruṁ vibudha-prasannaruṁ dêva-brāhmaṇa-pādôdaka-pavitraruṁ sujanaika-mitraruṁ śishṭ-êshṭa-jan-ādhāra-

[12] ruṁ êkāṁga-vīraruṁ anêka-ratna-maṇḍaḷī-ratna-maṇḍanaruṁ kadana-prachaṇḍanaruṁ nānā-dêsī(śīya)-samuddharaṇaruṁ Sarasvatī-karṇṇa-ku-

[13] ṇḍaḷābharaṇaruṁ sā(śā)p-ānugraha-samarttharuṁ samasta-dharmma-purôvri(vṛi)ddhi-kara-kri(kṛi)tārttharuṁ sa(śa)raṇagata-vajra-paṁja-

[14] raruṁ vairi-dikkuṁjararuṁ grāma-nām-ôttamar=(ruṁ)=vvai(vai)śya-kuḷa-kamaḷa-divākararuṁ satya-ratnākararuṁ chatussamaya-samuddha.

[15] raṇaruṁ śrīmaj-Jagadêkamalladêva-prasād-āsādita-chchhatra-chāmara-sā(śā)san-ādi-mahimônnatar=appa śrīmad-Dharmma-

[16] voḷala padinaṛuvaru(var=) sse(=sse)ṭṭigaḷu mahānagaramuṁ(mu)m=irddu tamma māḍisida bauddha-vihārakke Śrī-Lokkiguṇḍiya va-

[17] dda(ḍḍa)-bya(vya)vahāri Saṁgavayya-seṭṭiyaru māḍisida Śrī-bhagavati Āryya-Tārādêvī-vihārī-pratibaddhav=āgi Svasti Śrī-

[18] Chāḷukya-Vikramavarshada 19neya Yuva-saṁvatsarada Māgha-su(śu)ddha-paṁchamī Ādityavārad-aṁdu uttarāyaṇa-

[19] saṁkrānti-vya[5]tīpātad-aṁdu śrīmat-Tārādêvigaṁ Buddhadêvarigaṁ pūjā-satkārakkaṁ gandha-puḥpa-dhūpa-dīpa-māllya(lya)-naivêdy-ādi-

[20] ka[kka*]ṁ pūjārigaṁ alliya bhikshugaḷge grās-āchchhādanakkaṁ nava-karmmādikakkaṁ ūriṁ mūḍalu Ponnakuṟuvada polada-

[21] l=oṁdu mattaru tôṁṭamumaṁ sarbba(rvva)namaśya(sya)v=āgi varsha-prati aruvaṇaṁ mūṟu gadyāṇa ponnaṁ tettu sukhadal=uṁb-ant-ā-

[22] gi koṭṭaru [||*] Int=ī dharmmamaṁ sva-dharmmadiṁ pratipāḷisuvaru [|*] ī dharmmamaṁ pratipāḷisidavargge Bāṇārasi Kurukshê-

[23] tra Prayāge Argghyatīrtthaṁ modal-āgi puṇya-kshêtraṁgaḷolu sāsira kavileya kôduṁ koḷagumaṁ ponnu-be-

[24] ḷḷiyaluṁ kaṭṭisi sāsirbba(rvva)r=chchaturvvêda-pāragar=appa brāhmaṇargge sūryya-grahaṇad-aṁdu dānaṁ-goṭṭa phaḷam=akku [|*]

[25] ī dharmmaman=upêkshisiy=aḷidavargge int=ī puṇya-tīrtthaṁgaḷoḷu sāsira kavile-yumaṁ sāsira chaturvvêda-pāra-

[26] gar=appa brāhmaṇaran=aḷida paṁchamahāpātakan(m)=akku ||* Svasti Samastabhuvana-vikhyāta-paṁchasa(śa)ta-vīra-sā(śā)sa-

[27] na-labdh-ānêka-guṇa-gaṇ-āḷaṁkri(kṛi)ta-satya-śauchā[chāra*]-chārucharitra-naya-vinaya-vijñāna Vīra-Baḷaṁja-dharmma-pratipāḷana

[28] visu(śu)ddha-guḍḍadhvaja-virājamān=ānūna-sāhasa-vīra-lakshmi(kshmī)-liṁgita-vaksha[ḥ*]-sthaḷa bhuvana-parākram-ônnata Vāsudê-

[29] va-Khaṇḍaḷī-mūḷa-bhadra-vaṁś-ôdbhavaruṁ
Bhagavatīdêvī-labdha-vara-prasādam=āge
dvātriṁsa(śad-) vê(-vê)ḷāvu(pu)ram=ashṭādaśa

[30] paṭṭaṇamuṁ chaushashṭi-yôga-pīṭhamuṁ chatur-
ddesey=āśri(śra)mamuṁ nānā-dês(ś)-
ābhyantaradavargge puṭṭa(ṭṭe)yuṁ Kri(kṛi)tayuga[ṁ*]
Trê-

[31] tê Dvāpāraṁ Kaliyugaṁ modal-āge Brahmā(hma)-
Vishṇu-Mahêśvarara maṁthadiṁd=āda Baḷaṁja-
dharmma-bya(vya)vahāra-varttana-prava-

[32] rttanaruṁ Ayvoḷe-puravar-êśvarar-appa śrīmad-
ubhe(bha)ya-nānā-dêsī(śīya)-samūham=irddu
Dharmmavoḷala padinaṟuvaruṁ

[33] mahānaka(ga)ramuṁ māḍisida Buddha-vihārakkaṁ Śrī-
Lokkiguṇḍiya Saṁgavayyaseṭṭiyaru samasta-dêsi(śī)ya-
dha-

[34] rmmav=āgi māḍisida Śrī-bhagavati Āryya-Tārādêvigaṁ
samasta-pūj-ārtthav=āgi teṁkaṇiṁ banda pasuṁbeyalu
pā-

[35] ga teṁka pôpa kāsaṭa biṇige maḷave pasuṁbege bêḷe
vaṁ[6] eraḍu sthānakkav=ā-chaṁdr-ārkka-sthāyi varaṁ
naḍev-ant-āgi kô-

[36] ttar=ī dharmmamaṁ pratipāḷisidavargge Bāṇārasi
Kurukshêtra Prayāge Argghyatīrtthadalu sāsira kavileya

[37] kôḍuṁ koḷagumaṁ suvarṇṇadalu kaṭṭisi sahasra
chaturvvêda-pāragar=appa brāhmaṇarige sūryya-
grahaṇa-

[38] dalu dānaṁ-goṭṭa phalam-akku [|*] ī
dharmmaman=upêkshisi kiḍisida[7] vaṁ sthāna-
garddabha chāṇḍālaṁ same(ma)ya-bāhiraṁ Baḷaṁ-

[39] jigaṁ gôlalu paṇaṁ-goṁḍava
paṁchamahāpātakan=akku ||*
Bā(ba)hubhir=vvasudhā dattā rājabhis=Sagar-ādibhiḥ

[40] yasya yasya yadā bhūmi[ḥ*] tasya tasya tadā phalaṁ ||
Sāmānyô=yaṁ dharmma-sêtu(tur=) nri(=nṛi)pāṇāṁ
kālê kā-

[41] lê pālanīyô bhavadbhis=sarbbā (rvvā) n= etān=bhāgi(vi) naḥ=pārtthivêṁdrā[n*] bhūyô bhūyô yāchatê Rāmabhadra[ḥ*] | | Sva-da-

[42] ttāṁ para-dattāṁ bā(vā) yô harêti(ta) vasundharā[ṁ*] shashṭi-rvva(va)rsha-sahasrāṇi vishṭhāyāṁ jāyatê krimi[ḥ*] | |

[43] Svalpa-mātraṁ pradāsyanti yê dānaṁ Buddha-sā(śā)sanê aśīti[8]-kalpa-sahasrāṇi mahābhôgā mahādhanā [ḥ*] | |

[44] Yatra yatr=ôpapadyantê nityaṁ dānaṁ smaranti tê êvaṁ mahāphalā hy=êshā gaṁbhīrā Buddha-dakshiṇā |(| |)

[45] Kṛitaṁ cha yan=mayā puṇyaṁ karshyê(rishyê) yach=cha kiṁchana têna mêjagataś=ch=āsya padaṁ siddhya(dhya)tu saugataṁ | |

The Verses Round the Top of the Stone

[46] Asarbba(rvva)-bhāvêna yadri(dṛi)chchhe(chchha)yā vā par-ānuvri(vṛi)ttyā vichikitsayā vā yê tvān=namaśyaṁ(syaṁ)ti Munīndra-bhadraṁ tê shyāṁmarīṁ[9] saṁpadam=āpnu[va*]nti | | Sarbbê(rvvé) satvās=sarbbê(rvvê) prāṇā[ḥ*] sarbbê(rvvê) bhūtāś=cha kêvalā[ḥ*] sarbbê(rvvê) vai sukhina[ḥ*] santu sarbbê(rvvê) santu nirāmayā[ḥ*] | |

[47] Pāthas(thaḥ)-pārtthiva-vahnishū(pū)ga-pavana-prakhyāta-bhīty-ākulā(la)-prāṇa-trāṇa-vidhāna-labdha-karuṇa-vyāpāra-chint-āturā prôdyat-tashka(ska)ra-sindhu-sindhura-hari-vyāl-ādi-saṁ(śaṁ)k-āpahā Tārā tūrṇṇa-vitīrṇṇa-vāṁchhita-phalā pāyāt-sadā Saṁgamaṁ | |

Translation

Reverence to Buddha! Reverence to thee, O holy Tārā,[10] who dost allay the fear of lions and elephants and fire and hooded snakes and thieves and fetters and water and the ocean and demons, and who dost bear a splendour like that of the rays of the moon! May that Tārā always bless you, who allays the misery of the affliction of existence; who sprang from the churning of the ocean of knowledge; who is called Prajñā;[11] who is the giver of the power of Buddha; who is the supreme form of perfect wisdom in the three worlds; and who dwells in the heart of Tathāgata,[12] just as the full digit of the moon dwells in the sky!

(L. 4.)—Hail! While the victorious reign of the glorious Tribhuvanamalladêva,—the asylum of the universe; the favourite of the world; the great king; the supreme king; the supreme lord; the most worshipful one; the glory of the family of Satyāśraya; the ornament of the Chāḷukyas,—was continuing with pérpetual increase, so as to endure as long as the moon and sun and stars might last:—

(L. 7)—Hail! And while the glorious chief queen Lakshmādêvī,—who shared the enjoyment of the thousand results of unceasing and supreme good fortune and prosperity; who was like a second (*goddess*) Lakshmī; who was the treasure-house of her retinue; who was a very philosophers's tone in charity' who was the chief ornament of all the women's apartments; and who dwelt upon the mighty breast of the glorious Tribhuvanamalladêva,— was governing the Eighteen *Agrahāras* and the city of Dharmāpura, and was ruling with the delight of pleasing conversations:—

(L. 10.)—Hail! The sixteen *Seṭṭis* of the glorious (*city of*) Dharmavoḷal,—who were endowed with truth and purificatory observances and pleasing conduct and morality and modesty and good character, adorned by innumerable good qualities; who were kindly disposed to learned men; who were purified by the water (*which had been sanctified by the washing*) of the feet of gods and Brāhmaṇs; who were the chief friends of good people; who were the supporters of excellent people and friends; who were brave even by themselves; who were the jewelled ornaments of many assemblages of jewels; who were bold in war; who were the supporters of the people of many countries; who were the earrings of the ears of (*the goddess*) Sarasvatī; who were capable of conferring favours in return for curses; who were successful in increasing all religion; who were a very cage of thunderbolts to those who took refuge with them; who were very elephants of the regions to their enemies; who were of the highest rank by the villages (*of their birth*) and by their names (?); who were the suns of the white waterlilies of the caste of Vaiśyas; who were jewel-mines of truth; who were the sustainers of the four observances; and who were ennobled by the greatness of the umbrellas and the *chauris* and the charters that they had acquired through the favour of the glorious Jagadêkamalladêva,[13] –constituting the large (*assembly of the*) town, gave, to the Bauddha *vihāra* which they themselves had caused to be made, and in connection with the large *vihāra* of the holy Śrī-Ārya-Tārādêvī which the *Seṭṭi* Saṁgavayya, the *vaḍḍa-vyavahārī*[14] of (*the city of*) Śrī-Lokkiguṇḍi had caused to be made: –

(L. 17.) – Hail! At the time of the sun's commencement of his progress to the north, on Sunday the fifth day of the bright fortnight of (*the month*) Māgha of the Yuva *saṁvatsara,* which was the nineteenth year of the Śrī-Chāḷukya-Vikramavarsha: –

(L. 19.) – To (*the goddess*) the holy Tārādêvī, and to the god Buddha, one *matter* of garden-land, as a *sarvanaṁasya* grant, in the field of Ponnakuṛuva to the east to the village, and one *aruvaṇa*[15] and three *gadyaṇas* of gold every year, to be levied as a tax and enjoyed in happiness, for the proper performance of the worship, for the purpose of providing perfumes and flowers and incense and lamps and garlands and the perpetual oblation and other things, for the (*support of the*) *Pūjāri,* to provide food and clothes for the religious mendicants of that place, and (*to pay*) for restorations.

(L. 22.) – They shall preserve this act of religion according to their own religion! May those who preserve this act of religion obtain the reward of fashioning the horns and hoofs of a thousand tawny-coloured cows from gold and silver, and giving them at the time of an eclipse of the sun to a thousand Brāhmaṇs, well versed in the four *Védas,* at Bāṇārasi and Kurukshêtra and Prayāga and Arghyatīrtha and other holy places! May those who neglect and destroy this act of religion incur the guilt of the five great sins of having slain a thousand tawny-coloured cows or a thousand Brāhmaṇs, well versed in the four *Védas,* at those same holy *tīrthas!*

(L. 26.) – Hail! To the *vihāra* of Buddha which was caused to be built by the sixteen (*Seṭṭis*) of (*the city of*) Dharmavoḷal, constituting the large (*assembly of the*) town, and being the assembly of people living in many countries on both sides of it, —who were endowed with truth and purificatory observances and pleasing conduct and morality and modesty, adored by innumerable good qualities acquired by five-hundred strict edicts celebrated over the whole world; who were the protectors of the Vīra-Baḷañja religion; who were decorated with the pure banner of a hill;[16] whose breasts were embraced by the goddess of perfect impetuosity and bravery; who were ennobled by their prowess throughout the world; who were born in the original and auspicious Khaṇḍaḷīvaṁśa, (*the lineage*) of Vāsudêva; who, having acquired the excellent favour of the goddess Bhagavatī, constituted thirty-two sea-side towns (?), and eighteen cities, and sixty-four seats of the *Yôga,* and colleges of the four points of the compass; who were born to those who belonged to many different countries; who were energetic in disseminating the practice of the Baḷañja religion which included the Kṛitayuga and the Trêtāyuga and the Dvāpārayuga and the Kaliyuga and sprang from the churning of (*the religions of the gods*) Brahmā and Vishṇu and Mahêśvara; and who were the lords of Ayvoḷe, which is the best of cities, —and to (*the vihāra of*) the holy Śrī-Ārya-Tārādêvī which had been caused to be built, as an act of religion for the people of all countries, by the *Seṭṭi* Saṁgavayya of Śrī-Lokkiguṇḍi, —to these two establishments, there was given, to be continued as long as the moon and sun might last, a *pāga*[17] on (*each*) bag coming from the south, and one *bêḷe* on (*each*) bag of . . . . . . or . . . . or . . . . . .[18] going to the south.

(L. 36.) —May those who preserve this act of religion obtain the reward of fashioning the horns and hoofs of a thousand tawny-coloured cows from gold and giving them at the time of an eclipse of the sun to a thousand Brāhmaṇs, well versed in the four *Vêdas,* at Bāṇārasi, and Kurukshêtra, and Prayāga, and Arghyatīrtha! May he who neglects and destroys this act of religion, —(*whether he be*) an ass of the place, or a Chāṇḍāla, or an outcaste, or a Baḷañjiga . . . . ,[19] —incur the guilt of the five great sins!

(L. 39.) —Land has been given by many kings, commencing with Sagara; he, who for the time being possesses land, enjoys the fruits of it! "This general bridge of piety of kings should at all times be preserved by you," —thus does Rāmabhadra again and again make his request to all future princes! He is born for 0the duration of sixty thousand years as a worm in ordure, who takes away land that has been given, whether by himself or by another! Those who may give even a small gift in a character of Buddha, they shall have great enjoyment and shall be very rich for eighty thousand ages! Wheresoever they find a perpetual gift, there they remember it; thus their offering to Buddha brings a great reward! Whatever religious merit I have acquired, and whatever I may acquire, —by that may be condition of myself and of this world be perfected as a condition of the Sugata religion!

The Verses Round the Top of the Stone

(L. 46.) —Those who do reverence to thee, who are propitious to Munīndras,[20] —(*even though it be*) with imperfect faith, or spasmodically, or from imitation of others, or through mistake, —obtain the good fortune of becoming Śambaras.[21] May all sentient beings, and all (*who have*) souls, and all who are mere existing beings, —verily may all of them be happy, and all be free from illness! May (*the goddess*) Tārā, —who is anxiously busied with her exercise of tenderness entailed by preserving (*persons possessed of*) souls who are distressed by the notorious fear of water and kings and volumes of fire and wind; who takes away the dread of bold thieves and oceans and elephants and lions and snakes,[22] &c.; and who quickly confers the rewards that are desired, —always preserve Saṁgama![23]

References

1. See Vol. VIII., p. 187.
2. *Seṭṭi,* or *śeṭṭi,* is a corruption of the Sanskrit *śrêshṭhin,* 'a head merchant; the head or chief of a company following the same trade; the president or foreman of a guild or corporation.
3. Other forms, in inscriptions, are *Baḷañju, Baṇañja,* and *Baṇañju.* The modern form is *Baṇajiga* and *Baṇijiga.* There is still a division of the Banajigas which is called Jaina-Baṇajiga.

4. Some correction is necessary here; probably *sphīt=êva* is what was intended.
5. Some other letter, probably *tī,* was engraved here, and then was corrected into *vya.*
6. Sc., *vaṁdu,* for *ondu.*
7. This letter, *da,* was at first omitted and then inserted below the line.
8. The metre is wrong here.
9. Some correction is needed here. I can only suggest that *śāṁbarīṁ* was intended.
10. One of the Jain *śaktis,* or 'female energies'.
11. Wisdom, – the *śakti* of the Ādi-Buddha.
12. A Buddha or Jina.
13. The Western Chālukya king Jayasiṁha III.
14. *Vyavahārin* is 'one whose occupation or trade is (*so and so*).' The meaning of *vaḍḍa* has not been settled yet, but it is probably another form of *vaṭṭa,* 'the difference in the exchange of money.' If so, *vaḍḍa-vyavahārī* means 'a money-changer.'
15. Half a *haṇa* or *paṇa.*
16. *Guḍḍa-dhvaja;* the meaning, however, is not quite certain. *Guḍḍa* is explained by Sanderson, and *guṭṭa* by Sanderson and C.P. Brown, as meaning 'a hill'. C.P. Brown also gives *guḍḍa* as meaning 'cloth'. But neither of these meanings seems quite satisfactory here. On the pedestal of a standing image of Buddha in a small and half-ruined Jain temple at Nêsargi in the Sampgaum Tālukā of the Beḷgaum District there is the following Old-Canarese inscription, in characters of the eleventh or twelfth century A.D.: –

Transcription

[1] Śrī-Mūlasaṁghada Baḷātkāragaṇada Śrī-

[2] Pārśvanāthadêvara Śrī-Kumudachaṁdrabhaṭṭāraka-dêvara

[3] guḍḍa Bāḍigasātti-seṭṭiyaru mukhyav-ā-

[4] gi nakha(ga ?)raṁgaḷu maḍisida nakha(ga ?)-

[5] ra-Jinālaya | |

Translation

The *Jinālaya* of the town (?), which was caused to be made by (*the people of*) the town (?), headed by the *Seṭṭi* Bāḍigasātti who was the *guḍḍa* of Śrī-Kumudachandra-bhaṭṭārakadêva, (*the priest*) of (*the god*) Śrī-Pārśvanāthadêva, of the Baḷātkāragaṇa of the Śrī-Mūlasaṁgha.

It is plain that here *guḍḍa* cannot mean 'a hill'; and it seems to mean 'a disciple, follower, or adherent.'

17. *Pāga* or *hāga,* a quarter of a *paṇa* or *haṇa.*

18. The meanings of *kāsaṭa, biṇige* or perhaps *bīṇige,* and *maḷave,* are not known.

19. The meaning of *gôlalu paṇaṁ-goṁḍava* is not apparent.

20. *i.e.,* Buddhas.

21. See note 9 above, Śambara or Sambara is the name of one of the Jain *Arhats* of the future period.

22. See *Rep. Arch. Sur. W. India,* vol. III, pp.75, 76.

23. *i.e.,* the *seṭṭi* Saṁgavayya of the body of the inscription.

28

Ḍambaḷ Buddhist Inscription of Ś. 1017

J.B.

At p. 185 *ante,* Mr. Fleet has published the text of an interesting inscription, which indicates that Buddhism still held a place among the natives of the Karṇāṭaka as late as the end of the 11th century A.D. In his remarks, Mr. Fleet seems to confound the Buddhists with the Jains; but though both sects used a very similar ecclesiastical nomenclature, it is almost always possible to discriminate clearly to which of them any image, inscription or document belonged; and it is very desirable that this should be carefully done, and the distinction attended to, —for no end of confusion has arisen from the mistake so frequently made, of regarding these two sects as almost identical. Even into books treating on mythology the error has found its way; in Birdwood's *Industrial Arts of India,* for example, (plate G, fig. 4) a figure of Pārśvanātha does duty for "the ninth avatār of Vishṇu as Buddha," though one would have thought the *Śêshaphaṇī* over his head and the jewel on the breast might have sufficiently distinguished the Tīrthaṁkara.

In the inscription under notice, the Dêvī, figured at the head of the stone and invoked after Buddha, is Tārā. This name is known, I believe, among the Jains, but she holds no prominent place in their mythology—is not a *śāsanadêvī* or *yakshiṇī* to any of the twenty-four Tīrthaṁkaras, —while among the Mahāyāna sect of Buddhists, Āryā-Tārādêvī stands almost first in favour among the female *śaktis*. She belongs to Amôghasiddha, the fifth of the Jñānātmaka Buddhas, and had temples dedicated to her worship at Buddha-Gayā and elsewhere, and she is figured in the Nāsik, Auraṅgābād and

Elurā Buddhist caves (*ante,* vol. IX, p. 115; *Archœol. Rep. W. Ind.,* vol. III, p. 78; *Cave Temples,* pp. 133, 371, 384). Like Avalôkitêśvara or Karuṇārṇava she is especially distinguished by her efforts for the salvation of men (Vassilief, *Bouddisme,* p. 125). Indeed in Népāl, and in the Kaṇheri caves, Ārya-Avalôkitêśvara is figured with Lôchanā (the *śakti* of Akshôbhya) at his right hand and Tārā at his left (see *Cave Temples,* pl. lv). She is represented on this slab, as usually among the Buddhists, holding a flower in her left hand, and an opening blossom apparently springs up behind her right side, while the hand, now broken, perhaps hung over the knee. It is curious to remark too that, in the inscription, she is addressed as delivering her votaries from these very eight forms of evil—the fear (1) of lions , (2) of elephants, (3) of fire, (4) of hooded-snakes, (5) of thieves, (6) of fetters, (7) of the ocean waves, and (8) of demons,—which Avalôkitêśvara is represented, in the bas-reliefs at Auraṅgābād, Ajaṇṭā, Elurā, and Kaṇheri, as saving men from. The inscription identifies Ārya-Tārādêvī with Prajñā, as does also the *Sarakādhāra* of Sarvajña-Mitrapāda. The words *Tathāgata* and *Sugata* are constantly applied to Buddha, but rarely used by the Jains. All the terms in the inscription are those in common use among Buddhists, and none of them specially Jaina,—for the conjectural reading of *śāṁbariṁ,* in the verses at the top, can hardly be admitted, since Śrī-Saṁvara, the 18th Jina of the future cycle, is never alluded to, except in the formal lists. Nor would Jains address Buddha at all in an inscription.

These remarks, I think, show beyond doubt that this inscription is purely Buddhist. Is there not a trait of the Bauddha scorn for the Jaina-Baṇajigas, in joining them with outcasts and Chāṇḍālas ? Buddhists, too, would not be likely to become converts to Jainism—the two sects hated each other too heartily—but as the Episcopalian of modern times, who leaves his church, rarely joins any closely allied form of worship, but goes to the extreme of Plymouthism—so the Buddhists when they changed at all, would go over at once to the popular Liṅgāyat religion.

29
A Chinese Inscription from Buddha-Gayā

At p. 193 *ante,* Professor Beal has given some account of two Chinese inscriptions discovered at Buddha-Gāya by General Cunningham, under whose instructions his assistant, Mr. Beglar, photographed them. We learn from the *Pioneer* that the Executive Engineer in charge of the works reports to the Magistrate of Gayā the discovery during last year (1880-81) of several more Chinese inscriptions, and Mr. Garrick, Assistant to the Archæological Surveyor, having been sent to photograph them, has obtained from Mr. H.A. Giles of the Chinese Consular Service, the following translation of one of the most perfect of them discovered, we believe, be Gen. Cunningham himself in the Mahant's house:–

"This pagoda was erected by the Emperor and Empress of the Great Sung dynasty, in memory of His Imperial Majesty, T'ai Tsung.[1]"

"By command of His Imperial Majesty, our divinely enlightened, most glorious, most virtuous, most filial sovereign of this Great Sung dynasty, and of Her Imperial Majesty, our most gracious, most virtuous, and most compassionate Empress,–I the Buddhist priest, Hui-wen, have been humbly commissioned to proceed to the country of Magadha, and to erect, on behalf of His departed Imperial Majesty, T'ai Tsung–the humane, the orthodox, the deserving, the divinely virtuous, the wise, the supremely filial,–a pagoda beside the Bodhimaṇḍa, the Diamond Throne. For His Imperial Majesty, T'ai Tsung, was humbly desirous of passing aloft to the

Dêvalôka – the Mansions of the Blest, there to receive the Word from Buddha himself, to witness the ranks of the Immortal Saints, and be enrolled for ever among the ranks of the faithful; hoping thus to secure to the House of Sung divine protection through all generations."

"Recorded this 19th day of the first moon of the 2nd year of *Ming Tao*" (A.D. 1033)."

The Pagoda or whatever the structure was, appears to have been constructed in honour of the second Emperor of the Sung dynasty (A.D. 976-998) and by order of Jen Tsung, the fourth emperor who came to the throne in A.D. 1023. The legend, so to speak, above the inscription, is engraved in what Chinese scholars know as the "lesser seal," used where an ornamental style is considered desirable. The inscription itself is in the usual style current since the 4th century of our era.

References

1. *Rawlinson's Herodotus,* Bk. IV, ch. 67.

30

A Buddhist Sanskrit Inscription from Kota[1]

E. Hultzsch, Ph. D.; Vienna

The subjoined Nāgarī inscription is edited from a slightly damaged paper-rubbling, which I owe to the kindness of Professor Bühler, who received it from Dr. Burgess. A label attached to the rubbing states that the inscription is engraved "on a stone built into a recess under a flight of stairs on the right hand as one enters the 'Barkhārī Gate' of the inner wall of the town of Shergaḍh in Koṭā."

The inscription consists of twenty Sanskṛit stanzas, in various metres, and in a very turgid style. It professes to be a *praśasti,* or eulogy, and records the building of a Buddhist temple and monastery to the east of mount Kośavardhana by the feudal chief (*Sāmanta*) Devadatta, in whose seventh regnal year the document is dated, and whose genealogy is given as follows :–

Bindunāga.

|

Padmanāga.

|

Sarvaṇāga,
married to Śrī.

|

Devadatta.

This pedigree does not enable us to connect the Nāgas here mentioned with the Nāga kings discovered by General Cunningham,[2] or with the Nāga family of the Gurjara grants.[3]

Both the composer of the *praśasti,* Jajjaka, and its engraver, Chaṇaka, have done their work so conscientiously, that there are almost no mistakes to be found throughout the inscription. In spite of this, the deciphering, and the translation of this small *Kāvya* has not been an easy task. To Professor Bühler I am indebted for several kind suggestions. The correct reading of the date, which I had perfectly misunderstood in my original paper, was pointed out to me by Paṇḍit Bhagwānlāl Indrajī.

References

1. Reprinted, after revision, from the *Journal of the German Oriental Society.*
2. *Archæol. Surv. Ind.* Vol. II, p. 310.
3. *ante* Vol. XIII. pp. 82 and 88.

31

The Date of the Kota Buddhist Inscription of the Samanta Devadatta

J.F. Fleet

This inscription has been edited by Dr. Hultzsch at page 45ff. (in Indian Antiquary Vol. 14) above. The reading of the date given there is—*Samvat śarāṅka* (read *samvatsarāṅka*) 7 *Māgha śudi* 6 |—"In the (*regnal*) year, in figures, 7; on the 6th day of the bright half of Māgha."

Even if only because of the peculiar way in which, according to this emendation, *aṅka* is compounded with *saṁvatsara,* this is not at all a satisfactory rendering of the date, and must certainly be abandoned. And, in his original edition of the inscription, in the *Jour. Germ. Or. Soc.* Vol. XXXVIII. p. 546ff., Dr. Hultzsch had interpreted the date differently,—*Samvat śa* 841 *Māgha śudi* 6 |; with suggestion that the *śa* might represent either *śata,* 'hundreds,' or the numerical symbol for 100, or *Śaka,* the name of the era.

I now give a lithograph of thc date, reduced from the lithograph given with Dr. Hultzsch's original notice, and compared by me with the paper-rubbing of the inscription:—

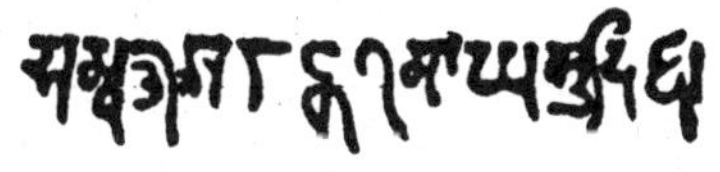

The date is rather a peculiar one, in containing a decimal figure combined with numerical symbol. But it seems plain to me that what follows the word *samvat,* is a late form of the numerical symbol for 100, followed again by the decimal figure

8; the two together representing 800. The next sign cannot be the symbol for 4, as, being followed by a third sign, it must be one of the tens, not a unit. Moreover, in the symbol for 4, the upward stroke in the left lower corner is not joined to the cross-stroke (thus forming a loop), as it is here. It is plainly a form of the symbol for 70. The third sign is not straight enough to be the decimal figure 1; it is plainly the symbol for 9. After *śu di* we have evidently a late form of the symbol for 20, – not the decimal figure 6, with a half mark of punctuation after it.

My reading of the date is *Samvat* 800 70 9 *Māgha śu di* 20, – "The year 800 (*and*) 70 (*and*) 9; (*the month*) Māgha; the bright fortnight; the day[1] 20."

The era is not specified, but, from the locality of the inscription, it must be the era of the Mālava tribe or kings, *i.e.* the Vikrama era. The date, accordingly, is A.D. 822-23.

References

1. Not of the fortnight, but of the month; and in accordance with the arrangement indicated by Hiuen Tsiang, – "The preceding dark portion, and the following light portion, together form a month" (Beal's *Buddh. Rec. West. World,* Vol. I. p. 71).

32

A Buddhist Stone-inscription from Sravasti, of [Vikrama]-Samvat 1276

F. Kielhorn, *C.I.E.; Göttingen*

I edit this inscription from two good rubbings supplied by Mr. W. Hoey, B.C.S., and forwarded to me by Mr. Fleet. The stone which holds that inscription was found by Mr. Hoey at Sêṭ-Mahêṭ,[1] the ancient Śrâvasti; "in the Jêtavana mound, in the ruins of an essentially Buddhist building with monastic cells; in a stratum which indicated that it had been placed in a restored building."

The inscription consists of 17 full lines, and one short line containing merely the date. The writing covers a space of about 2' 8½'' broad by 1' 2½'' high, and is throughout well preserved.—The size of the letters in from 5/8'' to ¾''.—The characters are Dêvanāgarī, and there is nothing remarkable about them except that the *anusvāra,* instead of being written *above* the *akshara* after which it is pronounced, is 11 times written *after* it, with the sign of *virāma* below the *anusvāra.*—The language is Sanskṛit, and except for the introductory blessing and the date at the end, the inscription is in verse. The name of the composer of the verses is Udayin (line 17). From a grammatical point of view I may draw attention to the wrong from *avamanya,* line 1; to the wrong compound *tatpaṁchamaḥ,* line 10; and to the unusual derivatives *janīna,* line 7, and *udarambharīṇa,* line 14.—In respect of orthography I would note the employment of the dental for the palatal sibilant in *saṁvara,* line 1, *sākya,* line 1, *vaṁsê,* line 3, *atisāyī,* line 3, *sakuni,* line 4, *vaṁsa,* line 5, *subhrair,* line 5, *paṁchasara,* line 10, *vahusō,* line 15, and *prasastim,* line 17; and the fact that *ba* is throughout denoted by the sign for *va.*

The inscription is dated in the year [of the Vikrama era] 1276; corresponding to A.D. 1219-20, and is of some interest as showing that Buddhism had not become extinct in northern India in the first half of the 13th century A.D. For it records that a certain Vidyādhara, son of Janaka, and grandson of Bilvaśiva, of the Vāstavya family, established a convent or Buddhist ascetics at the town where the inscription was originally put up. Janaka, the father of Vidyādhara, is described (line 8) as the counsellor of Gôpāla ruler of Gādhipura or Kānyakubja; and Vidyādhara appears to have held a similar position under the prince Madana (line 13), probably a successor of Gôpāla. The town where the convent was established, is called Jāvṛisha (or possibly Ajāvṛisha), it is said to have been built by Māndhātā, of the solar race, and to have had "its protection entrusted to Karkôṭa."

We know that Jayachchandra of Kanauj was defeated and Kanauj taken by the Muhammadans in A.D. 1193; and it is therefore interesting that our inscription, like another inscription pointed out by Sir A. Cunningham, *Archæol, Survey of India,* Vol. XI, page 128, should speak "of the Hindu kingdom of Kanauj as if it were still in existence."

The place Jāvṛisha (or Ajāvṛisha) mentioned in the inscription, I am unable to identify at present. In my opinion, there is just a possibility that it may be Jaunpur or some place close to it. According to Sir A. Cunningham, *loc. cit.* pp. 163 and 104, Jaunpur had an older name which is as yet unknown; there is near it a fort overhanging the river which was called Karārkôṭ, and "four miles to the South-east of Karārkôṭ, on the site of the present Zafarābād, stood the palace of the later kings of Kanauj, with whom this was a favourite residence." But my difficulty is that Jaunpur is about 130 miles distant from the place where the inscription was actually found.

Text[2]

1. Ōṁ namō Vītarāgāya || Mārān[3]=ashṭa niyamya dikshv=adhipatīn=āyvôjya sat[t*]v-ôdayê durllaṁghyāṇy(ny)=avamanya[4] Sa(śa)ṁva(mba)ra-ripôr=ājñ-āksharāṇy=ādṛitaḥ | uddharttuṁ yatatê sma yaḥ karuṇayā śrī-Sā(śā)-

2. kya-siṁhô jagad=vô(bô)dhīṁ prāpya cha Vu(bu)ddhatām=abhigataḥ sa tvāṁ paritrāyatāṁ || Saṁsār[5]-āṁbhôdhi-tārāya Tārām=uttāra-lôchanāṁ | vandê girvvāṇa-vāṇīnāṁ Bhāratīm=adhidêvatām ||

3. Māṁdhāt[6]-ākhyaḥ śatru-jich=Chhakra-tulyô vaṁsê(śê) Bhānôr=bhānu-têjô-tisā(śā)yī| nityānandī sādhu bhôktā trilôkīṁ rājñām=ādyaś=chakravarttī va(ba)bhūva || Svêchchhaṁ[7] bhrāmyan=kadāchit=sara-

4. siruha-rajô-rāji-chitrīkṛit-āmbhaḥ samyag-dṛishṭvā sarô=ntar-madakala-sa(śa)kuni-vrātarāv-ābhiramyaṁ| karttuṁ kīrttêr=vitānaṁ sucharita-muditô mṛidbhir=āpūrya yatnāt=Karkkôṭ ādhīna-ra-

5. ksharṁ sva-puram=idam=athô nirmamê Jāvṛish-ākhyaṁ || Tasminn[8]=abhūvan=dhaninô=tidhanyāḥ śrī-pūrvva-Vāstavya-kula-pradīpāḥ | ady=āpi yad-vaṁsa(śa)-bhavair=yaśôbhir=jjaganti su(śu)bhrair=dhavalī-

6. kriyantê || Têshām[9]=abhūd=abhijanê jaladhāv=iv=êndur=iṁdu-dyutiḥ prathita-Vi(Bi)-lvaśiv-ābhidhānaḥ | yasya Smarāri-charaṇāṁvu(mbu)ja-vatsalasya lakshmir=dvijāti-sujan-ārthijan-ôpabhô-

7. gyā || Saujany[10]-āṁvu(mbu)n dhêr=udāra-charita-pratyasyamān-ainasaḥ sādhūnām=udayaika-dhāma jananī-sthānaṁ śriyaḥ sat[t*]va-bhūḥ | tasy=āsīj=Janakô janīna-hṛidayaḥ putraḥ satān=a-

8. graṇīr=mānyô Gādhipur-ādhipasya sachivê Gôpāla-nāmnaḥ sudhīḥ || Tên=[11]ôchchakair-abhijan-āmvu(mbu)nidhêḥ prasūtā Lakshmīr=iv=achyuta-vibhūshaṇa-kānta-mūrttiḥ | ānanda-kanda-ja-

9. nanī jananī-kulānāṁ Jijj=êti saṁbhṛita-kulasthitin=ôpayêmê || Tābhyām[12]= abhūvaṁs= tanayāḥ shaḍ=êva shaḍbhir=mukhair=êka-tanur-ya êkaḥ | jyāyān=sutaḥ Pippaṭa-nāmadhê-

10. yô dhīmān=iv-Āgni-prabhavaḥ Śivābhyāṁ || Tat[13]-paṁchamaḥ Pāṁchasa(śa)r-āṇukārī tayôs= tanūjô= tanu-kīrtti-kaṅdaḥ | vidy-āvavô (bô)dhād=anukīrttyatè yô Vidyadharô nāma yathārtha-

11.nāmā || Rasādhikam[14]=abhivyāpi Girīśa-charaṇ-āśritaṁ| haṁs=īva mānasaṁ yasya jahāti sma na Bhāratī || Mādhuryaṁ[15] madhunô mudhā himaruchêr=ānanda-mêdhāvitā mi-

12.thy=aiv=āmvu (mbu)nidhêr=ggabhīrima-guṇas=tuṁgatvam= adrêr=alaṁ | yasy=aikaika-guṇādhirôhaṇa-girêḥ saujanya- sāṁdr-ô[|*]asat-pīyūsh-aika-nidhêr=gguṇêna guṇinaḥ sarvvê=py=adhaś=chakrirê|| Yasmai[16]

13.gaj-āgama-rahasya-vidê gajānāṃ=ānandanīṁ kalayatê dhuram=uddhurāya | bhūpāla-mauli-tilakô Madanaḥ pradāna-mān-ādibhiḥ kshitipatiḥ spṛityahāṁ-va(ba)bhūva | Dêvā-

14.layaiḥ prathayatā nija-kīrttim=uchchaiḥ pushya[d*]-dvija-vrajam=udêtum=alam=va(ba)-bhūva | yên=ārijjitaṁ draviṇam=ārttajan-ôpakāri jīvātu-sambhṛita-mudām=udaram-bharīṇaṁ || Sat[t*]va[17]-sārtha pe-

15.ritrāṇa-kṛita-kāyaparigrahaḥ | abhūd=a-bhūtapūrvô=yaṁ Vô(bô)dhisat[t*]va iv=āparaḥ | Ātmajñāta(na)[18]-kṛitôday[ê]na vigalad-rāgādi-dôsh-āśraya-prôdgachchhan-manasā vichārya va(ba)husô(śô)

16.madhyasthatāṁ Saugatê [|*] tên=ārādhita-satpathêna yaminām=ānanda-mūl-ālayō nirmm[ā*] py=ôtsasṛijê vihāra-vidhinā kīrttêr=iv=aik-āśrayaḥ || Sadvō(dbô)dha[19]-vaṁdya-chari-

17.tasya nay-aika-dhāmnaś=chaṁdr-āvadāta-hṛidayaḥ sumatiḥ kalāvān | asya priyêshu nirataḥ subhagaṁbhavi[sh]ṇuḥ samva(mba)ndha-va(ba)ndhur=Udayī vidadhê prasa(śa)stim ||

18.Saṁvat 1276 [||*]

Translation

Ōm!

Adoration to him

who is free passions!

May the illustrious Śākya lion protect you!—he who, having at the rising of truth (*first*) restrained the eight Māras, (*and then*) attracted to himself the lords over the regions,[20] having treated with contempt the difficult-to be-transgressed words of command of the enemy Śambara, full of zeal through compassion exerted himself to deliver the world; and who, having reached to Bôdhi-tree, attained the *status* of a Buddha!

To cross the ocean of worldly existence, I adore the saving Bhāratī, whose eyes have protruding pupils,[21] the goddess presiding over the utterances of the gods.

(L.3)—In the race of Sun there was, surpassing the splendour of the sun, the universal sovereign, the first of kings, named Māndhātā,[22] conquering the enemies, equal to Indra, ever gladdening, well protecting the three worlds.

Once upon a time roaming about at his pleasure, he saw a pleasant lake whose waters were variegated with lines of the pollen of lotuses, (*and which was*) charming with the cries of flocks of sweetly singing birds in it; and having strenuously filled it with earth, he, who delighted in good conduct, to make a canopy for his fame, then built this town of his, named Jāvṛisha,[23] the protection of which was entrusted to Karkôṭa.

(L.5)—In it there were wealthy (*and*) very fortunate (*people*), lights of the illustrious[24] Vāstavya family, by the splendid fame of whose race the worlds are rendered white even now.

As the moon (*is born*) from the ocean, so in their family there was (*a personage*), shining like the moon, whose name Bilvaśiva was famous; devoted as he was to the lotus-feet of (Śiva) the enemy of the god of love, his wealth was an object of enjoyment to the twice-born, to virtuous people, and supplicants.

(L.7)—He, an ocean of benevolence, who was counteracting sin by his noble conduct, had a son Janaka, a unique home of the elevation of the good, a birthplace[25] of fortune, a site of goodness, with a heart kind to people,[26] the foremost of the good, the honoured wise counsellor of the ruler of Gādhipura,[27] named Gôpāla.

He, who well maintained the prosperity of his family, married the daughter of a noble race, named Jijjā, who was causing joy[28] to her mother's family, (*and who*), inasmuch as her lovely body possessed imperishable ornaments, was like Lakshmī, born from the ocean, whose lovely body beautifies Achyuta (Vishṇu).

(L.9)—From these two there were born no less than six sons, just as the intelligent progeny of fire called Pippaṭa, who one, with one body, is endowed with six faces, (*was born*), as the elder son, from Śiva and his consort.[29]

Their fifth son of those[30] (*six*), resembling the five-arrowed (Kāma), (*and*) the root of no slight fame, who is celebrated for his knowledge of wisdom, is named, with an appropriate name, Vidyādhara, 'the holder of wisdom.'

(L.11)—Whose comprehensive mind, full of taste (*and*) attached to the feet of Śiva, Bhāratī (the goddess of eloquence) never abandoned, just as the swan never leaves the extensive Mānasa lake, full of water (*and*) situated at the foot of the lord of mountains (Himālaya).

Vain is the sweetness of honey (*and*) the proficiency in (*creating*) joy of the cool-rayed (moon); a sham indeed is the quality of depth of the ocean (*and*) the height of the mountain;—(*but*) enough! by the excellent qualities of this mountain for the ascent of every single excellency, of this unique receptacle of the abundant sparkling nectar of benevolence, everything whatever that is endowed with excellent qualities has been surpassed!

Him, who knew the secret doctrine regarding elephants, (*and*) who, unrestrained, bore the burden of elephants that was causing pleasure (*to him*), the head-ornament of princes, the lord of the earth, Madana, sought to attach to himself by gifts, honours, and so forth.

(L.13)—The wealth acquired by him, who spread his fame aloft by (*building*) temples,—(*wealth*) which gave relief to people in distress, (*and*) filled the bellies[31] of those filled with joy at (*the receipt of*) food,—was sufficient to exceed the multitude of the twice-born supported (*by it*).

He was as it were another Bôdhisattva, such as had never existed before, having assumed a human body for the protection of the multitude of living beings.

(L.15) – Elevated by the knowledge of the soul, (*and*) with a mind rising above the attachment to passion and other sins of which he was getting rid, having again and again pondered on the indifference towards the doctrine of Sugata, he, having resorted to the good path, caused to be built and granted to the ascetics, after the manner of convents, a dwelling causing joy, a unique home as it were of (*his own*) fame.

Taking delight in whatever is dear to him, the unique home of prudence, whose conduct is an object of adoration for people of true knowledge, Udayin, (*his*) kinsman by association, whose heart is pure like the moon (*and who is*) wise (*and*) accomplished (*and*) becoming prosperous, has composed (*this*) eulogy.

The year 1276.

References

1. Ordinarily written *Sāhêt-Māhêt;* see *e.g. Archæol. Survey of India,* Vol. I, page. 333; Beal, *Si-yu-ki,* Vol. II, page 1; Legge, *Fa-hien,* page 55. The above spelling I owe to Mr. Hoey, who writes as follows: "Our earliest settlement inquiries found the Jêtavana mound named *Sêṭ* सेट and the city mound Mahêṭ महेट. This, too is the spelling adopted by local Paṇḍits, and by Pāṭwārīs who write Hindi. The form *Sahêṭ-Mahêṭ* (सहेट महेट) is a corruption for the sake of the rhyme. It is curious that some Nepalese who visited the ruins while I was excavating, called the place *Mahês* (महेस)." One the map of the ruins of Śrāvastī, *Archæol. Survey of India,* Vol. I, Plate L, *Māhêṭ* is given as the name of the Jêtavana Monastery mound, and *Sāhêṭ* as the name of the town.
2. From the rubbing.
3. Metre, Śārdūlavikrīḍita.
4. Read *avamatya.*
5. Metre, Ślôka (Anushṭubh).

6. Metre, Śālinī.
7. Metre, Sragdharā.
8. Metre, Upajāti.
9. Metre, Vasantatilakā.
10. Metre, Śārdūlavikrīḍita.
11. Metre, Vasantatilakā.
12. Metre, Indravajrā.
13. Metre, Upajāti.
14. Metre, Ślôka (Anushṭubh).
15. Metre, Śārdūlavikrīḍika.
16. Metre, Vasantatilakā; and in the next verse.
17. Metre, Ślôka (Anushṭubh).
18. Metre, Śārdūlavikrīḍita.
19. Metre, Vasantatilakā.
20. Compare Kern, *Buddhismus,* German Ed. Vol. I. pp. 88, 89. It is difficult to say why the author of the verse should speak of *eight* Māras; the number eight would be more appropriate for the guardians of the four regions and the four intermediate regions.
21. The original contains a play on the word *tāra;* and there is clearly an allusion to the *Tārās,* or wives (*śaktis*), of the Dhyāni-Buddhas, one of whom is called Lôchanā. See Kern, *ib.* Vol. II. pp. 215 and 216; and *e.g., ante,* Vol. X. p. 187.
22. *Māndhātā,* of course, is the Nom. case of *Māndhātṛi;* but we have the same form, instead of the base of the word, in *Māndhātā-pura.*
23. In the original, the name may be either *Jāvṛisha* or *Ajāvṛisha.*
24. *Śri-pūrva*—I take in the sense of *śrī-yuta,* or simply *śrī.* A *śrī-Vāstavya-mahāvaṁśa* we find *e.g.* in the Mahôba inscription, of Saṁvat, 1240, *Arch. Survey of India,* Vol. XXI. Plate XXII. line 12, and in another Mahôba inscription, *ib.* Plate XXIII, line 12; and a *Vāstavya-vaṁśa* in line 27 of an unedited Malhār inscription of [Chêdi] Saṁvat 919.
25. *Jananī-sthāna* I take to be used in the sense of *utpatti-sthāna.*
26. The word *janīna* I cannot find anywhere else; it is formed from *jana,* as *viśvajanīna* (*i.e., viśvajanêbhyô hitam*) is from *jana,* as *viśvajana.* See Pāṇini V. 19.
27. Gādhipura is Kānyakubja. See *ante,* Vol. XV, pp. 8, 41, etc.

28. One of the two words *kanda-jananī* is superfluous, Jijjā may be called *ānanda-kandaḥ* (see *e.g. ante,* p. 202, line 1), or *ānanda-jananī.*

29. From this verse it appears that Pippaṭa, is another name of Skanda or *Kārttikêya.* The writer, though he makes Kārttikêya the son of Śiva and Pārvatī, at the same time alludes to the legend according to which Kārttikêya was son of Śiva without the intervention of his wife, Śiva's generative energy being cast into the fire.

30. *Tat-pañchama* is an irregular compound.

31. *Udarambharīṇa,* which is not found in the dictionaries, is used in the sense of *udarambhari.*

33

A Buddhist Stone-Inscription from Ghosrawa

F. Kielhorn, *C.I.E.; Göttingen*

This inscription was discovered in March 1848, by Captain M. Kittoe, in a mound from which the people were then digging bricks, at a village about 7 miles south-east of the town of Bihār, in the Paṭna district of the Province of Bengal; and it was first edited, with an English translation by Dr. Ballantyne, remarks by Captain Kittoe himself, and a note by Mr. J.W. Laidlay, in the *Journ. Beng. As. Soc.* Vol. XVII. Part I, pp. 492-501. The exact spelling of the name of the village where the inscription was found, has been somewhat difficult to make out with certainty. In Captain Kittoe's remarks, *l.c.* p. 495, the place is called 'Pesserawa,' but this must be an error. For, in the Hindī heading of the Sanskṛit text, p. 492, we have 'Gusarāna,' and in Mr. Laidlay's note, p. 500, 'Gusserawa' instead; and in the volumes of the *Archæol. Survey of India* and in Sir A. Cunningham's *Ancient Geography of India,* Vol. I, p. 44, as well as in a paper by Mr. A.M. Broadley, which will be mentioned below, the name of the village is given as either 'Ghôsrāwā' or 'Ghôsrāwan'. According to information which I owe to Mr. E.H. Walsh and to Mr. Grierson, the name of the place, in all the village-papers etc., is written घोसरावान, but it is invariably pronounced घोसरावाँ, *i.e.* Ghôsrāvaṁ.

The importance of the inscription for the later history of Indian Buddhism was fully recognised by Captain Kittoe, who assigned it to the 9th or 10th century A.D.; and Mr. Laidlay rightly identified some of the places which are mentioned in the inscription. Captain Kittoe removed the slab on which the inscription is, to Bihār, where he took facsimiles and returned it afterwards to the village, where he had it fixed in a niche in the other wall of a modern temple, having first engraved in English on the margin the date its being recovered and set up (by Captain Kittoe) for preservation on account of Government.[1]

Afterwards, the inscription was prominently referred to by Sir A. Cunningham, in his Reports for 1861-62 and 1871-72, *Archæol. Survey of India,* Vol. I. p. 38, and Vol. III. p. 120, as well as in his *Ancient Geography of India,* Vol. I. p. 44. But the original edition and translation, as well as these references to them, appear to have entirely escaped the attention of Mr. M. Broadley; for, in a paper on 'the Buddhistic remains of Bihār,' which he published in the *Jour. Beng. As. Soc.,* Vol. XLI. Part I., and in which on pp. 268-174 he gave two transcripts and translations of this very inscription, one by Dr. Rājêndralāl Mitra and the other by Dr. R.G. Bhāṇḍārkar (accompanied by a rather useless photozincograph), he treated the record as if it had never been brought to public notice before. One cannot wonder at the somewhat severe tone, caused by the entire omission of Captain Kittoe's name by Mr. Broadley, which pervades Sir A. Cunningham's latest remarks on the antiquities of Ghôsrāwā, in *Archæol. Survey of India,* Vol. XI. p. 171 ff.; here it is sufficient to say that the stone containing the inscription, which longer bears Kittoe's name,[2] has been transferred to the Bihār Museum, where it is at present.

Though the inscription has been edited and translated three times, a critical edition of it appears still to be desirable, and I therefore re-edit it, at Mr. Fleet's request, from an excellent impression supplied by him.

The inscription contains 19 lines. The writing covers a space of about 1' 11'' broad[3] by 1' 2'' high, and it is in a state of perfect preservation almost throughout—The average size of the letters is about 7/16''—The characters belong to the northern class of alphabets, and they present a further development of the characters which we meet, *e.g.*, in the Bôdh-Gayā inscription of Mahānāman, of which a photo-lithograph has been given *ante,* Vol. XV. p. 358. This is clearly shown by a general comparison of the forms of the consonants and the signs for the medial vowels; and it is proved in particular, *e.g.*, by the form of the initial *ā* in *āchārya,* line 7, and of the conjunct *ry* in *āchārya-varyam,* in line 7, and *audāryam* and *vīryam,* in line 16 (but not in *sthitêr=yaḥ,* in line 11), compared, *e.g.*, with the initial *ā* of *āmradvīpa* in line 9, and with the *ry* of *yatir=yataḥ* in line 7, of the Bôdh-Gayā inscription.[4] Exactly the same alphabet appears to be employed, *e.g.,* in the short Nālandā inscription of Gôpāla, of which a photozincograph is given in *Archæol. Survey of India,* Vol. I. p. 15; and a still further development of the same alphabet we have in a short inscription of Mahīpāla, which is in the Bihār Museum. As regards the present inscription, I may also perhaps draw attention to the forms of the final *t* and *n* (followed by the sign of *virāma*) in *asmāt,* line 17, *sakalān,* line 7, and *bhikshūn,* line 9, and to the exceptional denotation of *tta* by the sign for *tu,* in *saṁkīrttanaṁ,* line 5, and *kīrtti,* line 13.—The language is Sanskṛit, and, except for the opening symbol representing *ôṁ,* the inscription is in verse throughout. In line 6 we find the wrong form *abhyupêtum* (for *abhyupaitum*), which is also met with elsewhere; otherwise the grammar calls for no particular remark. As regards lexicography, I would point out that the *kīrti* has in line 17 been employed in the sense of 'an edifice' or 'a temple,' a meaning which has been assigned to the word *kīrti* by Hêmachandra—As regards orthography, *v* has throughout been used for *b;* instead of *anusvāra* the dental *n* has been employed before the dental sibilant, and the guttural *ṅ* before the palatal sibilant, in *sansāra,* line 1, *dhvansī,* line 18, *vaṅśa,* line 4, and *vaṅsau,* line 17; and the rules of *saṁdhi* have been neglected in *bhikshūn śrī-,* line 9, and in *samvṛitêna,* line 12, and *êtam=vidhāya,* line 17.

The inscription is a Buddhist inscription; and it records (line 14) the erection, probably at the place where the stone containing the inscription was found, of an edifice for a *vajrāsana* or diamond-throne,[5] by a personage named Vīradêva, an account of whom takes up by far the greater part of this record. Vīradêva, the son of Indragupta and his wife Rajj[ê]kā, was born in a noble Brāhmaṇical family, at

Nagarahāra (in the Jalālābād valley) in Uttarāpatha (or Northern India). Anxious to follow the teaching of Buddha, he went, after he had studied the Vêdas and the Śāstras, to the great Kanishka vihāra (in the neighbourhood of the modern Pêshāwar), where he became the disciple of the teacher Sarvajñaśānti, and, as it appears, formally embraced to Buddhist faith. He subsequently visited the diamond-throne at Mahābôdhi (or Bodh-Gayā), and from there went to a vihāra, called Yaśôvarmapura, 'the town of Yaśôvarman,' where he stayed for a long time, enjoying the patronage of the king Dêvapāla. Vīradêva erected two *chaityas* on the hill Indraśaila (or Giryêk, about 5 miles south-west of Ghôsrāwā); and he was elected by the *saṁgha,* or assembly of monks, probably in succession to a monk named Satyabôdhi, to preside over the monasteries at Nālandā (the modern Baragaon, about 9 miles west of Ghôsrāwā).—It is hardly necessary to say that, with the exception of Yaśôvarmapura, which by Sir A. Cunningham has been identified with the town of Bihār, but which may be an older name of Ghôsrāwā itself; all the places mentioned here are well known from the records of the Chinese pilgrims. Nor need I point out what valuable proof is furnished by the above short narrative, in support of the fact that Buddhism was still flourishing in the famous localities mentioned, when this inscription was composed.

Unfortunately, the inscription is not dated, and we therefore are left to determine its age approximately from the characters in which it is written, and from the statement contained in it, that Vīradêva was patronised by a king Dêvapāla. The test of the characters is, under any circumstances, a vague one; and although there can be no doubt that the Dêvapāla spoken of is the Pāla king of that name, one of the more immediate successors of that Gôpāla of whom we have a short inscription at Nālandā, the chronology of the earlier rulers of the Pāla dynasty is still so doubtful that even a seemingly valuable statement like the mention of one of their number, in the present instance, leads to no very satisfactory result. I therefore can only repeat here, what has been stated already by Captain Kittoe, that our inscription was probably composed some time between the

Ghosrawa Buddhist Insctipriton (Facing Page 262)

middle of the 9th and the middle of the 10th centuries A.D. Judging merely from the characters, the forms of which appear to me considerably earlier than those of an inscription of Mahīpāla, of which I have an impression before me, I would assign it to the latter half of the 9th century; while the latest researches by Dr. Hoernle,[6] on the chronology of the Pāla dynasty would rather bring it down to about the middle of the 10th century. I do not think that the inscription can possibly be later.

Text[7]

Ōṁ[8]

1. Śrīmān[9]=asau jayati sat[t*]va-hita-pravṛitta-san-mānas-ādhigata-tat[t*]va-nayô Munīndraḥ| klêś-ātmanāṁ durita-nakra-durāsad-āntaḥ sansā(ṁsā)ra-sāgara-samutta-

2. raṇ-aika-sêtuḥ|| Asy[10]=āsmad-guravô va(ba)bhūvur=ava(ba)lāḥ sambhūya harttuṁ manaḥ kā lajjā yadi kêvalô na va(ba)lavān=asmi trilôka-prabhau| ity=ālôchayat=ê-

3. va Mānasabhuvā yô dūratô varjitaḥ śrīmān=viśvam=aśêsham=êtad=avatād=Vô(bô)dhan Savajrāsanaḥ| Asty[11]=Uttarāpatha-vibhūshaṇa-bhūta-bhūmir=dêś-ôttamô Na-

4. garahara iti pratītaḥ| tatra dvijātir=udit-ôdita-vaṅśa(ṁśa)-janmā nāmn=Ēndragupta iti rāja-sakhô va(ba)bhūva|| Rajj[ê]kayā dvija-varaḥ sa guṇī gṛi-

5. hiṇyā yuktô rarāja kalayā [ś]malayā ya[12]th=ênduḥ| lôkaḥ pativrata-kathā-paribhāvanāsu saṁkīrttanaṁ prathamam=êva karôti yasyāḥ|| Tābhyām=ajā-

6. yata sutaḥ sutarāṁ vivêkī yô vā(bā)la êva kalitaḥ para-lôka-vu(bu)ddhyā| sarvv-ôpabhôga-subhagê=pi gṛihê 0viraktaḥ [pravra]jyayā Sugata-śāsanam=abhyupê(pai)-

7. tuṁ|| Vêdān=adhītya sakalān kṛita-śāstra-chintaḥ śrīmat-Kanishkam=upagamya mahā-vihāraṁ[13]| āchārya-varyam-atha sa praśama-praśayaṁ Sarvvajñaśāntim=anugamya-

8. tapaś=chachāra || Sô=yaṁ viśuddha-guṇa-sambhṛita-bhūri-kīrttêḥ śishyô ऽ nurūpa-guṇa-śīla-yaśô-bhirāmaḥ| vā(bā)lêndu-vat=kali-kalaṅka-vimukta-kāntir-vandyaḥ

9. sadā muni-janair=api Vīradêvaḥ|| Vajrāsanaṁ[14] vanditum=êkadā ऽ tha śrīman-Mahāvô(bô)dhim= upāgatô ऽ sau| drashṭuṁ ta[t]ô ऽ gāt=sahadêś[i][15]-bhikshūn śrīmad-Yaśôvarmma-

10. puraṁ vihāraṁ|| Tishṭhann[16]=ath=êha suchiraṁ pratipatti-sāraḥ śrī-Dêva[17]pāla-bhuvanādhipa-lavdha(bdha)-pūjaḥ| prāpta-prabhaḥ pratidin-ôdaya pūrit-āśaḥ pūsh=êva dārita-

11. tamaḥ-prasarô rarāja|| Bhikshôr[18]=ātma-samaḥ suhṛid-bhuja iva śrī-Satya-vô(bô)dhêr=nijō Nālandā-paripālanāya niyataḥ saṅgha-sthitêr=yaḥ sthitaḥ| yên=aitau sphu-

12. ṭam=Indraśaila-mukuṭa-śrī-chaitya-chūḍāmaṇī śrāmaṇya-vrata-sam(ṁ)vṛitêna jagataḥ śrêyô ऽ rtham=utthāpitau|| Nālandayā cha paripālitay=êha satya śrīma-

13. d-vihāra-parihāra-vibhūshit-āṅgyā| udbhāsitô=pi va(ba)hu-kīrtti-vadhū-patitivê yaḥ sādhu sādhur=iti sādhu-janaiḥ praśastaḥ|| Chintā-jvaraṁ śamayatā ऽ rtta-jana-

14. sya dṛishṭyā Dhanvantarêr=api hi yêna hataḥ prabhāvaḥ| yaś=ch=êpsit-ārtha-paripūrṇṇa-manôrathêna lôkêna kalpataru-tulyatayā gṛihītaḥ|| Tên=aitad=a-

15. tra kṛitam=ātma-mano-vad=uchchair=vajrāsanasya bhavanaṁ bhuvan-ôttamasya| saṁjāyatê yad= abhivīkshya vimānagānāṁ Kailāsa-Mandara-mahīdhara-śṛiṅga-śaṅkā|| Sarvva-

16. sv[20]-ôpanayêna sat[t*]va-suhṛidām= audāryam= abhyasyatā samvô(mbô)dhau vihitaspṛihaṁ saha guṇair=visparddhi vīryan-tathā| atrasthêna nijê nijāv=iha vṛi(bṛi)hat-puṇy-ādhikārê

17. sthitê yêna svêna yaśô-dhvajêna ghaṭitau vaṅśā(ṁśā)v=Udīchīpathê|| Sôpāna-[21]mārgam=iva mukti-p[uras]ya kīrttim=êtām(ṁ)=vidhāya kuśalaṁ=yad=upāttam=asmāt|

18. kṛitv=āditaḥ sa-pitaraṁ guru-vargam=asya śamvô(mbô)dhim=êtu jana-rāśir=aśêsha êva||
Yāvat[22]=kūrmmô jaladhi-valayāṁ bhūta-dhātrīṁ vi(bi)bhartti dhvānta-dhvansī(ṁsī)

19. tapati tapanô yāvad=êv=ôgra-raśmiḥ| snigdh-ālôkāḥ śiśira-mahasā yāmavatyaś=chayāvat=tāvaṭ =kīrttir=jayatu bhuvanê Vīradêvasya śubhrā|| ||

Translation

Ōṁ

(L. 1)—Triumphant is that glorious chief of sages (Buddha), who with his excellent mind, striving for the welfare of the beings, found out the system of truth; (*and who*), to those whose nature is affliction, (*is*) the one bridge for crossing the ocean of worldly existence, (*a bridge*) the ends of which are difficult of approach for (*those*) alligators—evils!

(L. 2)—May the glorious (*Buddha*), who has his diamond-throne by the Bôdhi tree,[23] protect this whole universe!—he, from whom the mind-born (Māra) drew far aloof, thinking, as it were, that if his betters had, united, been powerless to captivate the mind of (*Buddha*), why need *he* blush for failing in strength, single-handed, against the Lord of the three worlds[24]!

(L. 3)—There is an excellent country, known by the name of Nagarahāra,[25] the land of which is an ornament to Uttarāpatha (the northern region). There, in a family which had risen higher and higher, was born a twice-born, Indragupta by name, a friend of the king.

(L. 4)—As the moon with its spotless digit, so shone that meritorious distinguished twice-born, united with his wife Rajj[ê]kā, of whom people make mention in the very first place, when they ponder on tales of devotion to husbands.

(L. 5)—To them was born a son, highly endowed with discernment, who, even as a child, was filled with thoughts concerning the other world. He gave up his attachment to his home, though it was blessed with every enjoyment, in order that, by going forth as an ascetic, he might adopt the teaching of Sugata.

(L. 7)—Having studied all the Vêdas (*and*) reflected on the Śāstras, (*and*) having gone to the glorious great Kanishka vihāra,[26] he then, following the excellent teacher Sarvajñaśānti,[27] (*who was*) praiseworthy for his quiescence, gave himself up to asceticism.

(L. 8)—This Vīradêva, (*being*) thus the disciple of one who by his pure qualities had accumulated great fame, (*and*) pleasing by the fame of corresponding qualities and natural disposition, (*was*) always, like the new-moon, an object of adoration, even to sages, inasmuch as his loveliness was free from the stain of the Kali-age.

(L. 9)—To adore the diamond-throne, he then once visited the glorious Mahābôdhi.[28] From there he went to see the monks of his native country,[29] to the vihāra, the glorious Yaśôvarmapura.[30]

(L. 10)—Then staying here for a long time, he, the quintessence of intelligence, being treated with reverence by the lord of the earth, the illustrious Dêvapāla, shone like the sun, endowed with splendour, filling the quarters with his daily rising, (*and*) dispelling the spread of darkness.

(L. 11)—He who, (*being*) a friend (*dear*) like his own self, being as it were the own arm of the holy monk Satyabôdhi,[31] by the decree of the assembly of monks (*saṁgha*) was permanently appointed to govern Nālandā; (*and*) by whom, engaged in the vow of a *Śramaṇa,* there were erected for the welfare of the world these two holy *chaityas,* clearly two crest-jewels in the diadem of Indraśaila;[32]—

(L. 12)—And who, on becoming the lord of the lady Great Fame, graced though he already was here by Nālandā, governed (*by and*) true (*to him and*) decorated by a ring[33] of famous *vihāras,* was well praised by good people as a good man:—

(L. 13) – Who, by (*his mere*) sight allaying the fever of anxiety of people in distress, verily eclipsed the power of even Dhanvantari,[34] and whom people, whose wishes he fulfilled by (*granting to them*) the objects desired, took to be equable to the tree of paradise; –

(L. 14) – He erected here for the diamond-throne, the best thing in the world, this habitation, lofty like his own mind, the sight of which causes those moving in celestial cars to suspect it to be a peak of the mountain Kailāsa or of Mandara.

(L. 15) – Practising the generosity of those who are friends of the beings, by offering up his all, as well as manliness, eagerly directed towards the attainment of perfect wisdom and vying with (*his other*) excellencies, residing here, while his high holy office was continuing, he hoisted the banner of his fame on the two poles[35] (*of his family*) in Udīchīpatha (the northern region).

(L. 17) – Whatever merit has been acquired by the erection of this edifice,[36] (*which is*), as it were, a staircase to the city of salvation, may through that the whole assemblage of men, headed by the circle of his elders (*and*) including his parents, attain to perfect wisdom!

(L. 18) – As long as the tortoise bears the ocean-girded mother of all beings; as long as the sun with its fierce rays is shining, dispelling the darkness; as long as the nights present a pleasing appearance with the cool-splendoured (moon); – so long may the bright fame of Vīradêva be triumphant in the world.

References

1. According to Sir A. Cunningham, *Archæol. Survey of India,* Vol. XI. p. 172, the slab was still at Ghôsrāwā in January 1862, with the following words engraved on the margin: – "Recovered and placed here by Captain M. Kittoe on part of Government, March 30, A.D. 1848."

2. *Loc. cit.*, p. 173. Although Kittoe's statement has been removed, traces of Roman letters can, to judge by the impression before me, be still recognized below the last line of the inscription.
3. The measurements of the stone given by Mr. Broadley are wrong.
4. The peculiar form of the sign for *ā*, and of that for *ry*, has misled Captain Kittoe to state that the inscription, in line 7, has *achāya* (instead of *āchārya*), and induced Dr. Bhāṇḍārkar to put a sign of interrogation after the words *audāryam* and *vīryan* in line 16. In Dr. Bhāṇḍārkar's impression the words *āchārya-varya* in line 7 were illegible; and Dr. Rājêndralāl has *prāptāya êva* instead.
5. See *ante*, Vol. XV. p. 357.
6. See *ante*, Vol. XIV. p. 164. The Dêvapāla of the 'huge Gwālior inscription,' mentioned on p. 165 and re-discovered at Sêrôn (Sīyaḍôṇī), is, in my opinion, not the Dêvapāla of the Pāla dynasty, and his date, Vikrama-Saṁvat 1005 (not 1025) is therefore useless for the chronology of that dynasty.
7. From the impression.
8. Expressed by a symbol.
9. Metre, Vasutatilakā.
10. Metre, Śārdūlavikrīḍita.
11. Metre, Vasantatilakā; and of the next four verses.
12. This *akshara, ya,* was originally omitted, and is engraved below the line.
13. The two *aksharas vihā* were originally omitted and are engraved below the line.
14. Metre, Indravajrā.
15. Perhaps this sign for *i* has been struck out, so that the *akshara* would be *sa,* not *śi.*
16. Metre, Vasantatilakā.
17. Originally *Dêvāpāla.*
18. Metre, Śārdūlavikrīḍita.
19. Metre, Vasantatilakā; and of the next two verses.
20. Metre, Śārdūlavikṛīḍita.
21. Metre, Vasantatilakā.
22. Metre, Mandākrāntā.
23. See Beal, *Si-yu-ki,* Vol. II. p. 115: 'In the middle of the enclosure surrounding the *Bôdhi* tree is the diamond throne (*Vajrasāna*).......It

is composed of diamond.....On this the thousand Buddhas of the Bhadra-kalpa have sat and entered the diamond *Samādhi;* hence the name of the diamond throne. It is the place where the Buddhas attain the holy path.'

24. See, *e.g.*, the opening verses of the *Nāgānanda,* Boyd's Translation, pp. 1 and 2.

25. In the immediate vicinity of Jalālābād. See Cunningham, *Ancient Geography of India,* Vol. I. p. 43; Beal, *Si-yu-ki,* Vol. I. p. 91.

26. The *Saṁghārāma,* which was built by king Kanishka in the neighbourhood of the modern Pêshāwar. See Beal, *l.c.,* Vol. I. pp. 103 and 109.

27. I cannot understand why this word should not have been taken as a proper name in the previous translations. Compare such names as *Buddhaśānti, Ratnākaraśānti, Dharmākaraśānti,* mentioned by Tāranātha.

28. *I.e.* either the great Bôdhi tree, or the Mahābôdhi *saṁghārāma* at Gayā, or Bôdh-Gayā itself. See Beal, *l.c.,* Vol. I. Introduction, p. x; Vol. II. p. 133; *Journ. Beng. As. Soc.,* Vol. XVII. Part I. p. 498; and *Archæol. Survey of India,* Vol. XI. p. 141, and Vol. XV. Preface, p. III.

29. I am not quite sure that this is the right meaning of the word *sahadêśin* (or, possibly, *sahadêśa*) of the original.

30. Comparing the passage in line 7 *śrīmat-Kanishkam...mahāvihāraṁ,* I ought perhaps to translate 'the glorious *vihāra,* [called] Yaśôvarmapura,' although the word *śrīmat* is prefixed to *Yaśôvarmapuram.* I am aware that Sir A. Cunningham has identified Yaśôvarmapura with the present town of Bihār (see *Archæol. Survey of India,* Vol. III. p. 120 and p. 135; and also Vol. VIII. p. 76), and it would be very tempting to take *vihāra,* in the above passage, as a proper name and to translate: 'From there he went...to Bihār, the town of the glorious Yaśôvarman,' I nevertheless believe that the word has been used in its ordinary sense, and that Yasôvarmapura was the name of the *vihāra* visited by Vīradêva. I do not deny that Yaśôvarmapura *may* have been a name of Bihār; but I consider it equally possible that it may have been the name of the very Ghôsrāwā, where the inscription has been found.

31 The beginning of the verses might also be translated: 'He, who, [*being dear*] to the monks like their own selves [*and being*], as it were, the own arm of the holy Satyabôdhi.' Satyabôdhi may have been Vīradêva's predecessor at Nālandā.

32. Nālandā has by Sir A. Cunningham been shown to be the modern Baragaon, and Indraśaila identified with the hill Giryêk—*Ancient Geography of India,* Vol. I, p. 469.

33. The dictionaries do not give this meaning for the word *parihāra;* but *parihāraka* means 'an arm-ring.'

34. The physician of the gods.

35. *Vaṁśau,* 'two poles,' or the two families (of his father and mother).

36. According to Hêmachandra's *Anêkārthasaṁgraha* the word *kīrti* also means 'a palace' or 'temple' (*prāsāda=kīrtana*), and this clearly is the sense in which it has been employed here. *Kuśala,* according to the lexicographers, also is synonymous with *puṇya.*